About Frithjof Schuon

"I knew when I was in his [Schuon's] presence that I was in the presence of a true saint and also the spiritual master that I was seeking. When I say 'true saint', I don't mean just a saintly man but a true saint of the first magnitude, such as one cannot expect to meet in the twentieth century. I mean a saint of the magnitude of St. Bernard, St. Francis, or St. Augustine in Christianity; of Ibn 'Arabī or Rūmī in Sufism; of Shankara in Hinduism; and of Milarepa in Buddhism. I knew this with a certainty."

—**Martin Lings**, author of *A Sufi Saint of the Twentieth Century: Shaykh Ahmad al-'Alawī*, describing his first meeting with Schuon

"I think Schuon has exactly the right view. . . . That I can be accepted in a personal and confidential relationship, not exactly as a disciple but at any rate as one of those who are entitled to consult him directly and personally. This is a matter of great importance to me. . . . It can have tremendous effects. I see that already."

—**Thomas Merton**, from *The Hidden Ground of Love* and *Merton and Sufism*

"[Schuon is] the most important religious thinker of our century. . . . [He] is the only person I have known who invariably made me feel on leaving him that I had been in the presence of a different order of human being."

—**Huston Smith**, author of *The World's Religions* and *Why Religion Matters*

"The highest praise that I can offer concerning the writings of Frithjof Schuon is that they are worthy of their subject matter—the teachings of the great spiritual traditions. Whether one's views are supported or challenged by these writings, any serious person will feel grateful to be confronted by such a generously discerning intellect and to witness the emergence of authentic contemplative thought in this darkening time."

—**Jacob Needleman**, editor of *The Sword of Gnosis*

"I have met with no more impressive work in the comparative study of Oriental and Occidental religion."

—**T. S. Eliot**, Nobel laureate for literature, on Schuon's first book, *The Transcendent Unity of Religions*

"Schuon's thought does not demand that we agree or disagree, but that we understand or do not understand. Such writing is of rare and lasting value."

—**Times Literary Supplement**

"[Schuon's] face was bright with the light of inner illumination. He possessed a regal bearing . . . but he was at heart so humble, simple, and loving. The love in his heart was manifest on his face. . . . [He was] a very prince among saints."

—**Swami Ramdas**, from a "Visit to a Sufi Saint" in *World is God*

About This Book

"Here, Michael Fitzgerald brings to the academic world and to serious seekers a wealth of reliable sources of information not only from Frithjof Schuon himself but from a quite impressive number of persons who knew him well: appropriate and concise quotations from articles, books, memoirs, correspondence, and an impressive array of photographs. This book provides the reader with a valuable tool necessary to deepen his or her understanding of Frithjof Schuon's works and life: a difficult but important task that Michael Fitzgerald carried out objectively and beautifully."

—**Jean-Pierre Lafouge**, Marquette University, editor of *For God's Greater Glory: Gems of Jesuit Spirituality*

"Intellection at its highest level, of which the sage was a providential locus of manifestation, is unveiled through the many quotations of Schuon's own description of his inspirations, and the message which resulted from his insights is presented in its essentiality."

—**Jean-Claude Petitpierre**, Schuon's long-time friend

"Like a skillful craftsman, the author manages to reflect the multiple facets of Frithjof Schuon through the German thinker's own words and those of his closest collaborators. The abundance of photographs and illustrations provide yet another way of assimilating the unique characteristics of this great sage of our times. A remarkable biography on a remarkable man."

—**Carlos Sugobono**, Schuon's long-time friend

"[Schuon's] gifts could only be the result of a lifelong cultivation of the spirit with an intensity of concentration almost beyond comprehension. Michael Fitzgerald's fine presentation of Schuon's message and his portrait of the messenger provide many keys for understanding Schuon's life and spiritual gifts."

—**Vincent Rossi**, Director of Education for the American Exarchate of the Jerusalem Patriarchate of the Orthodox Church

"Frithjof Schuon's extraordinary discrimination, as seen through his two dozen books, has the power to cut the Gordian knot of our illusions and errors. For the reader who wants to know more about this great man's life and wisdom, Michael Fitzgerald's biography is the best answer. It provides an enormous amount of organized and clear information, some hitherto unknown."

—**Mateus Soares de Azevedo**, editor of *Ye Shall Know the Truth: Christianity and the Perennial Philosophy*

World Wisdom
The Library of Perennial Philosophy

The Library of Perennial Philosophy is dedicated to the exposition of the timeless Truth underlying the diverse religions. This Truth, often referred to as the *Sophia Perennis*—or Perennial Wisdom—finds its expression in the revealed Scriptures as well as the writings of the great sages and the artistic creations of the traditional worlds.

Frithjof Schuon: Messenger of the Perennial Philosophy appears as one of our selections in the Spiritual Masters: East & West series.

Spiritual Masters: East & West Series

This series presents the writings of great masters of the past and present from both East and West. Carefully selected essential writings of these sages are combined with biographical information, glossaries of technical terms, historical maps, and pictorial and photographic art in order to communicate a sense of their respective spiritual climates.

Schuon's English Language Works

Books by Frithjof Schuon

The Transcendent Unity of Religions (1953, 1984)
Spiritual Perspectives and Human Facts (1954, 1970, 1987, 2007)
Gnosis: Divine Wisdom (1959, 1978, 1990, 2006)
Language of the Self (1959, 1999)
Castes and Races (1959, 1982)
Stations of Wisdom (1961, 1980, 1995)
Understanding Islam (1963, 1972, 1986, 1998)
Light on the Ancient Worlds (1965, 1984, 2006)
Treasures of Buddhism (In the Tracks of Buddhism) (1968, 1989, 1993)
Logic and Transcendence (1975, 1984, 2009)
Esoterism as Principle and as Way (1981, 1990)
Sufism: Veil and Quintessence (1981, 2006)
From the Divine to the Human (1982)
Christianity/Islam: Perspectives on Esoteric Ecumenism (1985, 2008)
Survey of Metaphysics and Esoterism (1986, 2000)
In the Face of the Absolute (1989, 1994)
The Feathered Sun: Plains Indians in Art and Philosophy (1990)
To Have a Center (1990)
Roots of the Human Condition (1991, 2002)
Images of Primordial and Mystic Beauty: Paintings by Frithjof Schuon (1992)
Echoes of Perennial Wisdom (1992)
The Play of Masks (1992)
Road to the Heart: Poems (1995)
The Transfiguration of Man (1995)
The Eye of the Heart (1997)
Form and Substance in the Religions (2002)
Adastra & Stella Maris: Poems by Frithjof Schuon (bilingual edition) (2003)
Songs without Names, Volumes I-VI: Poems by Frithjof Schuon (2006)
Songs without Names, Volumes VII-XII: Poems by Frithjof Schuon (2006)
World Wheel, Volumes I-III: Poems by Frithjof Schuon (2006)
World Wheel, Volumes IV-VII: Poems by Frithjof Schuon (2006)
Primordial Meditation: Contemplating the Real (2007)
Autumn Leaves & The Ring: Poems by Frithjof Schuon (bilingual edition) (2010)

Anthologies of Frithjof Schuon's Writings

The Essential Frithjof Schuon, ed. Seyyed Hossein Nasr (1986, 2005)
Songs for a Spiritual Traveler: Selected Poems (bilingual edition) (2002)
René Guénon: Some Observations, ed. William Stoddart (2004)
The Fullness of God: Frithjof Schuon on Christianity, ed. James S. Cutsinger (2004)
Prayer Fashions Man: Frithjof Schuon on the Spiritual Life, ed. James S. Cutsinger (2005)
Art from the Sacred to the Profane: East and West, ed. Catherine Schuon (2007)
Splendor of the True: A Frithjof Schuon Reader, ed. James S. Cutsinger (forthcoming)

Schuon's Works in Their Original Languages

Written in French

De Quelques aspects de l'Islam (1935)
De l'Unité transcendante des religions (1948, 1958, 1979, 2000)
L'Oeil du cœur (1950, 1974, 1995)
Perspectives spirituelles et faits humains (1953, 1989, 2001)
Sentiers de gnose (1957, 1987, 1996)
Castes et races (1957, 1979)
Les Stations de la sagesse (1958, 1992)
Images de l'Esprit (1961, 1982)
Comprendre l'Islam (1961, 1976)
Regards sur les mondes anciens (1968, 1997)
Logique et transcendance (1970, 2007)
Forme et substance dans les religions (1975)
L'Ésotérisme comme principe et comme voie (1978, 1997)
Le Soufisme, voile et quintessence (1980, 2006)
Christianisme/Islam: visions d'oecuménisme ésotérique (1981)
Du Divin à l'humain (1981, 1993)
Sur les traces de la Religion pérenne (1982)
Approches du phénomène religieux (1984, 1993)
Résumé de métaphysique intégrale (1985, 2000)
Avoir un centre (1988)
Racines de la condition humaine (1990)
Les Perles du pèlerin (1991)
Le Jeu des Masques (1992)
La Transfiguration de l'Homme (1995)

Written in German

Urbesinnung: Das Denken des Eigentlichen
(Leitgedanken zur Urbesinnung) (1935, 1989, 2009)
Sulamith (1947)
Tage-und Nächtebuch (1947)
Von der inneren Einheit der Religionen (1981, 2007)
Adastra & Stella Maris: Sinngedichte (2001)
Herbstblätter & Der Ring: Sinngedichte (2002)
Lieder ohne Nahmen I, II, III: Sinngedichte (2002)
Lieder ohne Nahmen IV, V: Sinngedichte (2003)
Lieder ohne Nahmen VI, VII: Sinngedichte (2003)
Lieder ohne Nahmen VIII, IX, X: Sinngedichte (2004)
Lieder ohne Nahmen XI, XII: Sinngedichte (2004)
Das Weltrad I, II: Sinngedichte (2004)
Das Weltrad III, IV, V: Sinngedichte (2005)
Das Weltrad VI, VII: Sinngedichte (2005)

Compiled or Written in English

Language of the Self (1959, 1999)
Treasures of Buddhism (In the Tracks of Buddhism) (1968, 1989, 1993)
The Feathered Sun: Plains Indians in Art and Philosophy (1990)
Images of Primordial and Mystic Beauty (1992)
Road to the Heart: Poems (1995)

Frithjof Schuon

Messenger of the Perennial Philosophy

by
Michael Oren Fitzgerald

Foreword by
William Stoddart

World Wisdom

Frithjof Schuon: Messenger of the Perennial Philosophy

Library of Congress Cataloging-in-Publication Data

Fitzgerald, Michael Oren, 1949-
Frithjof Schuon : messenger of the perennial philosophy / by Michael Oren Fitzgerald ; foreword by William Stoddart.
p. cm. -- (Spiritual masters. East & West series)
Includes bibliographical references (p.) and index.
ISBN 978-1-935493-08-2 (pbk. : alk. paper) 1. Schuon, Frithjof, 1907-1998. 2. Religion--Philosophy. 3. Tradition (Philosophy) I. Title.
BL51.F539 2010
200.92--dc22

2009049252

Printed on acid-free paper in China.

For information address World Wisdom, Inc.
P.O. Box 2682, Bloomington, Indiana 47402-2682
www.worldwisdom.com

Cover photograph of Frithjof Schuon by Roland Michaud, circa 1990

Even if our writings had on the average no other result than the restitution, for some, of the saving barque that is prayer, we would owe it to God to consider ourselves profoundly satisfied.

Frithjof Schuon,
The Play of Masks,
"Foreword", vii

CONTENTS

Frithjof Schuon, 1965

FOREWORD

Although almost all of Frithjof Schuon's books have been available in English for many years, one can hardly say that his name is a household word. To people with special interests, however, in such fields as philosophy, theology, comparative religion, and the spiritual life, a great deal has been known about him for a long time.

The present biography provides, in an engaging and fascinating manner, a detailed background to his life, his writings, and his ideas, but I will summarize here some of the essentials in order straightway to give a hint as to the nature and character of this man.

Frithjof Schuon (1907-1998) was born in Basle, Switzerland of German parents. His parents were of Catholic origin, but did not practice, and they sent their son to a Lutheran school. Throughout his long life, Schuon remained profoundly grateful to a beloved school teacher of his early years for his "wonderful Bible lessons". At the same time, the child Schuon was enthralled by reading the Arabian Nights and folk tales from all over the world. Also as a child, he was already aware that what he admired and yearned for above all were the four universal qualities: "the holy, the noble, the beautiful, and the great". At about the age of 11 or 12, he unexpectedly had a deep and lasting spiritual experience when he viewed, and was overwhelmed by, the three great Japanese Buddhist statues in the Ethnological Museum in Basle. This experience was pivotal for him, and taught him how wisdom and holiness are inseparable from beauty, and how they can be conveyed to the heart of man by the peaks of sacred art.

After the death of his father in 1920, his mother and her two sons moved to Mulhouse (Mülhausen) in Alsace, which had been annexed by France in 1918. His father's death and the move to Alsace were extremely traumatic for the young Schuon, but at Mulhouse he attended a convent school run by aristocratic French nuns, under whose influence the young adolescent happily and willingly became a Catholic. At the same time he learned French, the language in which he was destined to write his many philosophical books.

Throughout these adolescent years Schuon continued his yearning for the four universal qualities mentioned above; and, even without explicit teaching, the youthful Schuon had developed a profound grasp of metaphysical, theological, and spiritual realities. But explicit teaching was also at hand. He eagerly read all holy Scriptures, and especially the *Bhagavad Gītā*, which was for him a revelation in every sense of the word. However, in all his understanding, inborn and acquired, he was alone. He was misunderstood by his family and acquaintances, and suffered much as a result. He continued to love his childhood Protestantism and his youthful Catholicism but, as he grew into adulthood, he loosened his attachment to them, and lived almost entirely in the uncompromising and implacable intellectual aura of Vedanta and Platonism.

In 1924, at the age of 17, he discovered the books of the magisterial French philosopher and orientalist René Guénon (1886-1951). This was for Schuon an immense consolation. Not only did he find in Guénon's writings a full confirmation of the views which he already profoundly held; he also found in them the precise metaphysical vocabulary and terminology with which to clothe and express his own understandings and insights. Some years later there began between Guénon and Schuon a prolific correspondence, which continued until the end of Guénon's life.

Several significant events and experiences in Schuon's life took place in the late 1920s and early 1930s, amongst them, his military service, his earliest travels, and finally his decisive encounter with the Algerian Sufi master the Shaykh al-'Alawī. But I will leave the details of these crucial and seminal events to the biographer, who deals with them copiously, and turn to the important matter of Schuon's long and intimate intellectual association with René Guénon.

René Guénon and Frithjof Schuon were the originators of what has subsequently become known as the "Perennialist" or "Traditionalist" school of wisdom. Guénon was the pioneer, and Schuon the fulfillment or quintessence. Schuon pointed out the analogy here with two other wisdom schools which had dual originators and expositors, namely, those associated with Socrates and Plato in fifth century B.C. Athens, and with Jalāl ad-Dīn Rūmī and Shams ad-Dīn at-Tabrīzī in thirteenth century Turkey.

Basically, the point of view of Guénon and Schuon is that of the "perennial philosophy". This term was made familiar to English-speaking readers by the publication in 1945 of Aldous Huxley's book of the same name.[1] The central idea of the perennial philosophy is that Divine Truth is one, timeless, and universal, and that the different religions are but different languages expressing that one Truth. The symbol most often used to convey this idea is that of the uncolored light and the many colors of the spectrum which are made visible only when the uncolored light is refracted. In the Renaissance, the term betokened the recognition of the fact that the philosophies of Pythagoras, Plato, Aristotle, and Plotinus incontrovertibly expounded the same truths as lay at the heart of Christianity. Subsequently the meaning of the term was enlarged to cover the metaphysics and mysticisms of all of the great world religions, notably, Hinduism, Buddhism, and Islam.

In point of fact, Huxley was not the first exponent of this idea in modern times. It had already been propounded by the Bengali saint Ramakrishna (1836-1886), who was intimately familiar—and at a much deeper level than Huxley—, not only with Hinduism, but also with Christianity and Islam. Given the "exotism" and unfamiliarity of the great Ramakrishna, however, and also the dubious religious credentials of the rather superficial and syncretistic Huxley, the term and the idea of the "perennial philosophy" did not get off to a good start with conservative religious seekers, Christian and other.

But a development that no one could have foreseen occurred. In the 1920s, the books of the French philosopher René Guénon began to appear. These expounded, in irrefutably Platonic fashion, the oneness of supra-formal Truth, and the multiplicity of the formal expressions thereof. From this one could perceive that the reason for being of the different religions is not that they are "all the same", but, precisely, that they are *all different*! The *essence* (concerning God, man, and salvation) is of course the same, but the *forms* are significantly different. Each religion—not only Christianity—makes an absolute claim, for the precise reason that it is an expression of the Absolute; this is its justification and its *sine qua non*. Red, yellow, and green are not darkness; on the contrary, each one of them is a refraction of the uncolored light. The principle of religious unity lies in God alone, and it is a rash man who declares that God has expressed Himself in only one language!

Guénon's works were followed, from the 1930s onwards, by the long series of articles and books by Schuon, who carried to incredible heights the exposition of timeless truth, *and its saving quality*. Schuon's message was indeed one of truth, beauty, and salvation.

It is difficult to dispute the profundity and genius of these two authors who were the originators of the current of intellectuality and spirituality known as the "Perennialist" or "Traditionalist" school.[2] Nothing can take away from the originality of vision of Guénon and Schuon, but it is appropriate to mention some of the great precursors to whom they most frequently refer. These include Shankara (Hinduism), Plato (Ancient Greece), Eckhart (Western Christianity), and Ibn 'Arabī (Islam). Yet the Perennialist vision does not require lengthy expression: it is summed up in the words of Christ: "Ye shall know the Truth, and the Truth shall make you free." For the perennial philosophy, this is indeed the whole story: timeless truth, and its liberating quality.

Perhaps because of the superficiality of early-twentieth-century Huxley and the fantasies of late-twentieth-century "new-age" ideas, the Perennialist school, with its universalist theses and extra-Christian references, is still in some quarters regarded with suspicion. Some people indeed tend to confuse two opposites: "new-age" ideas and the perennial philosophy.[3] Others, again, think that the perennial philosophy has to do only with something which is pejoratively referred to as "Eastern mysticism", forgetting that the term itself is of Christian origin, and that it was brought into service in the first place by the Christian recognition of the eternal truths of Platonism. These eternal truths are precisely what the perennial philosophy is all about.

The perennial philosophy is not for fools, and it is precisely this that the modern sophisticated man needs to know. The perennial philosophy—which is true universalism and true ecumenism—is a recognition of the divine origin of each religion. The essence of each religion is pure truth, and the various religious forms clothe that truth in garments of different designs and colors. "In my Father's house are many mansions." This saying of Christ applies not only to Heaven, but also to earth. The function of the various religions is to express the truth, and to offer a way of salvation, in a manner suited to the needs of the different segments and ethnicities of mankind. Each religion comes from God, and each religion leads back to God. Each religion, moreover, comprises a doctrine and a method, that is to say, it is an enlightening truth coupled with a saving means. Were this not so, it would not be a question of religion, but of an empty man-made ideology (such as Freudianism, Jungianism, Teilhardism, and many others) that can save no one.

— ·:· —

Frithjof Schuon sometimes summarized his message in a highly succinct fashion. For example:

His complete teaching in four words: Truth, Prayer, Virtue, Beauty.

The three concomitants of the Love of God: Virgin Nature, Sacred Art, Holy Company.

The *doctrine* of Shankara, the *method* of Hōnen, and the *primordiality* of the Red Indians.

As regards the last of these summaries: Shankara was the pinnacle of Hindu wisdom, a master of universal metaphysics in the form of *Advaita Vedānta* ("non-duality"); Hōnen, a Japanese Amida Buddhist Master, was the preeminent exemplar of total trust in the saving power of the revealed Name; as for the great Indian Chiefs, they evoke the qualities of dignity, courage, frugality, sacrifice, and closeness to Virgin Nature.

In Christian terms this ternary is: the *doctrine* of Meister Eckhart, the *method* of Saint Bernardino of Siena, and the *love of nature* (the *primordiality*) of Saint Francis of Assisi.

In Islamic terms it is: *Tawhīd* (the doctrine of unity), *Dhikr* (the remembrance of God), and *Fitra* (primordial nature or the state of the *hanīf*).

Each of the various expressions of each of the three components of this ternary (doctrine, method, and primordiality) derives from the same (respective) archetype. The first example mentioned above (referring to Shankara, Hōnen, and the Red Indians)—formulated by Schuon himself—is a particularly felicitous, evocative, and memorable expression of the three archetypes concerned.

Personally, Schuon was a combination of majesty and humility; of rigor and love. He was made of objectivity and incorruptibility, coupled with compassion. In meeting with him many times during a period of nearly five decades, the immediate personal qualities which constantly struck me were his infinite patience and his infinite generosity.

May this informative and well-documented biography successfully convey to readers the precious and unique phenomenon that was Frithjof Schuon.

William Stoddart
Windsor, Ontario

PREFACE

The present work is a biographical portrait of Frithjof Schuon, composed for the benefit of those who have encountered his written message. What color has been painted into this picture comes, for the most part, from the philosopher's own hand. In the text, all of Schuon's words, whether written or spoken, are displayed in colored lettering;[1] my wish is to emphasize the value of listening to Schuon himself when considering his life's story and its meaning. To supplement his self-witness, I have also frequently relied on statements made by those who knew him well, and in a few instances, I myself have provided observations about the people and events in his life.[2] In many cases, however, it will be left to later biographers to fill in the details that surround the emerging framework of principal figures and themes. While the approach of the biography is generally chronological,[3] in three places we step away from the sequence of events in order to consider certain leitmotifs of Schuon's life: a view of his daily life; his special interest in the American Indians; and his artistic genius. We close with an Afterword that presents some reflections on his legacy.

This book is in some ways a companion to the forthcoming documentary film of the same name; indeed, the film and the book share some of the same photographs and interview comments by Schuon and a number of his friends and admirers.[4] The origin of both projects goes back to 1991 when I co-directed and co-produced a documentary film about Schuon's life, based in large part upon video interviews between a newspaper reporter and the then eighty-four year old philosopher.[5] The following year, I asked Schuon's permission to create a longer and more complete documentary film. This process allowed me to ask him several direct questions about what he considered to be the most important aspects of his life and message. He eventually approved the proposed documentary film and a written biography about his life and work, but with the caveat that both projects be postponed until after his death. During this process he reviewed various possible titles for the project and eventually wrote out his preference in his own hand:[6]

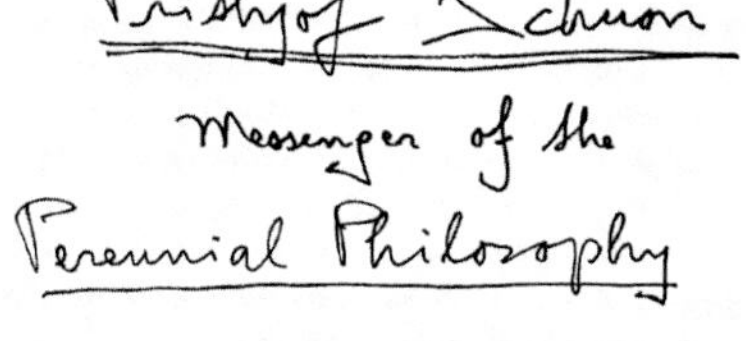

Schuon deliberately chose a relative anonymity throughout his life, which allowed him to repose in "holy solitude"[7] while creating his remarkable body of written work. He often noted the importance of his personal privacy and added that, were he to become too well known, he would not have sufficient time to complete his writing, emphasizing: "my message is in my books".[8] Nonetheless, he was remarkably open regarding formerly private aspects of his life in the poems he penned in his final years.[9] This only reflects the fact that:

What I think and what I am,
I should not keep begrudgingly within me;
For my existence has a meaning for others —
And the secret powers of the Spirit belong to God.[10]

History shows that the lives of great sages have often been the subject of diverse interpretations and the life of Frithjof Schuon will be no exception. It seems safe to say, therefore, that there will never be a single, definitive biographical portrait of him. Each biographer's situation is somewhat analogous to a painter looking at a mountain that soars above the surrounding landscape: the painter must attempt to render a "true" portrait of the mountain, but from only one point of view and from one point in time; yet no single work can provide a "complete" picture of the entire mountain as it is seen through the course of the seasons and during the course of its earthly existence. Hokusai's (1760-1849) famous response to this limitation—his forty-six "Views of Mount Fuji"—informs the approach of this work, which offers a series of views of a towering figure within whose one life, many lives are contained. As Schuon wrote in his ninetieth year:

When one has wandered through nearly a century,
One has lived more than one single life
Here below; one is a "we" inside an "I" —
Destiny was able to weave one and all.

One has lived in a fairy-tale world,
Which for others is no longer real nor graspable;
So this play may elude us too — what counts
Is that the heart forget not the Most High.[11]

Michael Fitzgerald
Bloomington, Indiana
September, 2009

INTRODUCTION

> [E]verything has been said already, though it is far from being the case that everyone has always understood it. There can therefore be no question of presenting "new truths"; what is needed in our time, and indeed in every age remote from the origins of Revelation, is to provide some people with keys fashioned afresh . . . in order to help them rediscover the truths written in an eternal script in the very substance of man's spirit.[1]

Based on an intellectual vision of the Real, Frithjof Schuon possessed the rare ability "both to speak and to understand the various dialects through which the Spirit has chosen to communicate itself".[2] His more than thirty books form the centerpiece of a school of thought that is focused on the enunciation and explanation of the perennial philosophy (*philosophia perennis*).[3] It is a philosophy in the original sense of that term, a "love of wisdom",[4] whose subject is the essential and hence universal Truth that underlies the diverse religions, together with the human consequences of this Truth. Schuon's writings, therefore, offer us the necessary keys to understand the nature of God, the metaphysical Absolute, as well as to restore our soul's proper relationship to God, who is also the Sovereign Good.

"The term *philosophia perennis*", writes Schuon, "signifies the totality of the primordial and universal truths—and therefore of the metaphysical axioms—whose formulation does not belong to any particular system." It is in the same sense that one can speak "of a *religio perennis*, designating by this term the essence of every religion; this means the essence of every form of worship, every form of prayer, and every system of morality, just as the *sophia perennis* is the essence of all dogmas and all expressions of wisdom."[5] While it is impossible to exhaust the meaning of such a message, it is nonetheless possible to state, along with the editors of a collection of his writings, that

> Schuon's message has three main dimensions: comprehension, concentration, conformation. Comprehension of the Truth; concentration on the Truth through methodical and quintessential prayer; conformation to these dimensions through intrinsic morality, which means beauty of character. Without this beauty, there can be no serious assimilation of the metaphysical truth, nor any efficacious method of orison. To these, we may add a fourth and more extrinsic element: the beauty of our ambience and hence our affinity with virgin nature. As Plato expressed it: "Beauty is the splendor of the True."[6]

This summary was confirmed by Schuon himself in a 1991 film interview: when asked, "If you had to boil your philosophy down to a few elements and if you wanted to recommend ways to follow that philosophy, what would you say?", he answered:

> Essentialism, because I must focus everything on the essential. There are four elements that are essential:
>
> There is first discernment between the Absolute and the relative. *Ātmā* and *Māyā*, reality and illusion.
>
> Then prayer, because if one understands what is essential and what is Absolute, one wants to assimilate it; otherwise one is a hypocrite. In order to assimilate the truth of the Absolute one must pray. Now there are three types of prayer: first canonical prayer—in Christianity it is the Lord's Prayer. Then free, personal prayer, like the Psalms in the Bible—the Psalms are David's personal prayer with God. The third type of prayer is prayer of the heart—essential prayer, which is an act of contemplation in the innermost self. This is esoterism and I am interested in this. I say to people you must pray, always pray. You must have at least one canonical prayer every day and then you must talk to God; but you must always pray like St. Paul said in an epistle, "pray without ceasing"—this is "prayer of the heart". The Eastern Church knows this practice very well—the Jesus Prayer—*japa-yoga* in Hinduism. This is the second thing.
>
> The third thing is intrinsic morality: beauty of the soul; nobility; humility, which means objectivity toward oneself; charity, which is objectivity towards the neighbor; domination of oneself; generosity—this is beauty of the soul, this is intrinsic morality.
>
> The fourth dimension is beauty: beauty of forms, of surroundings, of dress, of comportment.

"Metaphysical truth, a life of prayer, moral conformity, interiorizing beauty: this is the essential, and this is our message."[7] Together, these principles can be said to make up a "fabric of elementary certainties that encompasses and resolves every human uncertainty and in this way reduces the whole problem of earthly existence to a geometry at once simple and primordial".[8] Schuon's article "*Sophia Perennis*", which appears as an Appendix to this biography, likewise contains a summary of these essential human dimensions. In this formulation the focus is placed on the first three of the elements identified previously, the fourth, beauty of forms and of surroundings, being implicit as a support for the others:[9]

> There is something that man must know or think; something that he must will or do; and something that he must love or be. He must know that God is necessary, self-sufficient Being, that He is That which cannot not be; and he must know that the world is only the possible, namely that which may either be or not be; all other discriminations

> and value judgments are derived from this metaphysical *distinguo*. Furthermore, man must will whatever directly or indirectly leads him to God, and thus abstain from whatever removes him from God; the main content of this willing is prayer, the response to God, and therein is included all spiritual activity, including metaphysical reflection. And then, as already mentioned, man must love whatever corresponds to God; he must love the Good, and since the Good necessarily transcends his own selfhood, he must make an effort to overcome this narrow and weak selfhood. One must love the Good in itself more than one's ego, and this self-knowledge and selfless love constitute the whole nobility of the soul.[10]

All this finds expression in the most essential way in one of Schuon's English poems, appropriately titled "Synthesis":

> Truth, Way, and Virtue: threefold is the Path
> From Earth to Heaven. First, discriminate
> Between Reality and Dream; then pray:
> Invoke the Name and reach the Godhead's Gate.
>
> Then Virtue: for we must conform our selves
> To That which we believe, adapt our soul
> To That which saves. Our very breath should be
> One with our Faith and with our highest Goal.[11]

Or again, with the inclusion of integral aesthetics or "the sense of forms" as the fourth dimension:

> There are principles that I constantly repeat,
> Because they belong to the sage who is without fault.
> First comes the doctrine concerning God;
> Then the invocation of the Highest Name,
> Which purifies and liberates the heart;
> Then comes the beauty of all virtue, nobility of soul;
> And finally the sense of forms, inward and outward.
> These are the four principles —
> God grant that they be never violated.[12]

Finally, we must never forget that a formal condition of any authentic spirituality is "a valid attachment to an intrinsically orthodox religion"; for "man is a form, and he cannot attain to the non-formal except in a form; otherwise the religions would not exist."[13] Schuon's message of Truth, Prayer, Virtue, and Beauty—far from replacing religion—can only be realized *within* the framework of a given religious tradition.[14] "The general conditions of our earthly world are such that these . . . elements, to be able to bear their fruits and to be sheltered from all deviation, need a framework of traditional orthodoxy, hence a religion; without this, wisdom would disappear; the path would enjoy no guarantee of authenticity."[15] According to Catherine Schuon, his wife, "[Schuon's] function in the world is really to bring people back to practice their religion . . . to bring them back to a path that leads to God. . . . [M]any people have gone back and practiced their religion very seriously after having read his books. He wants to help us to go back to where we belong."[16]

Each of the aspects of Schuon's message is woven into the very fabric of his being—the man being inseparable from his message. A review of his biography bears witness to his crystalline discernment of the truth, his ceaseless practice of prayer, and his impeccable nobility of soul. In addition, his life testifies to the significance given to the beauty of surrounding forms, and to the importance placed on attachment to an orthodox religious tradition. There is, in short, undoubtedly a "connection between the work and the personality" of Frithjof Schuon, given that "the depth . . . and essentiality of Schuon's doctrinal message was a mirror image of his personal life as a spiritual master and spokesman of the *Religio Perennis*. . .".[17] It is proper, therefore, before turning to his biography, to present the essential elements of his message in further detail.

Metaphysical Truth

Schuon's point of departure is pure metaphysics such as it has been expressed, for example, by Plato in the West and by Shankara in the East.[18] It should be clearly stated, however, that Schuon's exposition of metaphysical truth cannot be reduced to the status of a historical interpretation of any particular figure or school. As he affirms in the Preface to one of his books, "it will be noted that we have in view, not traditional information pure and simple so much as intrinsic doctrinal explanations; that is to say the expression of truth of which the traditional dialects are the vestitures; hence it is not as a historian of ideas, but as a spokesman of the *philosophia perennis* that we expound diverse formulations of the truth that is everywhere and always the same."[19]

"The key to the eternal *sophia*", Schuon declares, "is pure intellection or in other words metaphysical discernment."[20] The nature of this discernment is aptly proclaimed by the Vedantic maxim ascribed to Shankara, "God is real, the world is appearance; the soul is not other than God" (*Brahma satyam, jagan mithyā; jīvo brahmaiva nāparah*).[21] "*Brahma satyam*—I cannot say anything better."[22] He expands on what is implied in the discernment of metaphysical truth:

> When speaking of discernment, we mean above all that between the Real and the illusory, *Ātmā* and *Māyā*, the Absolute[23] and the relative, necessary Being and possible Being; a distinction that implies on the one

hand the prefiguration of the relative in the Absolute, and on the other the projection of the Absolute into the relative, hence all the degrees and modes of universal Reality. The "prefiguration" of the relative in the Absolute is the Creator-Being with all the potentialities contained therein; the "projection" of the Absolute into the relative is the "Spirit of God", the celestial world, the universal Intellect, the *Avatāra*, Revelation; but also, the theomorphic microcosm, the human Intellect, the "naturally supernatural" prodigy of intellection; the organ of the *Sophia Perennis*, precisely.[24]

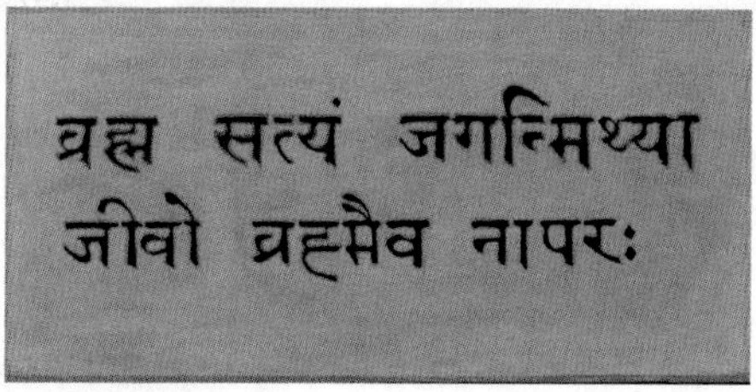

Sanskrit calligraphy in the Schuons' home

"The entire message of the *Upanishads*, of the *Brahma-Sūtras* of Bādarāyana, and finally of Shankara, may be condensed into the following words: '*Brahman* alone is real; the world is illusion, *Māyā*; the soul is not other than *Brahman*.'" (*To Have a Center*, "David, Shankara, Hōnen", 135)

These formulations are extended even further in a typically magisterial passage which covers nearly the entire arena of metaphysics and cosmology:

> The fundamental content of the Truth is the Unconditioned, the Metaphysical Absolute; the Ultimate One, which is also the Absolutely Good, the Platonic *Agathón*. But it lies in the nature of the Absolute to be Infinity and All-Possibility, and in this sense St. Augustine said that it is in the nature of the Good to communicate itself; if there is a sun, then there is also radiation; and therein lies the necessity of the cosmos which proclaims God.
>
> However, to say radiation is also to say separation from the source of light. Since God is the absolute and infinite Good, whatever is not God—that is to say, the world as such—cannot be absolutely good: the non-divinity of the cosmos brings with it, in its limitations, the phenomenon of evil or wickedness which, because it is a contrast, emphasizes all the more the nature of the Good. "The more he blasphemes", as Eckhart said, "the more he praises God."

> The essential here is discrimination between *Ātmā* and *Māyā*, between Reality seen as "Self", and relativity seen as "cosmic play": since the Absolute is infinite—failing which it would not be the Absolute—it must give rise to *Māyā*, a "lesser reality" and in a sense an "illusion". *Ātmā* is the Principle—the Primordial Principle, one might say—and *Māyā* is manifestation or effect; strictly speaking *Māyā* is in a sense also *Ātmā*, since in the last analysis there is only *Ātmā*; both poles therefore must impinge on one another and must be bound up with one another, in the sense that, in *Ātmā*, *Māyā* is in a way prefigured, whereas, contrariwise, *Māyā* in its own fashion represents or reflects *Ātmā*. In *Ātmā*, *Māyā* is Being, the Creator of the world, the Personal God, who reveals Himself to the world in all His possibilities of Manifestation; in *Māyā*, *Ātmā* is any reflection of the Divine, such as the *Avatāra*, the Holy Scriptures, the God-transmitting symbol.
>
> In the domain of *Māyā* or relativity, there is not only "space", there is also "time", to speak comparatively or metaphorically: there are not only simultaneity and gradation, but also change and succession; there are not only worlds, but also "ages" or "cycles". All this belongs to the "play" of *Māyā*, to the well-nigh "magical" unfolding of the possibilities hidden in the Primordial One.[25]

Schuon's poems often speak to the reader in a language at once simple and profound. Several of them relate to the fundamental discernment between Reality and illusion, including the following, which expresses "in few words" the doctrine of the *advaita* (or non-dualist) school of *Vedānta* associated with the great Shankara:

> *Advaita*
> *Māyā* is radiation from *Ātmā*,
> For *Ātmā* radiates: It is the Highest Light.
> In *Māyā* lie the cycles of the worlds —
> But they are illusions, they touch not *Ātmā*.
>
> Worlds and cycles arise and vanish —
> Before *Ātmā*'s Reality nothing endures.
> What you experience of places, times, and things
> Is but a dream. This is the doctrine in few words.
>
> However, O man: from *Ātmā* fell a spark
> Mysteriously into the stream of thy heart.
> Thy deepest depth is not blinded by *Māyā* —
> It is none other than *Ātmā* —
> *Shānti Om.*[26]

Life of Prayer

"We must know that God is Real—*Brahma Satyam*", Schuon observed in a 1991 interview, "but it is not enough to think it, we must assimilate it." While a sufficient degree of doctrinal knowledge is indispensable, "theoretical knowledge, even if perfect and hence unshakable, always requires a volitive element, which contributes to the process of assimilation or integration, for we must 'become what we are'".[27] This leads to the second element of Schuon's essential message, operative concentration or prayer.

Schuon provides this summary of prayer, encompassing all its possible modalities: "Prayer—in the widest sense—triumphs over the four accidents of our existence: the world, life, the body, the soul; we might also say: space, time, matter, desire. It is situated in existence like a shelter, like an islet. In it alone we are perfectly ourselves, because it puts us into the presence of God. It is like a miraculous diamond, which nothing can tarnish and nothing can resist."[28] He identifies three kinds of prayer: personal prayer, canonical prayer, and prayer of the heart.[29]

"The most elementary mode of orison—of contact between man and God—is no doubt prayer in the most ordinary sense of the word, for it is the direct expression of the individual, of his desires and fears, his hopes and gratitude."[30] This is what Schuon calls free or personal prayer—the prayer of David in his Psalms:

> The aim of this prayer is not only to obtain particular favors, but also the purification of the soul: it loosens psychological knots or, in other words, dissolves subconscious coagulations and drains away many secret poisons; it externalizes before God the difficulties, failures, and crispations of the soul, which presupposes that the soul be humble and genuine, and this externalization—carried out in the face of the Absolute—has the virtue of reestablishing equilibrium and restoring peace, in a word, of opening us to grace.[31]

Despite the personal character of this prayer, and the fact that it can be free and spontaneous in the manner of its expression, it is important to realize that this "does not imply that it is free from rules, for the human soul—as the Psalms admirably show—is always the same in its miseries and joys, and therefore in its duties towards God; it is not enough for a man to formulate his petition, he must express also his gratitude, resignation, regret, resolution, and praise."[32]

These teachings are summarized in Schuon's poem "Petition":

> Praise of God and thanks to God; and then another
> Prayer arises from our soul: petition.

Ask not only for thyself, but for thy neighbor too;
One asks not only for our daily bread.
And do not think that thy plea is not needed —
It too is remembrance of the Highest.

And ask for the ultimate Good: for God.[33]

The second form of prayer that Schuon indentifies is canonical prayer, such as the Lord's Prayer in Christianity and the *Fātihah* in Islam. It is a "discourse addressed to God", whose particular form is fixed by revelation or by traditional authority. Its purpose "is to tirelessly recall truths which man needs if he is not to become lost".[34] While the character of personal prayer is individual, the character of canonical prayer is universal "due to the fact that God is its author and that the reciting subject is not a particular individual, but man as such, the human species". Schuon further makes the point that "Canonical prayer shows its universality and timeless value by being expressed very often in the first person plural and also by its preference for using a sacred or liturgical and therefore symbolically universal language, so that it is impossible for whoever recites it not to pray for all and in all."[35] Canonical prayer, in short, "is not only a human discourse; it is also divine, which means that besides its literal value it has a sacramental import. It is on our level, yet at the same time beyond us."[36]

Man needs canonical prayer —
God wills that we think of Him in a rhythm;
Certainly, we can go freely to the Most High —
Nevertheless, God wills to guide the steps of the people.

For if the individual wishes to enjoy the Lord,
There must be a framework for all:
The Lord's Prayer and the *Fātiha* —
And long before these, the *Shemā*.

If there were not divine bread from which to live —
The possibility of wine would not exist.[37]

The third form of prayer is "prayer of the heart", that is to say the invocation of a sacred formula or Name of God.[38] "We have distinguished canonical prayer from individual prayer by saying that in the latter it is a given individual who is the subject, while in the former the subject is man as such; now there is an orison wherein God Himself is in a sense the Subject, and that is the pronouncing of a revealed divine Name."[39] In Christianity the doctrine and method of invocatory prayer is best preserved in the Eastern Church in the form of the "Jesus Prayer", but is to be found in the Western Church as well, for example, within the Rosary.[40] This practice is further to be found in Hinduism (as *nāma-japa* or *japa-yoga*), in Islam (as *dhikr Allāh*), in Buddhism (as the *Mani mantra* in Tibetan Buddhism and the *nembutsu* in Pure Land Buddhism), [41] and in other traditions as well.[42] "The foundation of this mystery is, on the one hand, that 'God and His Name are one' (Ramakrishna) and, on the other hand, that God Himself pronounces His Name in Himself, hence in eternity and outside all creation, so that His unique and uncreate word is the prototype of ejaculatory prayer and even, in a less direct sense, of all orison."

A passage from one of his earliest published books succinctly articulates the meaning of invocatory prayer:

> [W]e must emphasize the fundamental and truly universal significance of the invocation of the Divine Name. This Name, in the Christian form—as in the Buddhist form and in certain initiatory branches of the Hindu tradition—is a name of the manifested Word, in this case the Name of "Jesus", which, like every revealed Divine Name when ritually pronounced, is mysteriously identified with the Divinity. It is in the Divine Name that there takes place the mysterious meeting of the created and the Uncreate, the contingent and the Absolute, the finite and the Infinite. The Divine Name is thus a manifestation of the Supreme Principle, or to speak still more plainly, it is the Supreme Principle manifesting Itself; it is not therefore in the first place a manifestation, but the Principle itself. [43]

And further:

> The sufficient reason for the invocation of the Name is the remembering of God; and this, in the final analysis, is not other than consciousness of the Absolute. The Name actualizes this consciousness and, in the end, perpetuates it in the soul and fixes it in the heart, so that it penetrates the whole being and at the same time transmutes and absorbs it. Consciousness of the Absolute is the prerogative of human intelligence, and also its aim.[44]

Schuon likewise sings of the glory of the divine Name in numerous poems, including this from his English-language collection, *Road to the Heart*:

The Name

Thy Name is wine and honey, melody
That shapes our sacred way and destiny.
Who is the Speaker and who is the Word?
Where is the song Eternity has heard?

The liberating Word comes from the sky
Of Grace and Mercy; and we wonder why

Such gift can be; the truth is not so far:
Thy Name is That which is, and what we are.[45]

Moral Conformity

Following upon metaphysical comprehension (or "truth") and methodical concentration (or "prayer"), the third essential dimension of Schuon's message is moral conformation (or "virtue").[46] These three elements are inseparably related, for "Virtue is the touchstone of our sincerity; without it, Truth does not belong to us and the Way eludes us. The Truth is what we must know; the Way is what we must do; Virtue is what we must love, become, and be."[47]

All too often the virtues are seen as so many qualities for us to acquire and possess, but according to Schuon "Virtue is less the effort of acquiring qualities than the absence of faults; for, when evil is dissolved from within and fought from without, virtue shines forth; from the beginning it has slept within man, given that it stems from his deiformity."[48] It is also clear that we must avoid any false personal identification with virtue.

> Every man loves to live in light and in fresh air; no one loves to be locked up in a dark, airless tower. It is thus that one ought to love the virtues; and it is thus that one ought to hate the vices. No man who enjoys light or air would dream of saying: "I am the sun", or "I am the sky"; one loves the atmosphere of light and air, and that is why one enters into it. It is thus that one must enter into the virtues: because they are self-evident by their nature and because one loves their ambience.[49]

While there are several possible ways to categorize the myriad virtues, Schuon often singles out three virtues which he considers to be of fundamental importance: humility, charity, and veracity, or "effacement of ego, gift of self, realization of truth".[50] In the following extended passage, he discusses first the meaning of humility and charity, and then veracity:

> Virtue consists essentially in humility and charity; these are the fundamental qualities from which all others derive, to which they all relate, and without which no sanctity is possible. Humility presents itself under two aspects: awareness of one's metaphysical nothingness in the face of the Absolute and awareness of one's personal imperfection; this second humility implies not only a relentless instinct for detecting one's own limitations and weaknesses, but also a simultaneous capacity to discern the positive qualities in one's neighbor, for a virtue which is blind to virtues in others destroys itself thereby. Consciousness of one's individual insufficiency springs from the necessarily fragmentary character of the ego; in other words, to say "ego" is to say partial imperfection in regard to other individuals. Humility is moreover owed to all creatures, since all

of them manifest qualities and glorify God after their manner; the first relation goes from God to the thing, and the second from the thing to God; man has a right to the things of creation only on condition that he respect them, that is to say on condition that he discern in each one both its divine property and its spiritual language; man never has a right to destroy simply for the pleasure of destroying. Among virtue the position of humility is a special one—like that of the apex in a triangle—because it conforms to God, not by "participation" but by "opposition", in the sense that the attitude of humility, poverty, or self-effacement, is analogically opposed to the divine Majesty; this opposition is however a relative one, since it rejoins the direct analogy through its intrinsic perfection which is, *mutatis mutandis*, the simplicity of the Essence. Humility, therefore, is distinguishable from the other virtues by the fact that it marks a relatively indirect participation in the divine Prototype, or in other words by the fact that it is, depending on the point of view, either "more" or "less" than the other fundamental virtues.

As for charity, it consists in abolishing the egocentric distinction between "me" and the "other": it is seeing the "I" in the "other" and the "other" in the "I". Humility and charity are the two dimensions of self-effacement: they are, to use a Christian symbolism, like the vertical and horizontal branches of the Cross. The one can always be reduced to the other: humility is always to be found in charity, and conversely. To these two virtues must be added the virtue of veracity: it is love of truth, objectivity, impartiality; it is a virtue that situates intelligence in the framework of the will—to the extent that the nature of things allows of this or demands it—and its function consists in keeping away every passional element from the intelligence. Discernment must remain independent of love or hate: it must see things as they are, firstly according to universal Truth which assigns to each thing its degree in the hierarchy of values, and secondly according to the truth proper to things in their immediate nature; when the alternative presents itself, preference must be given to essential aspects, for which accidental aspects must not be substituted, and so forth. This serenity and this precision exclude neither love nor holy indignation, because these arise parallel to intellection and not within it: holy indignation, far from being opposed to truth, derives from truth as from its enabling cause. Truthfulness corrects any arbitrariness that might result from a humility or charity regarded in too subjective a way: it prevents humility from becoming an end in itself and thus sinning against intelligence and the nature of things; it likewise controls charity and determines its various modes. One has to be humble because the ego tends to think itself more than it is; and one has to be truthful because the ego tends to prefer its own tastes and habits to the truth.[51]

Finally, brief mention should be made of the way in which Schuon elucidates the complementary relationship between virtue and morality:

[Moral laws] are styles of action conforming to particular spiritual perspectives and to particular material and mental conditions, while

> the virtues on the contrary represent intrinsic beauties fitted into these styles and finding through them their realization. Every virtue and every morality is a mode of equilibrium. . . . Morality is a way of acting, whereas virtue is a way of being—a way of being wholly oneself, beyond the ego, or of being simply That which is. . . . This could also be expressed as follows: the various moralities are at the same time frameworks for the virtues and their application to collectivities. . . . Moralities are diverse, but virtue as it has been here defined, is everywhere the same, because man is everywhere man.[52]

And again in this poem, entitled "Virtue":

> Morality can be of different kinds:
> With devout feelings it can soar to Heaven,
> Shaped by the pious customs of society.
> It can also lie in the nature of things,
> In being, not feeling — in discerning
> The deep roots of good and evil,
> And not merely in naming them according to whim.
> Prescriptions are of use; but better still is virtue
> Which rises from mankind's primordial youth.
>
> The good as such comes from the beauty of God.[53]

Interiorizing Beauty

Schuon recalls, in the Platonic sense, the deeper dimensions inherent in the beauty of natural and artistic forms. "The message of beauty is both intellectual and moral: intellectual because it communicates to us, in the world of accidentality, aspects of [Divine] Substance, without for all that having to address itself to abstract thought, and moral because it reminds us what we must love and, consequently, be."[54] The moral message of beauty—its relationship to virtue—becomes clear once one understands that "Virtue is a presence of the divine Being in the will and in sentiment just as beauty is the presence of the Divine in form",[55] while the intellectual message of beauty—its relationship to truth—becomes clear through an understanding of the saying ascribed to Plato, "Beauty is the splendor of the True", to which Schuon added a commentary in saying that "Truth is the essence of the beautiful".[56] Truth, virtue, and beauty, "Only these three make life worth living."[57]

> *Truth*
> "In Beauty is the splendor of the True":
> If Truth we know, we will know Beauty too.
> And if in Beauty we can see the Good,
> Our spirit understands all that it should.

Words in our earthly language may be weak,
Yet Truth is strong; with Heaven's Heart we speak
To show a path to living's inmost duty.

"Allah is beautiful and He loves Beauty":
There is a Splendor we can hear and see;
A mirror of the True we ought to be.[58]

Schuon insists that beauty and art are natural and necessary dimensions of our human existence, so much so that not to feel the need for beauty is an infirmity. "[N]o religion is situated outside Beauty, every religion expresses itself through it; every traditional world is necessarily a world of Beauty, and this proves Beauty's interiorizing virtue."[59] One of the most insidious aspects of the modern world is precisely this lack of a sense of beauty and even a despising of it, and then replacing it with counterfeits of beauty—art for art's sake. In a 1992 film interview Schuon was asked, "What is the role of art in the spiritual life?" His response takes the understanding of art, and therefore of beauty, to its most profound level:

> [M]an needs beauty and he needs also symbolism. It is not enough to think about metaphysics, one wants also to see and to hear metaphysics in visible forms and this is symbolism. Symbolism coincides with beauty. If a thing exists it must be beautiful. So when God created man He was obliged, metaphysically speaking, to create him beautiful, because beauty is the norm. This is the metaphysical transparency of phenomena. One must look beyond the form at the essence. If I see something beautiful, a landscape, or a beautiful piece of music, or a human being, I see the *Rahmah*, I see *Ānanda*, I see the Principle.

To understand the meaning of beauty and symbolism is also to understand the importance of ambience, understood in its broadest sense:

> As for the environment which surrounds us and with which we surround ourselves, it is important because form is important; for we live among forms and we are a form, a form "made in the image of God". To affirm that "the spirit alone counts" is a hypocritical and unrealistic "angelism"—as if matter did not exist and as if an existing and ubiquitous thing could have no spiritual significance whatever. This is a typically profane error and thus as far removed as possible from esoterism, which insists not only on the symbolism of things—in art or handicrafts as well as in nature—but also on their aesthetic, moral, and quasi-musical message. The environment is an indirect element of intelligence and beauty in the spiritual life.[60]

At the same time, Schuon was well aware of the double-edged nature of beauty. The perception of beauty affects individuals differently and depends upon a person's nobility of soul, his receptivity, and his degree of spirituality.

> [E]very beauty is both a closed door and an open door, or in other words, an obstacle or a vehicle: either beauty separates us from God because it is entirely identified in our mind with its earthly support which then assumes the role of idol, or beauty brings us close to God because we perceive in it the vibrations of Beatitude and Infinity which emanate from Divine Beauty. . . . Virtue cut off from God becomes pride, as beauty cut off from God becomes idol; and virtue attached to God becomes sanctity, as beauty attached to God becomes sacrament.[61]

It follows that to benefit from an earthly beauty we must fulfill a condition: "We must live the experience of beauty so as to draw from it a lasting, not ephemeral, element, hence realizing in oneself an opening towards the immutable Beauty, rather than plunging oneself into the current of things; it is a question of viewing the world, and living in it, in a manner that is sacred and not profane; or sacralizing and not profanating."[62]

There is a spiritual way that accentuates the element of sacrifice as a support for a life of prayer. While never denying the validity of this penitential perspective—"the narrow way of renunciation"[63]—Schuon points out that,

> . . . In our age of ugliness we more than ever
> Need the beautiful in order to live
> As men should live.
> In order to lift the soul
> From the din of the world, up to Heaven.[64]

Schuon's own path was one "of Truth and Beauty"[65]—"the noble path of equilibrium"[66]—in which it is recognized that:

> Beauty would have no sense in the eyes of God,
> If it did not have a meaning for our spirit —
> If it did not summon to interiorization,
> To nobility, and to the abode of the Most High.
>
> Many believe they must flee from seduction;
> I am far from blaming this misunderstanding,
> Because people are what they are able to be;
> Fortunate are those who through beauty are ennobled.[67]

— ·:· —

Mention must also be made of Schuon's close association with the phrase he coined, "the transcendent unity of religions"—the metaphysical thesis that there exists a single Unity underlying the diverse religions. In the Preface to his book, *The Transcendent Unity of Religions*,[68] Schuon writes: "If the expression 'transcendent unity' is used, it means that the unity of the religious forms must be realized in a purely inward and spiritual way and without prejudice to any particular form. The antagonisms between these forms no more affect the one universal truth than the antagonisms between opposing colors affect the transmission of the uncolored light."[69]

The starting point of this concept is the acknowledgment that there are diverse religions which apparently exclude each other.[70] Some think this means that one religion is true and that all the others are false; others conclude that all are false. "It is as though certain persons, when faced with the discovery of other solar systems, continued to maintain the view that there is only one sun, our own, whereas others, perceiving that our sun is not the only one, denied that it was a sun and concluded that there was no such thing, since none was unique."[71] Schuon's writings demonstrate a third possibility—that all religions are right, not in their dogmatic exclusivism, but in their unanimous inner meaning.

Many modern writers who propound a belief in a universal Truth conclude that one can ignore or strip away the outward differences in the religions, in order to focus solely on their inner similarities.[72] Schuon rejects this notion and instead demonstrates that the outward distinctness in the forms is necessary and providential. He writes in a letter of the Divine Will underlying the divergences between religions:

> I must call your attention to an important aspect of universality or unity: the *divergence between religions* is not only due to the incomprehension of men; it is also in the Revelations, hence in the divine Will, and this is why there is a *difference between exoterism and esoterism*; the diverse dogmas contradict one another, not only in the minds of theologians, but also—and *a priori*—in the sacred Scriptures; in giving these Scriptures, however, God at the same time gives the keys for understanding their underlying unity. If all men were metaphysicians and contemplatives, a single Revelation might be enough; but since this is not how things are, the Absolute must reveal itself in different ways, and the metaphysical viewpoints from which these Revelations are derived—according to different logical needs and different spiritual temperaments—cannot but contradict one another on the plane of forms, somewhat as geometrical figures contradict each other as long as one has not grasped their spatial and symbolic homogeneity.[73]

The exoteric, or outward, dimension of each religious form has its own unique aspects that correspond to the human collectivity to which it is addressed. The need for the diversity of religious forms corresponds to the diversity of human types, as one of Schuon's commentators has explained:

> He [Schuon] perceives humankind neither as a monolithic psychic entity nor as an amorphous agglomerate, but as being long since divided into several distinct branches, each with its own peculiar traits which determine its receptivity to truth and shape its apprehensions of reality. Needless to say there is no question here of any kind of racialism or ethnocentrism which attributes a superiority or inferiority to this or that ethnic collectivity. Nor, however, is there any sentimental prejudice in favor of the idea that the world's peoples are only "superficially" and "accidentally" different: "We observe on earth the existence of diverse races, whose differences are 'valid' since there are no 'false' as opposed to 'true' races." Each branch of humanity exhibits a psychic and spiritual homogeneity which may transcend barriers of geography and biology. . . .
>
> To the diverse human collectivities are addressed Revelations which are determined in their formal aspects by the needs at hand. Thus, "What determines the differences among forms of Truth is the difference among human receptacles. For thousands of years already humanity has been divided into several fundamentally different branches constituting as many complete humanities, more or less closed in on themselves; the existence of spiritual receptacles so different and so original demands a differentiated refraction of the one Truth."[74]

Schuon puts this consideration more succinctly in one of his poems:

> Why are there so many religions?
> Because God talks to men, not to angels.
> If there were only one religion in the world,
> Humanity, precisely, would not be human. . . .[75]

Schuon's writings show that every religion, in addition to its literal—exoteric—meaning, has an esoteric dimension which is essential, primordial, and universal. He describes the subtle relationship between esoterism and exoterism, or between a religion's essence and its form, as follows:

> The word "esoterism" suggests in the first place an idea of complementarity, of a "half" as it were: esoterism is the complement of exoterism, it is the "spirit" which completes the "letter". Where there is a truth of Revelation, hence of formal and theological truth, there must also be a truth of intellection, hence of non-formal and metaphysical truth; not legalistic or obligatory truth, but truth that stems from the nature of things, and which is also vocational since not every man grasps this nature.
>
> But in fact this second truth exists independently of the first; hence it is not, in its intrinsic reality, a complement or a half; it is so only extrinsically and as it were "accidentally". This means that the

> word "esoterism" designates not only the total truth inasmuch as it is "colored" by entering a system of partial truth, but also the total truth as such, which is colorless. This distinction is not a mere theoretical luxury; on the contrary, it implies extremely important consequences.
>
> Thus esoterism as such is metaphysics, to which is necessarily joined an appropriate method of realization. But the esoterism of a particular religion—of a particular exoterism precisely—tends to adapt itself to this religion and thereby enter into theological, psychological, and legalistic meanders foreign to its nature, while preserving in its secret center its authentic and plenary nature, but for which it would not be what it is.[76]

Schuon's philosophy thus provides a metaphysical framework that allows one to appreciate "the profound and eternal solidarity of all spiritual forms",[77] while respecting and maintaining the integrity of the outward forms themselves—forms which, in their turn, have always drawn their nourishment from the underlying esoteric teachings.

— ·:· —

It is important to have an outline of Schuon's point of view on modernity and the contemporary human condition, which is primarily based upon the traditional understanding of cosmic cycles. Hinduism offers a particularly well formulated expression of this universal doctrine, which is "diverse, but nonetheless homogeneous with regard to the essential":[78]

> [T]he world, or the manifested universe, the creation . . . is like the "breathing" of the Divinity; it is essentially subject to phases, to "divine lives", as the Hindus would say. There is firstly the *para*, which is the "life" of the demiurge itself and which lasts one hundred "years of Brahmā"; the "days of Brahmā"—the *kalpas*—each represent the duration of a world, hence a "historical creation", the "night of Brahmā" being the "divine void" between two creations *ex nihilo*. Each *kalpa* comprises one thousand *mahā-yugas*, each of which is divided into four ages or *yugas*, namely: the *Krita-*, the *Tretā-*, the *Dvāpara-*, and the *Kali-yuga*; these are, analogically speaking, the golden age, the silver age, the bronze age and the iron age. Doubtless, there are variations in the different cosmological symbolisms of India, but the fundamental pattern remains identical. . . .[79]

According to Schuon, we must not lose sight of the fact that "we are in the 'iron age', the 'dark age', the *Kali-yuga*, or even at the end—particularly disgraced—of that age foreseen by all the traditional doctrines".[80] He draws our attention in this regard to the remarkable concordance between the views of orthodox Hindus and the Plains Indians of North America:

> A most striking feature of the North American branch of the Primordial *Sanātana Dharma* is the doctrine of the four *yugas*: the sacred animal of the Plains Indians, the buffalo, symbolizes the *mahā-yuga*, each of its legs representing a *yuga*. At the beginning of this *mahā-yuga* a buffalo was placed by the Great Spirit at the West in order to hold back the waters which menace the earth; every year this bison loses a hair, and in every *yuga* it loses a foot. When it will have lost all its hair and its feet, the waters will overwhelm the earth and the *mahā-yuga* will be finished. The analogy with the bull of Dharma in Hinduism is very remarkable; at every *yuga*, this bull withdraws a foot, and spirituality loses its strength; and now we are near the end of the *kali-yuga*. Like the orthodox Hindus, the traditional Red Indians have this conviction, which is obviously true in spite of all the mundane optimism of the modern world.[81]

This traditional view, however, has been turned on its head by today's prevailing ideology, which views the course of human history as an evolutionary progression from a benighted past to an enlightened present.[82] As a society we have concluded, based largely upon our increased quantitative understanding of the material world, that we must be "wiser or better or both than our predecessors".[83] This anti-traditional belief focuses primarily—one could even say solely—on an increase in material pleasures, not on a reforming of the human soul.[84]

> [I]n the name of humanitarian egalitarianism, vocations are crushed and geniuses wasted, by schools in particular and by official worldliness in general; every spiritual element is banished from professional and public life. . . . On the other hand, by a kind of compensation, professional life more and more assumes a "religious" air in the sense that it claims the whole of man, his soul as well as his time, as though the sufficient reason for the human condition were some economic enterprise and not immortality.[85]

In response to such a view, Schuon writes:

> The world is miserable because men live beneath themselves; the error of modern man is that he wants to reform the world without having either the will or the power to reform man, and this flagrant contradiction, this attempt to make a better world on the basis of a worsened humanity, can only end in the very abolition of what is human, and consequently in the abolition of happiness too. Reforming man means binding him again to Heaven, re-establishing the broken link; it means tearing him away from the reign of the passions, from the cult of matter, quantity, and cunning, and reintegrating him into the world of the spirit and serenity, we would even say: into the world of sufficient reason.[86]

This is not to say that there is in the current age no connection with the Golden Age of Truth and Goodness. One of Schuon's poems, entitled "Points of Rest", provides a concise picture:

> The *Kali-yuga* is not merely a fall
> Downward; it stands still at certain points:
> Cosmic values can appear everywhere,
> If the Most High will.
>
> Truth and the power of Good are at work;
> The *Krita-yuga* shimmers through the night.[87]

Schuon's writings acknowledge the paradox that we live in the most irreligious era in history, while at the same time esoteric truths and spiritual practices that were previously safeguarded within the formerly "closed world" of each religion are now everywhere on public display and in many cases detached from living traditions:

> There is indeed something abnormal in this, but it lies, not in the fact of the exposition of these truths, but in the general conditions of our age, which marks the end of a great cyclic period of terrestrial humanity—the end of a *mahā-yuga* according to Hindu cosmology—and so must recapitulate or manifest again in one way or another everything that is included in the cycle, in conformity with the adage "extremes meet"; thus things that are in themselves abnormal may become necessary by reason of the conditions just referred to. . . . [I]t must be admitted that the spiritual confusion of our times has reached such a pitch that the harm that might in principle befall certain people from contact with the truths in question is compensated by the advantages that others will derive from the self-same truths.[88]

Schuon recognized the grave difficulty confronting the revealed religions, each of which is under assault from various modernistic forces: "Exoterism is a precarious thing by reason of its limits or its exclusions; there arrives a moment in history when all kinds of experiences oblige it to modify its claims to exclusiveness, and it is then driven to a choice: escape from these limitations by the upward path in esoterism, or by the downward path, in a worldly and suicidal liberalism."[89] He also recognized that one response to the pressures of modernity is religious fundamentalism with its inevitable result that "the outward and readily exaggerated incompatibility of the different religions greatly discredits, in the minds of most of our contemporaries, all religion".[90] By providing the metaphysical explanation for the differences in the outward forms of religions, Schuon has restored an understanding of their necessity, one could even say of their "divine right", to existence.

By the same token, the dissolution of the natural barriers that formerly enclosed religious worlds,[91] combined with the proliferation of profane ideologies, has consequences for the faithful and for spiritual seekers who seek out sufficient answers to the flood of doubts and questions raised by these unusual conditions. Schuon's writings respond to this need in a comprehensive manner; he recognized that those who have the ability to speak with authority about esoteric truths are obliged to do so. "One of the paradoxes of our times is that esoterism, discreet by the force of things, finds itself obliged to assert itself publicly for the simple reason that there is no other remedy for the confusions of our time. For, as the Kabbalists say, 'It is better to divulge Wisdom than to forget it.'"[92] His mission was to unveil esoteric truths in order to provide the fundamental principles that can resuscitate each individual's faith in response to Truth: "Only esoterism can . . . restore the lost truth by referring to the total truth. . . . Just as rationalism can remove faith, so esoterism can restore it."[93]

These remarks provide an outline of certain key elements in Schuon's philosophy. Further discussion of the sage's thought is interwoven into the discussion of the events of his life, while the three appendices to this work present his essential message in his own words. Of course, to grasp the entire scope of his message, nothing can replace the in-depth study of his body of published writings. For those looking for an introduction to this corpus, Professor Harry Oldmeadow has written a valuable guide, *Frithjof Schuon and the Perennial Philosophy*, which complements the present work.[94] With this background, let us now turn to survey the life of Frithjof Schuon, a messenger of that "one and universal wisdom"[95] called the perennial philosophy.

1. Childhood

From my father came a mystical disposition,
That lived on music, romanticism, and beauty;
And from my mother an energetic nature,
That vibrated for the Real and the True.
Directly from God came an element
That knows a Way to Spirit and to God.

Not without trials is the holy Path;
The wheel of destiny is in God's Hands.[1]

Of his forefathers, Frithjof Schuon has related that the "Schuon family is a branch of the widespread Walser Juon family from Graubünden [a region of Switzerland], which after the Reformation emigrated to Württemberg [a region of Germany], flourished for centuries in Heilbronn and is still to be found in Ulm. In Germany the Romansh name Juon was changed to Schuon."[2] His father, Paul Schuon, was born near the middle of the nineteenth century in the Swabian region of southern Germany. As a young man he moved to the region of Alsace, then a part of France, where he met and married Margarete Boehler, whose mother was of Alsatian ancestry and whose father was from the Rhineland.[3] Around the turn of the twentieth century the couple moved to Basle, Switzerland where Paul Schuon, an accomplished violinist,[4] began to teach at the Basle Conservatory of Music and to play with the Basle Symphony Orchestra.

The Schuons had two sons, both of whom were destined, in different ways, to devote their lives to prayer. Their first son, Erich, born on August 3, 1906, was to find his calling as a monk, entering a Cistercian Trappist monastery in his youth. Their second son, Frithjof, came into the world in Basle on June 18, 1907 amidst the thunder and lightning of a raging storm. The precise moment of his birth—five minutes before midnight—was marked by a simultaneous strike of lightning that stopped all the hospital's clocks.[5]

"At birth", Schuon recounts, "I received the name Frithjof and also Fred, that is Alfred". The name Frithjof, he notes, is of Nordic origin and was given in remembrance of a friendship Paul Schuon formed with a Norwegian ship's captain named Frithjof Thorsen.

My late father, who played the violin in Oslo,
Had a friend, called Frithjof Thorsen —
A captain on the stormy fjords,
Which promised me a stormy destiny;
For I received this name from the North —

And something of the northern urge for freedom
And its snow-covered paradise.[6]

Concerning the etymology and significance of his names, Schuon wrote that "Frithjof means 'Peace-Disturber', and Alfred means 'Noble Peace'. . . . For me, the significance of these names is that the Primordial Tradition came from the North. I was always called by the first-mentioned name only; its meaning for me is the disturbing of the evil, deceptive peace of this world, that is to say of God-forgetting worldliness. The 'noble peace' presupposes the battle against the worldly soul."[7]

The brothers were raised in an ambience of German romanticism,[8] a dream-world "nurtured by the Middle Ages, at once chivalrous, enchanted, and mystical."[9] "Almost every evening our parents read to us stories of knights or Red Indians, as well as fairy-tales and myths, and then once a year came an intimate, radiant Christmas celebration. . .". They received, in addition, a certain flavor of the Oriental world. "Both of my parents loved the Arabs in particular and the East in general; they also loved the North American Indians. My mother's father had told her with enthusiasm about the Emir 'Abd al-Qādir;[10] my father loved Arab tales and the Islamic world in general. In the year preceding my birth my parents had worked themselves into a kind of romantic infatuation with the Islamic world and India. . .". Throughout these childhood years the two brothers were profoundly happy, being steeped in the ideals of virtue and beauty.

Frithjof Schuon often spoke with deep fondness and appreciation of his father's interest in traditional cultures and his dignified and aristocratic manner. Paul Schuon was an occasional poet[11] and his mystical sensitivity left a deep impression on his son, particularly the reverential ambience of his father's special reading room, which was especially reserved for the sacred scriptures from the various religions of the world, including the *Veda*s, the Koran, and the Bible. Schuon describes his first encounter with Hinduism in this way: he took a book, the *Bhagavad Gītā* or "Song of the Exalted One", from his father's library, opened it, and read: "The Exalted One spake." The beauty of this one sentence "made upon me a powerful impression that was never to leave me; it was as if in these words I had recognized my deepest, truest being."[12]

The religion of the brothers' childhood was one of deep piety, though of the utmost simplicity in its outward manifestation. While both parents were raised as Catholics, neither was actively observant, and Paul Schuon had more or less distanced himself from the Catholic Church. "My father did not go to church, but he loved the Holy Virgin and taught us to love her; we were brought up as evangelical Christians [Lutherans], but not in hostility towards the Catholic Church." His parents taught young Frithjof two prayers that he recited daily: "I am little; my heart is pure; may none dwell therein save Jesus alone." (*Ich bin klein; mein Herz ist rein; darf niemand drin wohnen als Jesus allein.*); and "Dear God, make me pious, so that I may come to Thee in Heaven." (*Lieber Gott, mach mich fromm, dass ich zu Dir in den Himmel komm.*) "In my early childhood I had no other religion but [these prayers]; then Psalms and Bible stories were added to it. . . . There was also our grace before meals, inviting the Lord Jesus to be our guest; that was all. Only later did I learn the Our Father." Above his bed there also hung "an image representing Christ and his Heart: a Sacred Heart image of embossed metal."

In later childhood, outside the home, the brothers received Lutheran Catechism, Schuon's first intensive study of the Bible. The "simple and intense piety of this first teacher"[13] left a deep impression on Schuon, who recalled him in a poem called "The Teacher", written more than seventy years later:

> The teacher Heinrich Jenny was a guidepost for me
> In my childhood. He taught us Bible history
> With a believing spirit — told us
> About God and prophets, miracles and visions.
>
> Once he related how Abraham
> Saw men, in the golden glow of evening,
> Kneeling before the sun — and I thought:
> How wonderful — would that I could be a heathen!
>
> He used to pray with us, with fervor and simplicity.
> My heart was open — I have never forgotten him.[14]

During these years, he was immersed in Biblical principles and discovered what was to become a lifelong love of the Psalms, for, as he later wrote, "David shows us how to speak to God".[15] He wrote of the Lutheranism of his childhood: "Its priorities are simplicity, inwardness, and trust in God; nothing else touched me in my early childhood."[16] While walking alongside the Rhine "on the long way to school", Schuon added, "I talked to God, and I thought that everyone else did the same."[17] In addition to this study of Biblical principles was the exploration of wisdom and philosophy often outside the Biblical world. A journalist later asked Schuon about the books he read in his youth, to which he responded, "Plato, Emerson, Germans like Goethe and Schiller, and then the *Upanishads* and *Bhagavad Gītā*." The interviewer commented, "Those are strong works for a young person to read." Schuon responded, "It was very easy; when I was ten years old I read Plato."

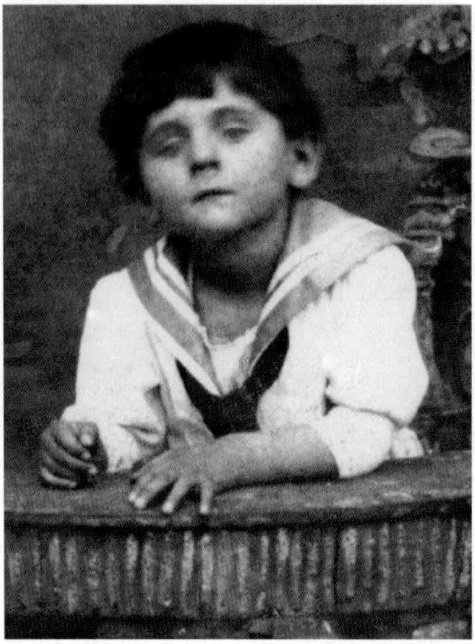 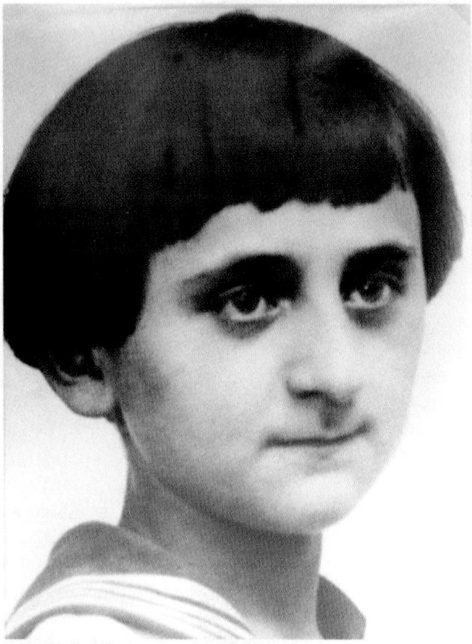

1912 1915

Frithjof Schuon

1916 1920

Left to right: Frithjof, Paul, Margarete, and Erich Schuon, 1917

Paul Schuon

One of his earliest friends, Johann Jakob Jenny, later recalled:

> It was at the age of eleven that I first met young Frithjof at the school. We often gathered in the cloister just behind the Cathedral. In this cloister we founded a society for the protection of the animals. He proposed to write to the Norwegian government to stop the killing of the whales. Often we would go to the forest in the neighborhood of Basle where we had our first philosophical speeches. I remember once he asked a question to our professor: "Are religion and art the same, or not?" The professor said "Oh, you are too young to solve this important question." This was at age eleven or twelve. Some years afterwards when I met this professor, he said to me, "I wonder what he will become, this boy Frithjof?"[18]

In a diary entry from 1923, Schuon quotes a passage he wrote years before, one of his earliest preserved written commentaries: "When I was a child, I wrote of the Divine All: 'Let one always bear in mind the image of a radiant sheaf of flames, spreading outwards and sending thousands of endless threads of light into the farthest reaches of the universe; and let one picture to oneself an eternal activity, like a golden wheel revolving around the Godhead, an ebb and flow, a harmony, a rising and sinking and blooming and rejoicing without end.'" It is, therefore, not surprising that even at an early age his friends came to him for spiritual advice:

> Already in my earliest youth,
> People came to me and emptied their hearts —
> They felt help. It is the same today;
> May the Lord illumine the house of my soul!
>
> As a child, I knew not how it happened with me;
> I heard myself speaking, and consolation was there.[19]

The young Schuon had an innate appreciation for all manifestations of the sacred. He said several times that "four things have always moved me most profoundly: the holy; the great; the beautiful; the childlike." One sees, for example, this love of sacred beauty when in 1919, at the age of twelve, he discovered three Buddhist statues in the Museum of Ethnology in Basle. "Our first encounter—intense and unforgettable—with Buddhism and the Far East took place in our childhood before a great Japanese Buddha of gilded wood, flanked by two images of Kwannon. Suddenly faced with this vision of majesty and mystery, we might well have paraphrased Caesar by exclaiming: *Veni, vidi, victus sum* [I came, I saw, I was conquered]."[20] Thus, from his childhood, Schuon loved museums. "I could spend hours visually assimilating the messages of the diverse traditional worlds. For me, visual assimilation came before conceptual assimilation; and here I have in mind not only sacred art, but handicrafts as well, including the most modest; for it can happen that an artifact may vehicle as much spirituality as does sacred art in the strict sense of the term."[21] These are early affirmations of an aesthetic intuition that showed itself prominently in later life.

Moments of profound illumination such as those in the museum in Basle occurred in a variety of situations and places during Schuon's childhood. As a youth walking in Basle's Zoological Gardens, he had a memorable first encounter with Islam in the form of a Senegalese marabout who had accompanied some members of his village for the purpose of demonstrating their culture. The venerable teacher drew a circle with many radii in the sand and explained, "God is the center, all paths lead to Him."[22] This metaphysical truth, so simply yet eloquently expressed, was to become a dominant principle of Schuon's thought, as indicated already by the title of his first major book, *The Transcendent Unity of Religions.* One of Schuon's later poems, entitled "Symbolism", recalls the meeting and sheds light on the innermost significance of the marabout's words:

A black holy man once said to me,
There are different paths that lead to Allah:
He is the Center, and the different faiths
Are like spokes on the Spirit's wheel.

And each human soul is a Way:
God wanted a thousand mirrors for the True.
O would that man, in his inmost heart,
Protect the deep meaning of the One —

Of the Self, whose countless rays shine forth —
Blessèd are they who reach "I am That I am"![23]

While still living in Basle, the twelve year old Schuon, influenced in part by his father's poetry, put pen to paper to transcribe his first poems. In his "Breath of the Night", one sees already the intensity of his spiritual longing:

Doth thy velvet arm bear me aloft to thee?
Doth thy mantle silently descend upon me?
Devoutly do I contemplate thy holy all;
I dissolve in the fragrance of thy soul.
To my heart dost thou softly open a door;
A quiet faith doth ripple gently down.[24]

This photograph (c. 1960) presents the three Buddhist statues Schuon saw in his youth in the Basle Museum. "The Museum of Ethnology in Basle—as it was at that time, for later it was ruined along the lines of modern 'museology'—had for me the meaning of an open window that afforded a view onto the wide and wonderful world; there I spent hours of longing and blissful contemplation, firstly in the room of Far Eastern art, then in the Indian room, and then in the sections dealing with Indo-Chinese and other peoples; North America was also represented. Unforgettable are all those golden and timeless hours, which gave me courage to live. . . ; unforgettable in the Museum are above all the three large, gilded Buddha statues from Japan. . . . In their presence I experienced the holy, and this for me was everything."

Schuon, 1920

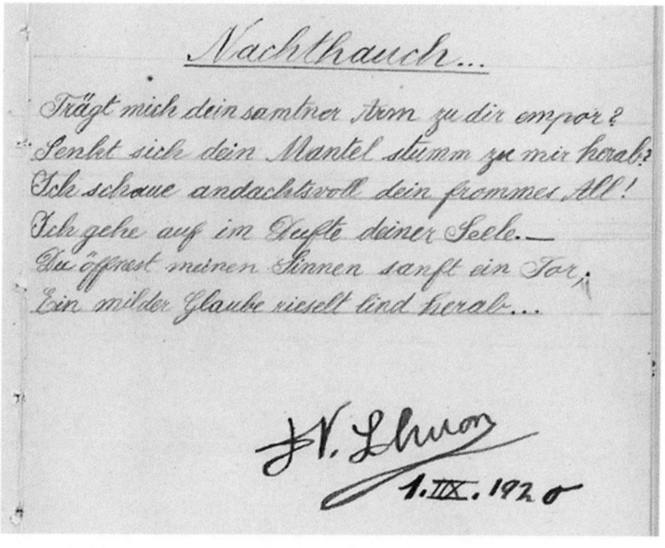

Nachthauch...

Trägt mich dein samtner Arm zu dir empor?
Senkt sich dein Mantel stumm zu mir herab?
Ich schaue andachtsvoll dein frommes All!
Ich gehe auf im Dufte deiner Seele.—
Du öffnest meinen Sinnen sanft ein Tor,
Ein milder Glaube rieselt lind herab...

F. Schuon
1. XII. 1920

Schuon's handwritten poem, "Nachthauch" ("Breath of Night"), December, 1920

2. A Time of Suffering

Paul Schuon was an inspiring and consoling presence in his young son's life, but that came to a wrenching end when Frithjof Schuon was just thirteen years old. Paul Schuon fell ill. As he was carried away to the hospital, the father bade a tearful farewell to his distraught sons, who, forbidden to visit him in the hospital, were never to see their father again. "In the hospital our father had opposite his bed an inscription: 'The Lord is my Shepherd, I shall not want'; he looked at this constantly; it was his viaticum into the hereafter."[1]

Following his father's death, Schuon lived completely in a "poetic world of myths and fairy-tales and in a kind of unconscious longing for Paradise." "I was happy with the red geraniums before our window, or on the banks of the Rhine amid the lawns and little flowers, or in the cloister of the Cathedral, where in the inner garden dark roses grew; and I wanted to have nothing more to do with the noisy world of people." The eloquent poems of the bereaved youth poignantly bear witness to his inward suffering:

Prayer on Golgotha

Be greeted on my part, O Golgotha,
Where reside my dreams and my prayers,
Whither hasten my thirsting thoughts;
O Christ, who makes my life sweet!

My heart is weary, my soul is weak,
I have trusted too much in humanity!
When my gaze turns to Thee, O Lord,
I find a place of repose and a shelter.

Golgotha, abode full of graces!
If my own strength would seem to suffice
And if my presumption should oppose Thee,
Thou wouldst be the refuge of my poor soul.

I end here my mortal song —
But shall eternally sing in beatitude;
Towards Thee I wish to ascend on wings
And put my trust in Thee, O Lord, throughout my life![2]

A short time thereafter, Schuon's mother moved with her two sons to Mulhouse, an Alsatian town that was then part of France, to be near her family. Here Schuon began his French-language education and was obliged to become a French citizen. He suffered from the bourgeois ambience of his mother's family, writing in his diary, "I have no father, no friend, on whose breast I can lay my head. My father is separated from me by the great door, and I know no beautiful human being who loves me. . . . All my strength was concentrated on one thing: to remain true to myself, to be what I wanted to be or become, not to become like the others, who were the opposite of what I was and who, consciously or unconsciously, wanted to force me to become like them." His suffering was intensified by the fact that his mother and her family, while being of good will, nonetheless so misunderstood him that, in his words, "they wanted to make of me something which I hated and despised, and they sought to eradicate in me everything that constitutes my deepest being." Schuon's aspirations rose away from the world and towards the Spirit:

When I was a child, they wanted to make me
Something very fine: a lawyer,
A doctor or a chemist — a gentleman for whom
The whole city would have the highest esteem.

Yet, I envied the man
In a poor cobbler's shop, who, all day long,
Could think of whatever he wanted,
Free from all learned lumber, and wholly unhampered —

He could dream he was a *yogī*,
Free from all the delusion of society.[3]

At the age of fourteen, Schuon was baptized and then confirmed in the Catholic Church. "Shortly before his death my father told us that if we wished to become Catholics he was agreeable to it; my brother thereupon took Catholic instruction, but I did not want to, as I feared it might be a narrowing. After the death of my father, however, we both had to become Catholics. . .". Though this choice was partly due to pressure from his mother, who had since returned to her Catholic faith, he also found consolation in this move to Catholicism, for he loved "the liturgical manifestation of the sacred, the beauty of the Mass in the Gothic-styled churches, the worship of the Blessed Virgin, and the rosary."[4] Something of the perfume of this love can be sensed in an untitled poem he then wrote:

Lost to the world I stand by the altar
My soul pervaded by the organ's roar
Subtly entwined with the waft of the years.
Outside one hears the autumn storm howling.

The altar's golden wine hangs on my lips
And lifts me up to the vault of Heaven.
The luminous tones of this holy hour
Flow down slightly from the dark pillars.

My prayer dissolves in those expanses
And embraces the All with shy aspiration.
Just as a ray of light breaks through the mist of dawn
So glide belovèd sounds into my soul.[5]

Nonetheless, he could not remain in Catholicism, for he had "already read, early on, the *Bhagavad Gītā* and had experienced the sacred art of East Asia in the deepest possible manner".[6] "At first he was very happy in the Catholic Church", his future wife, Catherine Schuon, explains, "but then he suffered from the fact that it was narrow-minded; he was always told that the only salvation was through Jesus Christ and he knew that this was not so—that there was also salvation through other religions."[7] At the age of fifteen he stopped attending church and poured himself into the study of the sacred scriptures of all the great religions, which became his primary consolation. Years later he was to write:

A Holy Scripture is not only great through its content,
It is also a sacrament: a heavenly gift,
A bread, a drink. Thou livest from its thoughts,
But also from its being — it frees thee from thy burdens
And the limitations of thy soul.[8]

3. Entry into Manhood

Schuon's childhood friend from Basle, Johann Jakob Jenny, recalls two different trips he made to Mulhouse in 1922 and 1923 to stay with his friend.

> Even as a boy of fifteen years, he was reading very much of philosophy and he spoke of what he read. His religious sense was very eminent at the age of fifteen when I visited him in Mulhouse. And when I went to visit him as a boy of sixteen years, I was very impressed with his mental and spiritual power. . . . But he wouldn't influence me when I was going still to church—I was taking confirmation. Then he told me "I don't want to influence you; I would like you to live in peace." Of course I knew that his way was not the way of the church. He was already oriented in philosophy and oriental science.[1]

Schuon left school at the age of sixteen to become a self-supporting textile designer—a profession which made only modest demands upon his energy and thus allowed him to continue his self-directed study of sacred writings.[2] The scriptures of all the world's religions and the writings of the great saints became his teachers for the next years. Plato and Meister Eckhart left a profound impression on the young man but, without question, the *Bhagavad Gītā* was his favorite text.[3] "For about ten years I was completely spellbound by Hinduism, without, however, being able to be a Hindu in the literal sense.[4]. . . I lived no other religion but that of the *Vedānta* and the *Bhagavad Gītā;* this was my first experience of the *religio perennis.*"[5] In his diary he wrote, "The most profitably and soundly based ascesis for me in these days of intense suffering is serious and difficult mental work: I consider the most profound sayings of Shankarāchārya from all angles and make myself thoroughly familiar with the most important of the European philosophers. Above all it is the limitless perspectives of the *Uttara Mīmānsā* that profoundly cheer and exhilarate me."[6]

His new-found independence allowed him to travel. "A liberating experience on the human plane", writes William Stoddart, "was Schuon's first visit to Paris in 1923, at the age of 16. This brought him encounters not only with the French (in contradistinction from the Germanic) genius, but also with people of Arab, Indo-Chinese, and Black ethnicity. This gave him a concrete human experience of their respective religions, with which he was already familiar theoretically."[7] As Schuon's diary entry from 1925 proclaims: "A loving empathy towards men of another race I consider to be an ethical obligation."

Schuon continued, however, to long for beauty and for grandeur, and to feel estranged from a milieu that tried to extinguish his "burning faith in a higher vocation".[8] In two poems looking back on this time of his life, he describes how the turmoil and suffering of his youth was overcome by remaining rooted in the unshakable ground of metaphysical Truth, something that self-evident to him at an early age and determined his essential character:

> In my childhood, those around me
> Would not believe that the sacred dwelt in me —
> That in a child, who was so unlike them,
> Something of the Highest Truth could be enthroned.
> So they sought to destroy my cast of soul —
> Whereas I could hear the words of God.[9]

— ·:· —

> In my childhood, I was obliged to dissimulate;
> The adult world did not understand me. Why?
> Because I bore within myself the kernel of wisdom —
> And this was vexing to others.
>
> It was not wanted; so I feigned dullness,
> And it made me ill. But Truth must always conquer —
> What God has given us, can never fail.[10]

The following diary entries from 1923 and 1924, when he was fifteen and sixteen years of age, present a few of Schuon's reflections on life and the ultimate principles of reality:

> I await my inner rebirth.
>
> The world passes away. Why despair at the view of the universe? My whole aim should be to plant the flowering branch in the individual soul. How great is the infinity of the individual soul!
>
> True knowledge and true virtue are one.
>
> Today I saw a flock of pitch-black ravens flying past with great wingbeats in front of the moon. The sight fascinated me; I had seen such a thing only in Japanese woodcuts. I love the gray sky with black branches with frost upon them, I love late autumn and winter, the silent speech of dead Nature. Now I understand the Chinese and Japanese winter landscapes, with their sharp contrasts and hazy, far-away mountain-ridges.
>
> I am now experiencing the wonderful, peaceful, and powerful gravity of the entry into manhood. I also feel how I am merging into the "Thou"; I mostly have an awareness that I am not really there as "I", that I am an impersonal eye in which the course of the world is mirrored.

I saw an African man in the town; he came walking along with a light, swaying step, holding his hands away from him almost as if in blessing, his head proudly tilted backwards; his mouth was open in a cheerful smile, and he sang something softly and casually to himself. . . . He made a strange and mysterious impression on me.

I suffer from the fact that my environment compels me to disavow it. Forgive me, O human beings made of beauty, if the bitter cup of my disavowal pains your hearts. My harp-strings are tangled and broken. Time passes over me with cruel tread, every hour is a wheel over my soul.

I love with a rare passion all good, simple, child-like, naively illusioned people who have nothing of the evil one in them and do everything with innocence, gentleness, and love.

When I see one of my fellow designers coming and going, I have the feeling that he is hemmed in by all the objects and mental images that daily surround him. I feel that these people adhere flatly to their mental images with all their soul, without any freedom of movement and without any possibility of taking up an objective attitude towards them.

Each sentence in our speech is a piece of life from an all-encompassing Truth—a fragment towards which we direct our attention, and which thereby loses some of its truth in that we break every connection with the All-Encompassing. The meaning of every word vibrates into the infinite, it becomes untrue when we utter it without the infinite and unfathomable with which it is organically united. When I say: "The one who is perfect is free", I pass over in silence the incontestable truth that all beings are free only to a certain degree, but otherwise are not free, and in general can only become freer, but not free; that only the Divine in its eternal state is perfect, and at the same time non-perfected, because perfection presupposes an antecedent, which the Divine cannot have.

I almost lose my mind in longing for the world of human beauty. All around me is frightful emptiness and wasteland—I become more and more lonely. I love the real, I love the expression of the human that has been intensely and lovingly penetrated by the soul. I have also understood the beautiful woman: her grace is for me the chalice of pure beauty wherefrom my lonely soul drinks rejuvenation.

Sometimes I think how beautiful it is to be a child, and to be wholly absorbed in the fragrance of beautiful human life. I have in me a longing for blossoming meadows, the longing of man for the feminine in the widest sense. I long for repose, beauty, purity, sun. I no longer have any passion for the gloomy and the tormented. I only want Truth and Light.

I call him enlightened who at every moment stands before God. He is the harp-player; he who perfects himself is he whose hands grow only for this playing.

It is the great error of modern Western culture that it should confuse living conditions with the meaning of life and take them to be life's only content. What do modern states do? They engage in trade, industry, and politics—not because they could not live without them, but because they do not know what to do with life.

I am more than ever certain that I must leave everyone and everything and live in solitude among strangers. Only in this way can that inner rebirth take place, for which I long and for which I am preparing myself.

Schuon with his maternal grandmother, c. 1924

Left to right: Frithjof, Margarete, and Erich Schuon, 1923

4. Introduction to René Guénon

In 1924, Lucy von Dechend, one of Schuon's earliest and lifelong friends, pointed him toward a book by the French metaphysician René Guénon (1886-1951), which presented a devastating critique of various modern ideologies.[1] Schuon characterized this discovery of Guénon's writings as "grist for my mill". According to one of Schuon's biographers, Guénon's works "served to confirm his own intellectual rejection of the modern civilization while at the same time bringing into sharper focus his spontaneous understanding of metaphysical principles and their traditional applications."[2] "I was called a dreamer and now I saw that my dreams were right; I saw that the true, the sacred, and the great were not only in my dreams."

Because the writings of Guénon were of such importance to Schuon, as well as to many others,[3] it is appropriate to devote some space to a description of these works. In an article written shortly after Guénon's death, Schuon subdivided Guénon's work into "four great subjects: metaphysical doctrine, traditional principles, symbolism, criticism of the modern world." Schuon describes these as follows:

> Let us speak first of metaphysical doctrine. Here, the merit of Guénon is not simply to have expounded it, but above all to have explained its true nature, by distinguishing it clearly from "philosophies" in the current meaning of this term. . . . Herein lies the great merit of the Guénonian thesis: to have recalled what modern thought, in the manner of "classical" thought, has forgotten or sought to forget, namely the essential distinction between intellectual intuition and mental operation or, in other words, between the Intellect, which is universal, and the reason, which is individual and even specifically human. . . .
>
> Basically, metaphysical doctrine is nothing other than the science of Reality and illusion, and it presents itself, from the starting-point of the terrestrial state—and thus with its cosmological extension—as the science of the existential or principial degrees, as the case may be: on the one hand, it distinguishes within the Principle itself between Being and Non-Being, or in other words, between the personal God and the impersonal Divinity; on the other hand, within Manifestation, metaphysics—now become cosmology—distinguishes between the formless and the formal, the latter being in turn divided into two states, the one subtle or animic and the other gross or corporeal.
>
> The second great subject treated by Guénon is tradition, or more precisely the aggregate of principles that constitute it, whatever its form; we can say that tradition is whatever joins all that is human to Divine Truth. Guénon emphasizes, not only the distinction between what is traditional and what is not, but also, on the level of tradition itself, the distinction between the two fundamental aspects of tradi-

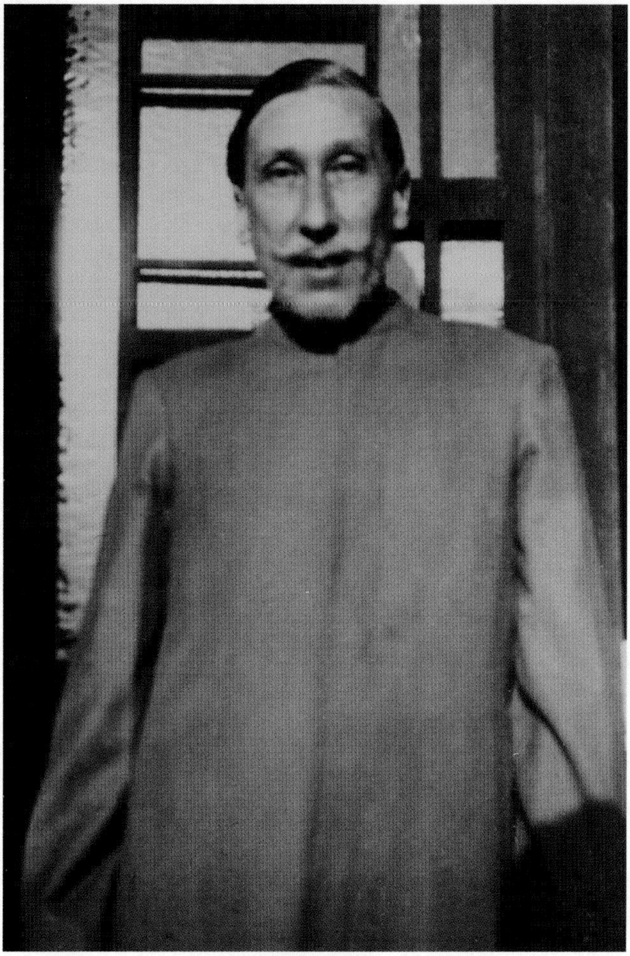

René Guénon

> tion, namely exoterism and esoterism, the latter directly rejoining metaphysical doctrine.
>
> As for symbolism, the third great subject of the Guénonian work, this is necessary because the natural and universal expression of metaphysics is the symbol. This expression is natural, because it resides in the nature of things, in other words, in real analogies, and it is universal in that it is capable of unlimited applications in the order of the Real. Symbolism has two advantages over ratiocination: first, far from artificially opposing what it expresses, it is in fact an aspect or an "incarnation" of it; second, instead of suggesting merely one aspect of a given reality, it manifests several of them at the same time and presents truths in their various metaphysical and spiritual connections, thus opening up incommensurable "dimensions" to contemplation.
>
> Finally, as the fourth great subject, the Guénonian work includes the criticism of the modern world; it cannot but include it, given on the one hand its intellectual and traditional character, and on the other hand its sphere of action which is precisely this world deprived of intellectuality and tradition as determining factors. This critique of modernism is presented under two aspects, one general and the other detailed; in other words, the author criticizes on the one hand the specific tendencies of the civilization in which we live, and on the other detailed expressions of this civilization, for example, the different forms of "neo-spiritualism".[4]

Schuon proceeds to explain that Guénon's writings correspond to the particular needs of the modern world in which we live:

> Now if, on the doctrinal plane, Guénon's work is of a unique kind, it is perhaps important to specify that this does not stem from a more or less "prophetic" nature, a proposition which Guénon himself already rejected in advance, but from an exceptional cyclical conjuncture of circumstances, whose temporal aspect is this "end of a world" in which we live, and whose spatial aspect . . . is the forced bringing together of the different civilizations; it can thus be said that for the West, Guénon is the providential interpreter of this conjuncture, at least on the level of doctrine. . . . [S]uch a work would have been without object in a period such as the Middle Ages, because the "end of a world" was still too far off and wisdom was not neglected as it is today as a result of modern tendencies; in addition, the spiritual perspectives of Asia were practically non-existent for Medieval Europe.[5]

This providential encounter with the works of Guénon helped provide Schuon with an intellectual language with which to express what, since childhood, had been his inclinations and intuitions. For Guénon's "presentation, both precise and profound, of crucial ideas", Schuon expressed "an unfailing gratitude".[6]

5. Beginning to Write

> Once, when very young, I was alone in a forest,
> And I said: "Ye Higher Powers, here I am,
> I wish to be an instrument of the sacred;
> Hear my prayer, and come soon."
>
> Heaven's answer did not fail —
> Had it not come, I would have written nothing.[1]

By the time he was eighteen, Schuon was surrounded by a group of friends who sought out his spiritual counsel. In a world still traumatized by the recent events of the First World War,[2] various occultist and spiritualist groups flourished. However, it is clear from a letter Schuon wrote during this time that he had already received a "touchstone against all false gold", which allowed him to see through the fallacies of these occultist groups and their practices. "I was granted", he explains, "an insight that is well able to distinguish the signs of darkness. No contract based on reciprocity is possible between me and spiritism. . .".[3]

This certainty was not based upon mere reasoning, but on a metaphysical vision of Reality arising from the transpersonal intellect. Such an intellectual intuition, as he was later to explain, "comprises in its essence a contemplativity that is in no way part of the rational capacity, this capacity being logical rather than contemplative; now it is contemplative power, receptivity toward the uncreated Light, the opening of the Eye of the heart, which distinguishes transcendent intelligence from reason. Reason perceives the general and proceeds by logical operations, whereas Intellect perceives the principial—the metaphysical—and proceeds by intuition."[4]

In November 1927, Schuon visited his brother, now "Father Gall", at the Abbey of Notre-Dame de Scourmont in Belgium. "My brother's reserved, ascetic nature", he remarked in a letter, "seems to have found its home here; he has found his way entirely in his mode of life and his faith."[5] In the same letter he refers to a "conversation with a young Chinese I met in the hotel", noting that, "When I confided to him . . . my respect for Chinese culture, the mask of mythical 'inscrutability' fell from him and he became positively cordial. He also showed me my errors in writing Chinese characters and we parted with deep mutual esteem."

Another letter written shortly thereafter contains both a calligraphic transcription of and commentary on the opening verse of the *Tao Te Ching*, demonstrating already at this age Schuon's notable ability to discern, at the level of both form and substance, the language of different spiritual worlds:

> [T]he conceptual gesture of the sentence, "The Tao that can be expressed is not the eternal Tao" has nothing to do with the words which clothe it. Lao Tzu confirms this himself in the second sentence of his book: "The Name that can be named is not the true Name." To understand the *Tao Te Ching*, one must bring each and every one of its sentences to bear on itself. The words here express values, and the sentences relationships, much more than they do concepts and ideas. Generally speaking, in the *Tao Te Ching*, as in the *Bhagavad Gītā*, the Gospels, and the Koran and all the profound writings of humanity, every sentence has several meanings, which correspond to applications in this or that domain. . . . I once rendered the above-mentioned first sentence of the *Tao Te Ching* [written in Chinese for the second time in this letter] as follows: "Definable knowledge is not true knowledge", or in the same way, "Discernible intelligence is not ultimate intelligence". One cannot learn to understand books such as the *Tao Te Ching* simply by reading them: one must in a sense understand them before one approaches them.[6]

By age twenty Schuon had begun his first book, disclosing to Lucy von Dechend that the text, "which probably will be called *The Doctrine of Deliverance*, has already been thought through in every detail and many thoughts essentially written down, but I have no time to perfect it—neither is it the time yet. . . . First part: 'Deliverance through inner script', second part: 'The Parable', third part: 'Visions and Songs'—philosophical, dithyrambical, and lyrical. But I must live my doctrine up to the last drop, experience in myself its deepest pain and triumph."[7]

In 1928, at age twenty-one, Schuon began his mandatory year-and-a-half of military service in the French Army. "He suffered tremendously", explains Catherine Schuon, "as the army tried to turn him into an infantry soldier. Eventually, the officers took pity on him and assigned him to a post as a military orderly which required him to work in a military hospital, as an accountant at the general office, and in the stables taking care of the horses."[8] This latter responsibility allowed him some freedom, including the opportunity to leave the barracks in the evening. He often found solitude by climbing up to the caves of Mt. Brégille, one of seven hills in the region.

Schuon did appreciate one aspect of military life—the self-discipline that was required by the training. "He often commented", Catherine Schuon informs us, "that he wished this or that person could experience military training in order to learn self-discipline."[9] When once asked in an interview, "What is the most important quality for a spiritual person to possess?", he responded, "Self-discipline, of course. . . . It is impossible to be happy without discipline", adding that it should be "without perfectionism and without pettiness; with grandeur and generosity. It must be a discipline like the sky."[10]

In the barracks in Besançon he had a second notable encounter with Islam: "I was alone in a room and an Arab soldier came in and said to me: 'When I awake I say: *Allāh.* When I go out I say: *Allāh.* When I come home I say: *Allāh.* When I go to sleep I say: *Allāh.*' Then he went away again. I did not know him and he did not know me; how did he have the idea to say this to me?" Schuon felt an affinity with the North Africans who lived in his barracks and he began to learn rudimentary Arabic. "I tried to speak Arabic with the Moroccans, and thought of far-away cities and people. . .".[11]

While fulfilling his military service, Schuon continued work on the manuscript of his first book, a process that would continue for almost four years. He also found time to write lengthy letters to his friends, who looked to him for advice. Excerpts from this 1929 letter indicate the inward trials Schuon underwent during his military training and the nature of a grace he received as a result of his intense spiritual longing:

> I have indeed been in error, and have been through the same errors whose effects now darken your world. It had to be: I had to find what I now possess without a master, alone, groping in the darkness; it was my destiny. No man has passed through more perplexity than I did last winter; and what saved me from destruction, from death, was the fact of my whole existence; not my ideas, not my wisdom, shaken and harrowed to the very core, not the art of my experiences, but rather the superhuman fact of that grace which led me into the darkness and raised me out of darkness. . . .
>
> I come to this subject because you are quite disconsolate about yourself; since you consider me healthy and strong—and not without reason, for I am so—perhaps it will not be without value for you if he who is liberated, affirming, speaks of last winter's valley of death and of the miracle by which he escaped a thousand-fold ruin. This man, who is now a teacher and master in the Spirit and feels the proximity of the Ultimate in every hour, who stands victorious in the present and found the deep mystery of Joy in the Divine, had to experience in sunless winter days the piece-by-piece paling and freezing of all that constituted the garden of his world; he had to see the icy hand of death strangle his dreams, and suffer the faltering existence of a living corpse. . . .
>
> And then the morning of deliverance, which came to me so soberly and yet with such painful sweetness, like the pensive countenance of a girl who would have tears in her eyes; and everything passed through my soul like a roaring vision, and I thought mostly of my earliest childhood. But enough said: I have tasted death and I know how the dying feel. There then came a time when I tried to realize naked knowledge and naked will and burned everything that was the content of knowledge or will. I wish to pass over the phases of my recovery; but one thing is certain and bears witness to the Omnipotence of ideas, or of the spiritual: had I then been an atheist or a worldly man, I would

In Paris, 1929

"The *Tao Te Ching* is for me a corroboration and illustration of the Truth that in other Scriptures is expressed more graphically, literally, less obscurely, but perhaps for this reason also more one-sidedly or otherwise inadequately." (letter to Albert Oesch, January 2, 1928)

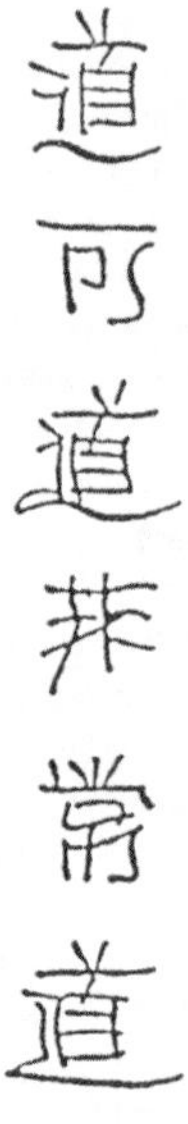

Schuon's calligraphic rendering of the opening line of the *Tao Te Ching*, 1928

c. 1929

> have fallen into incurable dementia or suicide; what guided and saved me was an idea, which I could not even grasp at that time, but which lay in me and worked liked a healing balm: my faith, my spirituality—Grace.[12]

Further in the same letter, Schuon confides to his correspondent that, "I feel Hindu, like a branch of this soul or of this spirituality, which spreads from the burning *Gopurams* of the Ganges to the red-gold shadows of the silent *Gompas* . . . as far as Angkor Wat and the Shivaite harmony of Mongolia and Cambodia, and which is still alive in pious Bali. This kinship is a fact and not a voluntary monomania; it corresponds to natural laws, to an elective affinity."[13]

After completing his military service in 1930, Schuon took up residence in Paris, where he began to work again as a textile designer,[14] while continuing to work on his first book. In order to deepen his understanding of the sacred scriptures of Hinduism and Islam, he studied both Sanskrit and Arabic, the former on his own, the latter with a Jewish immigrant from Syria and then afterwards at the Paris mosque.[15] He narrowly missed the opportunity to meet with René Guénon, who had left Paris for Cairo a few months before his arrival. In early 1931, however, Schuon initiated a correspondence with Guénon which would continue until the latter's death two decades later.

During his years there, Schuon came to love Paris, "with its dream-streets and museums, with Notre-Dame and the Luxembourg Gardens and the Latin Quarter. . . . [D]espite some painful experiences, Paris had become for me a second home." In an event that captures some of this love mixed with pain, he relates his experience as he stood in front of a full-scale replica of the Temple of Angkor Wat, built in 1931 for the International Exhibition at Vincennes:

> I am still filled with the tender pain of a vanished world; O that I might be consumed and made ready for the challenge that has now suddenly burst upon me! The West seeks to extinguish my spirit and steal my heart. I want to give both of them back to God, even if only in death. My heart wounds me, I must tear it out and throw it from myself. I must be melted down and recast. Thy Will, not mine, be done, O Lord.[16]

6. The Shaykh al-'Alawī

I was a fabric designer in Paris;
My comrades came from Alsace;
I was content, but I dreamt much,
Until I rent this miserable little corner of happiness

And fled to Algeria — to obtain
What my longing sought; and praise be to God —
The Shaykh al-'Alawī said: it is good that thou hast come —

From him I received the light of the Path.[1]

For Schuon the most precise explicit formulation of universal truth or doctrine is to be found in the *Advaita Vedānta*, especially in the writings of Shankara.[2] Metaphysical discernment must, however, be accompanied by a valid means of spiritual realization, and for this reason Schuon sought out a spiritual way and a master to guide him along this way. In a letter written in his old age, Schuon explains the nature and result of his search:

> Being *a priori* a metaphysician, I have had since my youth a particular interest in *Advaita Vedānta*, but also in the method of realization of which *Advaita Vedānta* approves. Since I could not find this method—in its strict and esoteric form—in Europe, and since it was impossible for me to turn to a Hindu guru because of the laws of the castes, I had to look elsewhere. . . . I finally decided to look for a Sufi master; the outer form did not matter to me.[3]

The method of realization he sought was the practice of the invocation, of which Shankara so beautifully sings: "Control thy soul, restrain thy breathing, distinguish the transitory from the True, repeat the holy Name of God, and thus calm the agitated mind. To this universal rule apply thyself with all thy heart and all thy soul."[4] In these lines, as Schuon notes, "The connection between metaphysical discrimination ["distinguish the transitory from the True"] and the practice of invocation ["repeat the holy Name of God"] is one of capital importance." Elsewhere he elaborates: "To realize the Absolute is to think of it, under one form or another as indicated by revelation and tradition, by a form such as the Japanese *nembutsu* or the Tibetan *Om mani padme hum* or the Hindu *japa-yoga*, not forgetting the Christian and Islamic invocations, such as the Jesus Prayer and the *dhikr* of the dervishes."[5] Thus it is that "The most diverse traditions agree that the best support for concentration and the best means to obtain Deliverance at the end of the *Kali-yuga* is the invocation of a revealed divine Name. . .".[6]

While in principle this universal path of the divine Name can be found in Christianity—in the Jesus Prayer of the Eastern Church and in the Latin Rosary[7]—in fact, however, its availability is limited and its significance often veiled. It is within the Oriental traditions where the invocatory practice is best maintained, and this is part of the reason why Schuon, who practically speaking could not become a Hindu, finally looked towards Sufism, the esoteric or mystical dimension of Islam, which lays stress on the remembrance of God and the invocation of the divine Name.[8] The ritual invocation of a divine Name requires the authorization and the direction of a qualified spiritual guide from an orthodox religious tradition. Therefore, as important as it was for Schuon to find a spiritual path within an orthodox framework, it was for him equally important to find a spiritual master to initiate and guide him in such a path, as well as to embody that path's supreme goal.

Within the span of less than a year, two events took place that caused Schuon to look more closely at Sufism as a possible home for his life of invocatory prayer. The first took place at the International Exhibition at Vincennes in 1931, when he found himself repeating the name of an unknown Sufi master, "Shaykh Nūr ad-Dīn".[9] This involuntary recitation took place even though, as he wrote later, "I was not yet a Muslim and I was not yet thinking of becoming one, although I was learning Arabic."

Then in early 1932 a second event took place pointing him toward Islam.

> [W]hen I was in the Luxembourg Gardens one morning, I asked myself the question whether I should enter Islam; and the thought suddenly came to me: if before midday you see a burnous, that will be the sign you should do so. Then I went wandering as usual through my favorite streets, dreaming, and forgot what I had been thinking in the public gardens—until all at once, as I came into the Boulevard Saint-Germain, I saw before my eyes a parade of Algerian troopers, every one in a burnous, and in a flash I remembered the thought I had had in the Luxembourg Gardens. On one of the houses there was a large clock; I looked at it and found that it was five minutes to twelve.

Nevertheless, these mystical events were not conclusive. Schuon delayed making the final choice of a religious framework until he could find the practical resolution to his search—a spiritual master. Shortly thereafter, having suddenly lost his job, he made the decision to leave for North Africa in search of both a spiritual method and a guide. "Everything is finished", he exclaimed. "I have sufficiently 'enjoyed' Europe. It has repelled me like dust. Next week, I shall already be in Algeria, without the least earthly hope, and even without money. What does it matter?"[10]

A friend, however, requested that he first visit Switzerland in order to reflect before taking the step to leave behind all that he had known. Schuon agreed, reluctantly, but considered the trip as no more than a means to bid farewell to his family and friends. He went first to the Abbey of Notre-Dame de Scourmont in Belgium to visit his brother, then proceeded to Basle, and finally to Lausanne, Switzerland, where he spent several months.[11] While in Lausanne, he continued to improve his Arabic and further his study of the Koran under the instruction of a young Persian mullah named Seyyed Hassan Imāmī, who also taught Schuon the Muslim canonical prayers.[12]

Throughout this time Schuon maintained a correspondence with several friends. In a letter to someone who had voiced the conclusion that Islam was the highest spiritual path, Schuon's response expresses a more universalist perspective:

> Have I ever said that the path to God passes through Mecca? If there is any essential difference between a path that passes through Benares and one that passes through Mecca, how could you think that I would wish to come to God "through Mecca", and thereby betray Christ and the *Vedānta*? In what way does the highest spiritual path pass through Mecca or Benares or Lhasa or Jerusalem or Rome? . . . Do I have to explain to you once again that either we are esoterists and metaphysicians who transcend forms . . . and who make no distinction between *Allāh* and *Brahma*, or else we are exoterists. . . ?[13]

His extended trip also afforded Schuon time to continue work on the book that he had begun four years earlier. In November of 1932, the twenty-four year old Schuon completed a revised manuscript called *Guiding Thoughts for Meditation on the Real*,[14] having "integrated many of my older aphorisms and added new ones that have become rather extensive treatises."[15] A comparison of this early book with his later works demonstrates that Schuon's foundational principles were already fully formed. His writings over the next seventy years can be seen as a development and clarification, both in breadth and in depth, of a philosophy already firmly established in the ground of his being.[16]

After completing the book, he left for the port city of Marseilles, France, in order to find passage to North Africa. While waiting to depart he wrote in his journal:

> I made a visit to the pilgrimage church of Notre-Dame de la Garde in order to pray. I no longer remember what I prayed; but what is certain is that I put all my distress into my prayer, whether I would go or not; and that I stood before God—the God of my childhood—with all that I aspired to and with all that I was. If God had willed, everything would have happened differently; He would have held me back there and

In Paris, c. 1931

With Father Gall (Erich Schuon) at the Abbey of Notre-Dame de Scourmont, Belgium, 1932

then. But in fact He smoothed the way for me in the most wonderful manner.

Subsequent encounters while still at port all pointed in the same direction, beginning with an Arab who "referred me to Shaykh Ahmad in Mostaghanem [Algeria] who, he said, was a holy man." This Arab introduced Schuon to a group of "Yemeni dervishes, who treated me with a touching hospitality and helpfulness and who likewise spoke to me of Shaykh Ahmad al-'Alawī." Shaykh Ahmad al-'Alawī (1869-1934) was a spiritual master in the *Shādhiliyyah-Darqāwiyyah Tarīqah*, one of the great Sufi orders dedicated to meditation and prayer, whose representatives trace their lineage in an unbroken "chain" (*silsilah*) back to the Prophet Muhammad.[17] Shortly after this event, in an Arab coffeehouse near the port, Schuon met an Indian from Peshawar who had just returned from spending three months in Mostaghanem with his master, the Shaykh al-'Alawī. Their conversation further confirmed the decision that Schuon had already made to seek out this Arab holy man. The Indian congratulated him on his resolution saying, "This Shaykh is one of the greatest Sufis in Islam and a spiritual leader whose influence reaches as far as Mecca."[18]

Schuon reached Mostaghanem in early December, 1932. Shortly after his arrival, he sought out the *zāwiyah*[19] of the Shaykh al-'Alawī, where he was received by a representative. "The same evening the Shaykh sent me word that he was pleased at my coming. The next day I was taken to him."[20] In an article written three years later in memory of the then recently departed Shaykh, Schuon writes:

> One could compare the meeting with such a spiritual messenger with what, for example, it would have been like, in the middle of the twentieth century, to meet a medieval saint or a Semitic patriarch; such was the impression given by him who, in our own time, was one of the great masters of Sufism. . . . Dressed in a brown *jellaba* and white turban—with his silver beard, visionary eyes, and long hands, the gestures of which seemed laden with the flow of his *barakah*—he exhaled something of the pure and archaic ambience of the time of Sayyidnā Ibrāhīm al-Khalīl (Abraham). He spoke in an enfeebled, gentle voice, a voice of cracked crystal, letting his words fall drop by drop. His eyes, two sepulchral lamps, appeared to settle on nothing, but, through whatever objects might lie in their path, to see only one sole reality, that of the Infinite—or perhaps, only one sole void, within the husk of things: a very straight gaze, almost hard in its enigmatic immobility, yet full of goodness. Often the long slits of his eyes would widen suddenly, as if captivated by a marvelous sight. The cadence of ritual songs, dances, and incantations seemed to be perpetuated in him in unending vibrations; his head sometimes moved in a rhythmic rocking, while his soul was plunged in the inexhaustible mysteries of the Divine Name, hidden

> in the *dhikr*, the remembrance of God. . . . An impression of unreality emanated from his person, he was so distant, closed, and unfathomable in his abstract simplicity. . . . He was surrounded by the veneration due to a saint, to a leader, to an old man, and to one who is dying.[21]

Schuon entered Islam a few days after his arrival in Algeria and was given the traditional name 'Īsā (Jesus).[22] In January 1933, he received "the light of the Path" through his initiation into the Sufi order of the Shaykh al-'Alawī:[23]

> [W]e reach the half-darkened room of the Shaykh. A breath replies to my softly spoken greeting. No one is in the room save the Shaykh lying there motionless, the *muqaddam*, and myself.
>
> The Shaykh slowly turns his head and says something in a weak and broken voice that sounds gentle and almost friendly. . . . Then the *muqaddam* speaks in a whisper with the Shaykh and turns to me again: "Draw near to our Lord so that he may give you the *Tarīqah*."[24] I crouch down very close to the slender, prophet-like figure and kiss his almost inanimate hand; large, dark eyes that are no longer of this world rest their gaze upon me. Then they stare beyond me into the void, and two cool hands with difficulty clasp my hand and hold it enclosed. In the room nothing stirs; only the barely audible words of the Koran, uttered by the Shaykh beside me, vibrate in the semi-darkness. He says prayers; the moments that go by while he prays are holy; something passes over into me from these waxen, other-worldly hands, like a current even into the heart. I am spiritually joined with him for life.[25]

In accordance with tradition, just before they clasped hands the Shaykh called Schuon's traditional name, 'Īsā, together with a second, initiatic name, Nūr ad-Dīn.

Much of Schuon's time for the duration of his stay in Algeria was spent in seclusion in his cell in the *zāwiyah*, punctuated by daily walks along the shore. He also wrote an article, dedicated to the Shaykh al-'Alawī, in which he described for the first time the idea of the essential and transcendent unity of the three monotheistic religions.[26] From time to time, he met with the Shaykh al-'Alawī himself. "Just now I was interrupted in my writing and taken to the Shaykh who, pale as death, was reclining on some rugs; he turned his large and mysteriously noble eyes towards me and held out his alabaster-like hand for me to kiss. As I knelt by his couch, he whispered: '*Marhaba*', 'Welcome'."[27]

Schuon's recollection of his encounters with a fellow disciple, the saintly Sidi Tāhir al-Mu'ammar, provides a glimpse into life at the *zāwiyah*:

> From the moment of my arrival at the *zāwiyah* I spent all my time in a semi-dark cell; at the beginning I was not alone, a dervish kept me silent company. He was a Kabyle, a grave man with a pale face and large, dark

eyes, and with a look of sharp disappointment about the mouth; he sat there, leaning against the wall, and looked straight forward unwaveringly into the void without speaking a word to me; at the end of some time he left; I do not remember how long he remained with me. He was one of the most remarkable disciples of the Shaykh, a saintly man who inspired in me the greatest respect; I even felt him to be a kind of master. He treated me with a proud reserve, sometimes with a kindliness which warmed the heart, sometimes also with a trace of disdain, at which I never took offense. I felt that he had experienced spiritual death; he seemed infinitely above all earthly things. When, at the beginning of my stay in the *zāwiyah*, I asked him if I could go into the town, he replied: "I have been here for many years and I have never yet gone into the town."[28]

In his later life Schuon wrote a number of poems relating to the person and the essential teaching of his spiritual master, with whom he forever felt a very direct and profound bond:

Shaykh Ahmad was a holy Sufi Shaykh
Who led souls to the kingdom of the Most High;
People flocked to him — the sage gave everything
That liberates us from the curse of the Fall;
He made the soul like unto a lark —
O sweet magic of the God-filled sound.[29]

— ·:· —

The town of Mostaghanem: dark blue sea,
A golden land with palm trees — and the mosque;
A few white houses. Pious people clad in white.
Then yellow sand, as far as eye can see.

The dervish brothers, who look toward the inward;
The holy Shaykh, to whom I had been brought.
Static dances and long litanies —
Radiant days; clear, star-filled nights.[30]

— ·:· —

'Ayn al-Qalb

The heart's eye, which sees *Allāh* —
The *'Ayn al-Qalb* — a shaykh described to me:
With mere thinking, one does not go far —
Who sees with the heart, learns to love *Allāh*.

For in the brain man hatches vain thoughts;
But in the heart doubts will not affect thee.[31]

—— ·:· ——

Shaykh Ahmad
What is faith, what is pious conduct?
The stern qualities of scholarship —
Disputing what is lawful, and what is not?
In the Great One the soul should rest.

Shaykh Ahmad said: the wealth of Revelation
Is fully contained in the Name of God;
In it are all the powers of Mercy —
Blessed is he who rests in *Allāh*'s Name.[32]

Not long after Schuon's arrival in Mostaghanem, the French colonial authorities—fearing political motives—became suspicious seeing a European living with the local Arabs. Schuon was thus forced to appear before the authorities and eventually both he and his venerable spiritual guide were summoned to Oran to provide further explanations. "Every time I have to go to the commissariat I am called to account in the most brazen way and may not even defend myself properly."[33] Protracted travels and legal inquiries were unthinkable for the aged Ahmad al-'Alawī, and in order to avoid such problems for his master and his new spiritual brothers, Schuon gave up his plan of remaining in their presence. A few days before his return to Paris, after nearly four months in Mostaghanem, he sent a letter lamenting, "I must now depart from my venerated, beloved Shaykh. I will never forget the touch of his blessed hands."[34]

Schuon's sketch of Shaykh Ahmad al-'Alawī, 1934

Shaykh Ahmad al-'Alawī

7. Descent of Responsibility

Once back in Paris, Schuon took a room near the Cathedral of Notre-Dame, found work as a textile designer, and again immersed himself in the reading and study of the world's scriptures and the writings of the great sages.[1] In the same year, 1933, he published three articles in French,[2] marking the beginning of his life as a published author.[3]

On July 11, 1934, just over one year after his return from Mostaghanem,[4] Schuon received an exceptional spiritual grace. "I was reading in the *Bhagavad Gītā*, when all at once I could read no more; the Supreme Name resounded within me and did not cease to vibrate powerfully within my breast." The Divine Name had descended upon him, "as an eagle swoops down on its prey".[5] Later, in the evening,

> I went out into the street and along the Seine, without the holy Name ever leaving my lips. Everything had become transmuted before my eyes. Everything was as if transparent, fluid, infinite. Everything was within me; I was in everything, and I felt myself in the farthest distance and the farthest distance in my heart. Now and then I would stand still and look at the world around me as if at a never before gazed-on sight.[6]

Two of Schuon's poems testify to the importance of this event in his life:

> The city of Paris was the love of my youth —
> The old streets near Notre Dame;
> Dream-wanderings full of longing songs —
> There it was that Heaven's grace came,
> In a small room, under the roof —
> It was there that a call from the Most High awoke in me.
> And then came Africa — God let destiny
> Weave several lives into my existence.[7]

—— ·:· ——

> *Bhagavad Gītā*, the Song of the Exalted One —
> Even as a child I loved it, for it meant India,
> And because it resounded in my own language;
> It is no wonder that I was reading in it
> When the greatest spiritual grace of my life entered into me.[8]

A few days later he learned that the venerable Shaykh Ahmad al-'Alawī had died on the very day this grace had descended upon him. "On the day of my Shaykh's death, the Supreme Name came upon me as rain comes upon a parched field. Until evening I walked along the banks of the Seine as if inebriated, almost floating on air, uttering the Name to myself. . . . The two preceding days, as I learned much later, the Shaykh had called my name."[9] One of Schuon's biographers, who interviewed members of the 'Alawī Sufi order, writes that, "According to members of the 'Alawiyyah *Tarīqah* at that time, two days before his death the Shaykh had, several times over, insistently called for his disciple 'Īsā Nūr ad-Dīn."[10] "The Shaykh al-'Alawī had told me that I could write to him and he would answer me. I wrote to him, but did not receive any letter. However, since a *murshid* always keeps his word—it cannot be otherwise—I did receive an answer, and that was when the Shaykh died: the grace of the Divine Name was his answer."

In early 1935 Schuon left his work in Paris to travel to North Africa, stopping first in Mostaghanem, where he was warmly received. He took an eight-day solitary retreat in prayer during which, he relates, "I could only leave with veiled face for my ablutions and prayers, without breaking my vow of silence. I received every evening a meal and slept on the ground. I also remained awake for part of the night in invocatory prayer."[11] The successor of the Shaykh al-'Alawī, his nephew, Shaykh Adda Ben Tounes (1898-1952), gave Schuon the additional name of Ahmad, in memory of the Shaykh Ahmad al-'Alawī. Toward the end of his visit, Schuon was presented with a formal certificate (*ijāzah*) signed by Shaykh Ben Tounes authorizing him to represent the 'Alawī Sufi brotherhood and to initiate aspirants into its spiritual lineage.[12] This authorization conferred on Schuon the right to act under the direction of Shaykh Adda, who maintained the primary responsibility for the spiritual aspirants in the branch of the *'Alawiyyah Tarīqah* centered in Mostaghanem.

After some weeks Schuon continued on to Fez, Morocco, where his childhood friend, Titus Burckhardt,[13] was then living. While in Fez he met Shaykh Mūlay 'Alī ad-Darqāwī, who led a branch of the *Shādhiliyyah-Darqāwiyyah Tarīqah* that is closely related to the *'Alawiyyah Tarīqah.* "I had a number of visits with Shaykh Mūlay 'Alī and other venerable Moroccans, spent one evening as a guest of the Squalli dervishes, and attended a festival in the Mūlay Idrīs mosque." In Fez, he fondly recalls, "the holy was discernible everywhere, in a sense it was in the air, one could not escape it." Soon, however, he had to return to Europe.

By the end of 1935 Schuon had published two metaphysical books and eleven articles—his first book was written in German and his second was a small book written in French.[14] His philosophical writings, however, did not provide income and the economic turmoil in France made it difficult for him to secure employment. He eventually found work as a designer in Amiens

1935

but his salary was modest and he occasionally had to borrow money to meet his expenses. Three months later he found a better paying position in Thann in Alsace, which also allowed him to save the expense of rent by living in the family home in Mulhouse, where his mother and aunt still lived. This living situation was sometimes problematic, but the residence was close to Switzerland, allowing him on a regular basis to visit the growing number of spiritual aspirants in Amiens, Basle, and Lausanne.

Then, at the end of 1936, the twenty-eight year old Schuon awoke one morning with the unshakable certitude that he had been invested with the function of spiritual guide. "This happened, moreover, at a time when I least expected such a thing. . .". During the same night, several of his friends had had visionary dreams of Schuon, all of which confirmed the receipt from on high of this new role. It was not Schuon but others who first announced this new function. "When next I went to Basle, the friends there told me, one after the other, that they had seen in the clearest of dream-visions that I had become Shaykh."[15]

Schuon was initially hesitant to accept the responsibility of guiding spiritual seekers in their lives of prayer. When René Guénon learned of Schuon's experience, he encouraged him to overcome his reluctance and accept the responsibility of aiding those who wished to follow him on a path towards God. Schuon, in writing of some of the reasons for his initial hesitation, also wrote of his ultimate certainty regarding his new function:

> I sometimes asked myself if I have the right to be Shaykh. I had forgotten, in those moments, that this function did not depend at all on my choice, that it had been placed on me at a given moment and completely unexpectedly. I became Shaykh at a providential time when I was in doubt about any spiritual possibility in the West, and when I was ready to give up everything. Heaven placed the function on me suddenly, without transition, like a ray of light falls in a dark room; it was totally contrary to my state of mind, but it was irresistible. . . . When I ask myself the question of knowing whether I am worthy of my function, the problem is unsolvable for me; but when I remember that this function was placed on me by Heaven, as also our method, there is no longer room for any uncertainty; praise be to God.[16]

Frithjof Schuon thus acceded to the responsibility of spiritual guide conferred on him by the providence of Heaven. As each Shaykh is effectively autonomous, this new function established a *de facto* separate and independent branch of the *Shādhiliyyah-Darqāwiyyah Tarīqah* under Schuon's direction, with Basle becoming the site of his first community of seekers. He never proselytized and knowledge of his function spread only from person to person.[17] For example, when spiritual aspirants sought guidance from Guénon, he would often refer them to Schuon, as Guénon himself rarely gave spiritual counsel and never had any disciples.[18] Word of mouth spread quickly and within a short time Schuon had spiritual communities in both Basle and Lausanne in Switzerland, and Amiens in France.

While from a certain point of view, "the outer form did not matter to me",[19] there are a number of reasons why, in fact, Sufism was a "providential ground" for Schuon's spiritual life of invocatory prayer. As has been discussed, Western Christianity has neither a well established tradition of invocatory prayer, or prayer of the heart, nor are there spiritual masters experienced in guiding aspirants interested in such a practice. In the Islamic form, moreover, access to metaphysical truth is particularly direct. The fundamental idea of Islam—as expressed in its testimony of faith, the *Shahādah*—is that of the Divine Unity, or of Non-Duality (*advaita*), to use the analogous Vedantic formulation.[20] "All metaphysics is in fact contained in the Testimony of Faith (*Shahādah*), which is the pivot of Islam. ['There is no divinity if not the (sole) Divinity (*Allāh*).' This may be compared with the Vedantic formulation: '*Brahman* is real, the world is an appearance.']"[21] "'The Doctrine—and the Way—of Unity is unique' (*al-Tawhīdu wāhid*): this classic formula", according to Schuon, "succinctly expresses the essentiality, primordiality, and universality of Islamic esoterism as well as esoterism as such; and we might even say that all wisdom—all *Advaita Vedānta* if one prefers—is contained for Islam within the *Shahādah* alone."[22]

Schuon also noted certain practical considerations that favored Islam: "Of paramount importance is the fact that each Muslim is his own priest, and then that the head of a *Tarīqah* owes reckoning to no one; a *Tarīqah* is an autonomous universe".[23] This fact enabled Schuon to espouse his universal metaphysical doctrine without fear of censure or curtailment by a clerical authority—an independence that would have been unthinkable had he been subject to a formal hierarchy within one of the branches of Christianity.[24] At the same time, as he emphasizes,

> The goal of the work is not the Islamic form as such, but precisely esoterism as such. . . . This is Islam not as the daily universe of Arab sentiments and passions, but as the manifestation at the end of time of the primordial religion: this is the Islam with its deep rootedness in the One God and its bringing back of all things to the One; with its direct relationship between God and man, whereby each individual becomes a priest or a priestess; with its opening toward Gnosis and with its emphasis on the perpetual remembrance of God, on the basis of the *Shahādah* and the Supreme Name.[25]

The following opening lines of Schuon's *Understanding Islam* define what constitute for him Islam's fundamental and universal premises:

Islam is the meeting between God as such and man as such.

God as such: that is to say God envisaged, not as He manifested Himself in a particular way at a particular time, but independently of history and inasmuch as He is what He is and also as He creates and reveals by His nature.

Man as such: that is to say man envisaged, not as a fallen being needing a miracle to save him, but as man, a theomorphic being endowed with an intelligence capable of conceiving of the Absolute and with a will capable of choosing what leads to the Absolute.

To say "God" is to say also "being", "creating", "revealing"; in other words it is to say "Reality", "Manifestation", "Reintegration"; to say "man" is to say "theomorphism", "transcendent intelligence", and "free will". These are, in our meaning, the premises of the Islamic perspective, those which explain its every application and must never be lost sight of by anyone wanting to understand any particular aspect of Islam.[26]

8. War Years

In 1938 Frithjof Schuon traveled to Cairo in order to visit René Guénon. "My first meeting with Guénon was at an appointed place; Guénon was waiting for me in the dress of an Egyptian man of learning—tall, thin, and distinguished like a Byzantine mosaic; he clasped my hand in both of his, closed his eyes, and murmured something in Arabic."[1] In this, as in subsequent encounters, the impression Guénon made upon Schuon was one of "self-effacement and of simplicity".[2] According to one of Schuon's biographers, "if Schuon was a little disappointed by the psychic lassitude that he thought he perceived in Guénon (he spoke later of a 'sort of mental exhaustion'), by the banality of his subjects of conversation (which others had also noted), and indeed, by his almost permanent restlessness, he nevertheless affirmed that 'the man was sufficiently fine and mysterious to make up for what might trouble or disappoint me in one way or another.' It is no doubt this impression that led him to note in his posthumous tribute to Guénon: 'The man seemed to be unaware of his genius, just as his genius, inversely, seemed to be unaware of the man.'"[3]

Although the two met nearly every day of the weeklong stay, most of Schuon's time in Cairo was spent in the district of the Sayyidnā 'l-Husayn Mosque. "[H]ere it was the Arab Middle Ages that predominated, with their merchants and craftsmen and their timeless, all-illuminating and all-reconciling piety. I also made the acquaintance there of two Shaykhs—Shaykh Haggāg and Shaykh 'Abd ar-Rahīm; the latter spoke to me about the 'tasting' (*dhawq*) of the mysteries, and the former gave me the blessing of the *Tarīqah Qādiriyyah*."[4]

The following year, in August of 1939, Schuon began a journey to India accompanied by two friends. A stop en route at Cairo gave Schuon the opportunity to visit Guénon a second and final time.[5] Guénon, who had taken ill, was forced to lie on a mattress on the floor; according to Schuon, "he radiated a kind of benevolence".[6] Continuing their journey, Schuon and his companions reached Bombay in September. "I felt something in the air like an immeasurable mystical inebriation which threatened to drink me in." He soon learned, however, of France's entry into the Second World War. As a reservist soldier in the French army, Schuon was therefore obliged to return to France and join his regiment. "[H]e left for India with the secret hope of disappearing there forever", writes Catherine Schuon.[7] Nevertheless, "It was obvious that the Almighty willed that the gifts He had put into this young man should be turned to account in the West, rather than be lost in the sands of the Sahara or the waters of the Ganges".[8]

At the pyramids, Cairo, 1938

Many years ago, by the pyramids,
I rode on a high dromedary,
Over golden sands, in the southern heat —
And I no longer knew where I had been born.
The day was unusually beautiful.
Why should I not put this into words?
I have mentioned so many other images,
I also wanted to let this one speak.

Days, like millennia, pass away —
The desert wind scatters them in the sand.
(*Songs without Names*, Eighth Collection,
CIII, 89)

With René Guénon in Cairo, 1938

One of Schuon's later poems, entitled "India", speaks to the lasting impact of his war-shortened stay.

> The air was heavy, filled with the Spirit's magic —
> Here was old India, rich in colors;
> Half-naked men and women, naked children;
> *Sādhus* who were earning karma's favor
> By murmuring *mantras* as they walk.
>
> A temple: a few beautiful women
> Stand, in golden saris, on its steps;
> The *vina* sings. Oppressively hot winds blow —
> And in the distance, one hears the peacock's call.[9]

He returned to France in late October of 1939, immediately joined his regiment, and was stationed by the Maginot Line near the Swiss border. While waiting for combat, he wrote numerous letters of counsel to his followers, which indicate his concern for their well-being. He also wrote his first article dealing with Christianity in a significant way: "Communion and Invocation". Here he draws out certain parallels between the Christian sacraments, particularly communion, and the Sufi practice of invocatory prayer.[10] This was the first of several articles that would eventually lead to a disagreement with René Guénon over the nature of Christianity; but that controversy would in fact be postponed until 1948, in part because communication was practically impossible during the wartime years.

In June 1940, Schuon's regiment was surrounded and forced to surrender to the advancing German Army; thereafter he spent a month in a German prisoner-of-war camp in Besançon, France. Because Germany claimed that Alsace formed part of its historic borders, prisoners of Alsatian ancestry[11] such as Schuon were granted relative freedom. Schuon realized, however, that he now faced forced induction into the German Army. To avoid this occurrence he made a daring night escape through the German lines, crossing rivers, barbed wire, and evading guarded check points. His solitary night flight took him over the ravines and forests of the rugged Jura Mountains toward Delémont, Switzerland, where he was arrested by Swiss soldiers. He was detained for two weeks and then released upon verification of his birth in Basle. Schuon received a Swiss residence permit in the summer of 1941 and eventually took Swiss citizenship.

He later spoke of an incident that occurred toward the beginning of his flight to Switzerland, as he was crossing the German lines. "When I fled into Switzerland there was a German policeman. He looked at me; he knew certainly that I wanted to flee, but he took pity on me—he let me run. I had a long beard and he thought I was a Jew. Many Germans saved the Jews. . . .

It is very curious; there was a German officer who told me, 'I hope we will lose the war, in order that this tyranny will cease'; so the Germans were not all Nazis, but nevertheless I fled, of course, into Switzerland."[12]

This return to the country of his birth took place twenty years after his father's death had caused his mother and her sons to leave Switzerland for France. Schuon remained in Lausanne, Switzerland, for the next forty years of his life. In June 1941, he was able to rent a small apartment in Lausanne on Chemin de Lucinge, an attractive and quiet residential street where he lived for almost ten years. Although World War II temporarily interrupted the publication of his articles and books, this move to new surroundings marked the beginning of a period of prolific writing that would continue until his death.

On board the ship to India, via Africa, 1938

On a ship on the boundless sea —
India and Africa, from world to world;
The keel cuts boldly through the ocean
Beneath the limitless sky.

Such is the ego as it traverses the universe
On the path prescribed by the Most High,
The Self, Pure Being — the most profound conjunction —
But both are subject to the One.

(*World Wheel*, First Collection, XCVI, 34)

With Father Gall (Erich Schuon) in uniform, 1939

In Lausanne, 1941

9. A Heavenly Gift

In the range of all possible thoughts
One thing alone is absolute: the Most High.
And then the way in which thou understandest this:
The enlightening theme of meditation comes next.

The Supreme Name and the theme of meditation —
These are the golden keys to Eternity.
Truth and then the Path — there is nothing more.
The life of Truth is immortality.[1]

For nearly ten years Schuon experienced a profound and contemplative love for a young woman named Madeleine. "[C]onsciously or unconsciously", he explains, "what we seek . . . in every love is that Divine element in which All-Goodness and All-Beauty coincide, and of which, in essence, the Universe is woven." In Schuon's case, his "inward attachment to the young girl was all the more intense because she embodied all that was different from these people [where he lived], namely, nobility, richness of soul, maternal warmth, and all this within the framework of her virginal beauty. . . . I felt that her faith in me would heal my soul, that it would give me what was cruelly lacking in my youth."

In 1941, however, she married another man. Schuon was still grieving when, on December 27, 1942, he received a gift from Heaven while in prayer—an illumination that brought him great peace[2] and provided a framework for his teachings on meditation and invocatory prayer. "A year passed [after her marriage].[3] Then came the liberating, great enlightenment, the Supreme Name took possession of me, and the Six Themes of Meditation stood like immovable stars in the firmament of my soul." As Schuon observed: "I had to experience what I had to experience. My friend was the outward, feminine manifestation of what I then lacked and what I now possess." A poem written in the last years of his life leaves no doubt as to the significance of the "themes of meditation" in his life:

The six essential themes of meditation,
I brought into the world many years ago;
But on the other hand — and this I must confess —
The themes of meditation are what made me.[4]

While it is impossible to pass over in silence this essential element of Schuon's life, the present setting does not require that his spiritual method be explained in any more detail than is presented in his published writings.[5] Suffice it to say that the purpose of these Themes of Meditation is to introduce and accompany the invocation of a divine Name or divinely inspired formula, each theme providing a means with which to actualize a particular attitude or intention in relation to God and the world. "Very schematically", writes Jean-Baptiste Aymard, "the Schuonian themes are expressed by the spiritual intentions that arise from the three fundamental planes of human nature—Will, Love, and Knowledge—each seen in its complementary polarity—Renunciation and Act, Peace and Fervor, Discernment and Union."[6] Schuon summarizes these six fundamental intentions in a 1961 article:

> One should enclose oneself in the Divine Name as in a shelter during a storm. One should also invoke it as though the Name were a miraculous sword in a battle, and thus conquer the enemies that we carry inside ourselves. At other times one should repose in the Divine Name and be perfectly content with it and abandon oneself to it with a profound composure, as though we were in a sanctuary wonderfully beautiful and full of benediction. Still at other times, one should cling to the Divine Name as though it were the lifeline thrown to a drowning man; one should call God so that He hears us and so that He saves us; we should be conscious of our distress and of the infinite Mercy of God. Another way of practicing the invocation is to concentrate on the idea that God alone is real, that neither the world nor ourselves are real; then it is as though we no longer existed and the Divine Name alone shines in us as in a great void. Finally, one should become united with the Divine Name as though we formed but a single substance with it; then we no longer have any ego, it being the Name which is put in the place of our heart; it is neither our body, nor our soul, which is "us", but the Name; and we are "ourselves" neither in such and such a thought, nor in such and such an act, but uniquely in the Divine Name, which is mysteriously identical with the One Named, or else in the sacred invocation, which unites us mysteriously with the One Invoked.[7]

Schuon also describes the nature of these "guiding thoughts" in several of his didactic poems, including the following:

Keys

Tell thyself that God is the Now and remain
In holy silence, God-consecrated stillness;
Another time tell thyself that the Now of God
Furthers the Spirit's activity; be thou His Will.

Then understand that God is the Center within thee —
Stay motionless within deep Peace;
Understand too that the Lord is Merciful —
Whoever firmly trusts will gain salvation.

And then, above all, know that God is One,
There cannot be two Ultimate Realities.
So, be thou one in the One, without "I" —
And may grace lead thee to the Self.

There is but one path to the Highest All;
Yet its Light is many-faceted — like a crystal.[8]

While Schuon emphasized the value of prayer of the heart as the spiritual means best suited to the present age, he nevertheless strictly followed the traditional principle that "he who invokes must have a right to this method, that is, he must have received it from a master who likewise received it, which presupposes an initiation regularly transmitted throughout the centuries since the origin of the corresponding Revelation".[9] Thus, the ritual invocation of a divine Name "is never practiced without the supervision or authorization of a spiritual master (the Sufi *shaykh* and the Hindu *guru*) of regular and orthodox lineage; if this condition is not fulfilled, the foolhardy man who gives himself up to attempts in this order of things exposes himself to extremely serious repercussions, such as mental disequilibrium or death, precisely because of his lack of qualifications."[10] He writes of the prerequisites for invocatory prayer in his poem "Condition":

It has been said that the Supreme Name saves us,
Despite the crushing weight of our sins;
True! However, to a base human being
The invocation of the Name is of no avail.

God does not hasten with miraculous powers;
Only noble souls does He make holy.
One should approach the Name with awe:
"Ye should not give what is sacred to dogs."

Be simple before God — He hears you. But also:
Be of noble mind! The way of Heaven requires it.[11]

The receipt of the Themes of Meditation coincided with the beginning of Schuon's role as a spiritual guide for adherents to other religions. Schuon's spiritual perspective and approach, as expressed and confirmed in the Themes of Meditation, corresponds to the three elements of esoterism, namely metaphysical discernment, methodic prayer, and intrinsic virtue. Thus understood, esoterism "contains in the final analysis the only things that Heaven demands in an absolute fashion, all other demands being relative and therefore more or less conditional. The proof of this is that a man who would have no more than a few moments left to live could do nothing more than: firstly, look towards God with his intelligence; secondly, call upon God with his will; thirdly, love God with all his soul, and in loving

Him realize every possible virtue."[12] Given the universality of his perspective, which transcends all denominational divergences,[13] it is not surprising that adherents from multiple religions sought out Schuon as their spiritual director.

As already observed, Schuon did not consider Islam to be intrinsically superior to other religions.[14] Martin Lings reports Schuon as having said, "If there was a religion which I did not love, I would not rest until I loved it."[15] Thus, Schuon did not oblige seekers to change from an orthodox religion of their birth or of their prior adoption. By the end of the 1940s he had a number of followers within Christianity and a few within Buddhism; he would eventually be a spiritual guide for disciples within Islam, Christianity, Hinduism, Judaism, and Buddhism. This is not unprecedented: among the most notable examples are Rūmī (1207-1273), who had Sufi, Christian, and Jewish disciples, and Kabīr (1398-1518), who had Hindu and Sufi followers.[16] In India it is also the case that many Sufi masters have accepted Hindu disciples.[17] In a letter to a Christian disciple, Schuon provides a concise explanation of the fundamentally esoteric understanding of forms that is required of a spiritual master who accepts followers of other religions: "If the spiritual master belongs directly and consciously to the *Religio Perennis* and if by this fact he is concretely situated beyond forms—which implies that he accepts them in practice and in knowing their value—and if the aspirant, whatever his formal religion, is situated in this same perspective, in this case there is no obstacle in the aspirant becoming the disciple of a master belonging formally to another religion."[18]

In this context it is important to underscore that Schuon adamantly excluded the establishment of any kind of "super-religion" formed from the blending of elements of more than one religion. "The affirmation of the spiritual equivalence of the great revelations", he writes, "cannot become the basis of a system and even less of a method, for this would be a contradiction and pleonasm."[19] In the following letter to a Christian disciple, Schuon makes it clear that there must be a strict separation of different religious practices:

> [Y]ou must get rid of the confused opinions expressed in your letter. There can be no question of esoteric Islam playing the role of a "spiritual coronation" in relation to a "Christian foundation". It is only too obvious that Muslim sages have something to offer Christians—and the reverse is true likewise—but Islam as such has nothing to add to Christianity; a traditional form is a closed system and is by definition perfect in its kind. Thus there is no possible "traditional complementarity" between the two religions; there can be no question of "grafting" the esoterism of Islam onto Christian practices. One must take great care to abstain from ambiguous speculations that risk compromising the efficacy of spiritual practices.[20]

10. Essentiality and Universality

> If, for the adept of the Heart or of Love, there is no question of abandoning religious practices, the principle of esoteric transcendence can nevertheless be manifested by a certain liberty with regard to these practices, especially by a tendency towards simplification, all the emphasis being put on contemplation and its direct supports; but this liberty or this objectivity will never be manifested by a dehumanization of the human on the pretext of metaphysical sublimity, for transcendent Truth puts each thing in its place and does not mix levels.[1]

Schuon deemed adherence to one of "the great and intrinsically orthodox religions"[2] as an unconditional human necessity, and he insisted that his disciples observe the indispensable legal requirements of their given religious form. At the same time, Schuon encouraged his disciples to place the emphasis on meditation and invocatory prayer rather than on the accumulation of meritorious practices, and in so doing, he upheld a principle espoused by spiritual masters of all times: that the essentializing practices of esoterism have certain rights over exoterism. It is here a question of the "letter which killeth" giving way—when need be—to the "Spirit that giveth life".[3] In the words of the Shaykh ad-Darqāwī, "The systematic pursuit of meritorious acts and the multiplication of supererogatory practices are habits amongst others; they pull the heart in all directions. Let the disciple therefore hold fast to a single *dhikr*, to a single action, each according to what corresponds to him."[4]

Martin Lings further observes that for Schuon and many of his disciples, the "changes of religious form" from Christianity to Islam "cannot possibly be called 'conversions' in the ordinary sense of the word, because the former religion is still loved and revered at the same level as the newly adopted religion."[5] Schuon expands in a letter on this idea and its implications:

> I will say that it would be quite abnormal, according to the nature of things and therefore "in the eyes of God", that men finding themselves objectively and subjectively in our situation be Muslims in exactly the same way as Muslim-born people, including esoterists; this is what explains in part that it is normal for the *sharī'ah* to be reduced, among us, to a strict minimum, a justification that results, on the one hand from a hostile ambience, and on the other hand from the graces of the Divine Name.[6] Since we have not "burnt what we had worshipped"—quite to the contrary, since we understand Christianity better than before—we cannot pretend not to know what we know, nor forget what we remember; we cannot feign "a selective lack of imagination" which in our case does not correspond to any reality. I will add that

life is too short for an extensive study of formal or "terrestrial" Islam, unless one sacrifices the "one thing needful", namely the one thing that is the sufficient reason for our traditional attachment.

So, what distinguishes us above all from Muslim born or converted individuals—"psychologically", one could say—is that our mind is *a priori* centered upon universal metaphysics (*Advaita Vedānta, Shahādah, Risālat al-Ahadiyah*) and the universal path of the divine Name (*japa-yoga, nembutsu, dhikr*, prayer of the heart); it is because of these two factors that we are in a traditional form which in fact—though not in principle—is Islam.[7]

A passage from *Understanding Islam* explains the *raison d'être* of his position, which draws its inspiration from the principle that the Divine Name contains the whole Law, and that it alone would suffice in principle to save us:[8]

> In Amidism[9] as well as in *japa-yoga* (the invocatory method, whose Vedic seed lies in the monosyllable *Om*), the initiate must abandon all other religious practices and put his faith in quintessential orison alone; this is the expression, not of an arbitrary opinion, but of an aspect of the nature of things; and this aspect is reinforced in the case of men who, in addition to this reduction as to method, base themselves on pure and total metaphysics. Moreover, knowledge of the various traditional worlds, and so of the relativity of doctrinal formulations and formal perspectives, reinforces the need for essentiality on the one hand and universality on the other. The essential and the universal are all the more imperative because we live in a world of philosophical supersaturation and spiritual disintegration.[10]

Titus Burckhardt describes the delicate balance that a spiritual master will strike: "The distinctive sign of a spiritual master is his awareness of the relativity of forms—as well as of their necessity. . . . A master whose spiritual outlook is limited by a particular formal or traditional framework is not a complete master (although a true master may in practice be unfamiliar with traditions other than his own); and a master who rejects all forms is a false master (although a true master may reduce traditional form to its essential elements, and he surely will.)"[11] While Schuon's writings constantly illuminate the myriad supports provided by the integral traditional civilizations that arose around each of the great religions, he encouraged his disciples to be discerning and cleave to the essential.[12] "[T]he plane of action", he reminds us, "is in itself entirely human, and insistence on a multitude of forms of action, belonging necessarily to a particular style, constitutes an absorbing *karma-yoga* (a path based on action) which has no connection with the Path of metaphysical discernment and concentration on the Essential."[13]

11. At Variance with Guénon

> In my early youth, my salvation was
> Shrī Shankara, and with him, spiritual virtue;
> And so I was able to learn: only inspiration,
> And not vain thinking, can give Wisdom.
> Then came the notion of tradition:
> Only the sacred may carry the sacred.
>
> All this Guénon wrote in his works with great diligence
> And zeal. But much still remained to be said![1]

Frithjof Schuon always respected the metaphysical and conceptual framework articulated by René Guénon, whose writings were particularly important to him at the time when he was beginning to formulate his own perspective. Starting in 1939 and continuing throughout the rest of his life, Schuon delved into many subjects that Guénon never considered or only touched upon lightly, including Buddhism and American Indian spirituality, sacred art in its diverse forms, and, especially, the operative aspects of spiritual realization—prayer of the heart and the human virtues. Martin Lings, who was Guénon's personal assistant in Cairo during the 1940s, later expressed an observation that first became apparent in these years: "There is nothing in Guénon that is not to be found in Schuon. There is much in Schuon that is not to be found in Guénon."[2] When, after the war, communication could be resumed between Guénon in Cairo and Schuon in Lausanne, Guénon was generally supportive of Schuon's point of view on these subjects and particularly appreciative of Schuon's interest in American Indian spirituality.

Schuon also began to express views on both Christianity and Buddhism that differed from the elder writer's well-established conclusions. Guénon had followed Shankara in condemning Buddhism as a heresy, an idea that Schuon, who had profoundly experienced Buddhism's spiritual perfume, could not possibly accept. Guénon corresponded on this issue with Schuon, Ananda K. Coomaraswamy, and Marco Pallis,[3] a Buddhist practitioner and one of Schuon's followers. In the final years of his life they persuaded Guénon to change his opinion on Buddhism and to accept it as an authentic religion, although he never had the opportunity to amend the many incorrect statements on Buddhism that occur in his earlier writings.[4]

On the subject of Christianity, Guénon was of the opinion that it had lost its original esoteric character in the third or fourth century, concluding that the Christian Church no longer possessed its original meaning and value; to the contrary, Schuon believed in the continued efficacy of the Christian

Ananda Coomaraswamy

"Coomaraswamy is an extremely precious author."
(letter to Martin Lings, April 4, 1956)

Marco Pallis

Martin Lings

rites. "[A]ccording to Guénon, the sacraments later lost their initiatic character, but this is impossible in principle and in fact: in principle, because God never gives less than He promises—rather it is the reverse that is true—and in fact, because it is technically impossible to operate such a change. . .".[5]

Despite his respect for Guénon, Schuon could not disregard his own convictions. The French edition of Schuon's *The Transcendent Unity of Religions* was published in January, 1948 and included several chapters on Christianity. It was followed in May by the article "Mystères Christiques" ("Christic Mysteries"), which emphasized the esoteric nature of the Christian sacraments.[6] Where the book presented a fundamentally different approach to Guénon on Christianity, the subsequent article implicitly disagreed with many of Guénon's positions. These publications marked the forty-year old Schuon's intellectual independence from Guénon.[7]

Nonetheless, the correspondence between these two originators of what would later be called the Perennialist (or Traditionalist) school,[8] remained cordial until Guénon's death in January 1951. In all of Guénon's letters to Schuon during the late 1930s and '40s, including the last one written three months before his death in October 1950, Guénon used the introductory expression, "Most Excellent Shaykh and Beloved Brother." However, it is also true that a "polemic [between Schuon and Guénon] was carried on by intermediaries who often did more than they were asked."[9]

The inevitable and unfortunate result of the open divergences between Guénon and Schuon,[10] including their public disagreement concerning the Christian sacraments, was that some people felt compelled to take one side or the other rather than recognize the many points upon which the two men were in agreement. "Once Guénon had published his article on the sacraments, with which I could not agree—and also because I knew myself to be spiritually independent and in many things felt and acted otherwise than Guénon wished—troubles broke out in my community; some members left me, a part of them going over to a false Hinduism and a part to Catholicism; in the Paris group there was a split because a number of them saw the master not in me but in Guénon."

Despite this break, the group in Paris under the direction of Michel Vâlsan continued to trace its lineage to the Prophet Muhammad through Schuon, who had initiated Vâlsan and many of his followers into Sufism. And in fact, the severity of the break proved to be temporary because in 1958 Vâlsan traveled to Lausanne to meet with his former spiritual guide, apologized to him, and asked to become again one of his disciples. Schuon declined the request because of Vâlsan's somewhat different point of departure, although he gave his blessing to Vâlsan's independent branch of the

Shādhiliyyah-Darqāwiyyah Tarīqah, which exists to this day. Schuon wrote to Vâlsan:

> If you feel a very direct and very profound bond with the person of René Guénon—somewhat like what I feel for the Shaykh al-'Alawī—I would be the last to reproach you for this; and likewise if, from a doctrinal point of view, you intend to follow as closely as possible the path set by Guénon; what I have in mind are certain particularities about which a choice can be made, not the great principles that apply to everyone. Your group must have a sufficient reason for being, and this reason can only be Guénon's particularity, and your affinities with it, or your natural desire not to follow another particularity of character. For this, I bless you; but do not ask me to follow you in this; I would not even have the right to do so.[11]

There are a number of letters between Schuon and Vâlsan during this time of reconciliation, which also resulted in the resurgence of *Études traditionnelles* under Vâlsan's leadership and with the participation of Schuon and many of his followers. In a letter written shortly after Vâlsan's death, Schuon claims "the highest degree of honor . . . for my former adversary Vâlsan, whose position I always respected—it was that of Guénon—and with whom, in spite of our divergences, I had good relations until his death."[12]

Vâlsan is representative of those individuals who disassociated themselves from Schuon in an honorable manner. However, there were others who, when unable to accept one of Schuon's principles, reacted with personal attacks against him. Calumnies were, therefore, a recurring part of Schuon's life, as is the case with almost all eminent persons whose opinions have an impact on the lives of others.[13] Though he keenly felt the pain of these disappointments,[14] he never lost that underlying serenity which is the touchstone of true faith, knowing full well that "It is necessary to accept 'God's Will' whenever evil may enter into our destiny and cannot possibly be avoided; indeed the partially paradoxical nature of All-Possibility requires of man an attitude that is in conformity with the situation, namely the quality of serenity, of which the sky above is the visible symbol. Serenity, so to speak, is to place oneself above the clouds, in an ambience of coolness and void, and far from the dissonances of this low world."[15]

12. Marriage and a New Home

In 1949, at the age of forty-two, Frithjof Schuon married Catherine Feer, the daughter of a Swiss diplomat, who was seventeen years younger than him.[1] Three years earlier, the then twenty-one year old Catherine Feer was living in Buenos Aires with her father, the Swiss Ambassador to Argentina. Schuon's followers in Buenos Aires included at that time the First Secretary of the Swiss legation, who introduced Feer to the writings of Guénon. Some months later, she became part of Schuon's spiritual community in Argentina. Never having been attracted to diplomatic life, she returned to Zurich, Switzerland. Shortly thereafter, she met Titus Burckhardt in Basle, who recommended that she move to Lausanne. She followed Burckhardt's advice and first met Schuon in Lausanne in March, 1947.

Schuon recounts the impression made upon him by his future wife:

> As soon as I became acquainted with her I was struck by her seriousness, her clear-mindedness, her sobriety, and her thoroughly contemplative nature; she possessed all the good qualities that Madeleine lacked, . . . and subjected herself to the duties of the spiritual life without any psychological difficulties; and since at the same time there was something of a Hindu dancer about her, I found myself more and more attracted to her, and in the end could do none other than make her a part of my life.

His mother had moved to Lausanne in the mid-1940s to be nearer to her son, but she died a few weeks before his marriage.[2] "The wedding", Schuon writes, "took place in the ancient little church at Wittikon, near Zürich; all of the large family of my bride were there, and, on my side, a few of my friends. There was an unforgettable bridal procession between blossoming trees to the little church, and, as Heaven would have it, the somewhat unpolished minister gave a very intelligent discourse on the notions of *eros* and *agapē*, with reference to the wonderful Thirteenth Chapter of the First Epistle to the Corinthians."

The newly married couple lived for a few months in Schuon's one-room apartment on Chemin de Lucinge, where he had lived for nearly ten years, before moving to a larger apartment on Chemin de Monribeau near the beautiful Parc Mon-Repos. Both locations were within walking distance of Lake Geneva, a place of blissful repose for Schuon. "[W]ith its calm surface and the majesty of the mountains in the distance", Catherine Schuon tells us, the lake "had become like an extension of his own soul."[3] The early morning would find him walking along its wooden shoreline, in search of solitude and "breath[ing] in deeply the Presence of God".[4]

With Catherine Schuon, 1950

Bridal procession, 1949

A short time later, two American-born disciples, Whitall and Barbara Perry, rented the apartment next to where the Schuons lived. "In their youth they had been seekers after truth, made the acquaintance of Coomaraswamy in Boston, and as a result wished to emigrate to India; they stopped short at Cairo, however, where they associated with Guénon and Martin Lings and joined my community. For a few years they lived in an Arab village at the Pyramids, then finally came to Lausanne, and since then they have always been our neighbors. . .".[5]

In 1953, with financial help from Catherine Schuon's family, the Schuons were able to purchase land and build a modest home. "We found in the vicinity of Lausanne an old abandoned orchard amidst vineyards, with a view of the lake and the mountains. We could not have dreamed of something better; it was a true little paradise that offered [my husband] the peace and space necessary for his activities."[6] As the Schuons' plot of land was larger than they required, they offered a part of it to the Perrys, who then built their home next door. This was to be where the Schuons and Perrys lived until 1980, when both couples moved from Switzerland to America. From his new home in America, Schuon reflected:

> Lake Geneva — here I lived for forty years.
> The lake, with mountain-peaks in the background;
> The path along the lake — all this is of the past.
> The world vanishes, as blow the winds.
>
> Life's garment is a web of dreams —
> The heart — in God — lives ever outside time.[7]

Schuon's combined bedroom and prayer room, Lausanne

The interior ambience of the Schuons' home was based upon his aesthetic principles. "In a traditional civilization, the question of the congenial ambience—dress and habitation—poses no problem; every formal element is a gift of Heaven and thus constitutes a pre-existent basis. In the modern world on the contrary, this basis practically no longer exists; the individual must consequently be aware of the problem and keep an eye on the formal integrity of his ambience, in order to avoid as far as possible the presence of forms that are contrary to the truth, the path, and virtue; hence to Grace." (text, "Specifications on the Question of the Ambience", partially quoted in James Cutsinger, *Advice to the Serious Seeker*, 132)

Left to right: Barbara Perry, Frithjof Schuon, Catherine Schuon, and Whitall Perry

The Schuons' home, near Lausanne

13. A View of Daily Life

In her article, "Frithjof Schuon: Memories and Anecdotes", Catherine Schuon succinctly describes her husband's daily routine and personal habits, which varied little throughout his life:

> [He] was leading a highly disciplined life, punctuated by the times of prayer; ever hard on himself, he was on the contrary indulgent with his disciples, taking into account the difficult work conditions of the modern world. He never changed his habits during all the years we lived together. He would get up at dawn and perform his prayers. "As long as one has not said one's prayers, one is not a human being." He also made his bed as soon as he was through with his morning prayers. After a simple breakfast, he would walk down to the lake alone, as he had always done before his marriage. He had a strict need for these hours of solitude outdoors. At ten o'clock he would receive visitors and in the afternoon, after having retired for an hour, he would write articles or letters. He answered all his mail with admirable patience and generosity, not hesitating to fill more than a dozen pages if necessary, to shed light upon all angles of a problem. Often he would write until late at night and would get up to go back and forth in his room, less to ponder what he wished to express than to remember God. Every day he would read at least one page in the Koran (in Arabic) and he also loved to read the Psalms—Psalms 23, 63, 77, 103 and 124 were his favorites, depending on circumstances.
>
> We would eat either sitting on the floor at a small Moroccan table or in the kitchen, in silence. "One should respect the food", and in fact my husband would always eat with recollection. He could not tolerate that people have intense conversations at table, and when I answered visitors out of courtesy, he would say: "Let them eat", which sufficed to impose silence on everybody. When seated, he would never lean back, and in any case we owned no chairs, only two stools, one for his desk and one for the kitchen; apart from this, we had a few Moroccan poufs. For visitors who were not accustomed to life *à l'orientale*, we had acquired two folding garden chairs which could be quickly produced from their nook. It was only during the last years of his life that he consented to sit in an armchair to receive his visitors, but he would avoid doing so as often as possible. He would always walk in a straight, upright fashion, even during the last months of his life, weakened though he was by three heart attacks. He would wash only with cold water; to take a hot bath occurred to him as little as to smoke a hookah! If it is true that some of his habits stemmed from the fact that he had always been poor, they correspond on the other hand to his ascetic nature. Everything he did, he would do well, without hurry, with recollected mien.[1]

Mark Perry,[2] the son of Whitall and Barbara Perry, recounts in a similar fashion his experience of traveling with and living nearby Schuon:

> It was quite fascinating, for those who had the opportunity to share some long journeys with Schuon, to see how he was always conscious of being in God's presence, to such an extent that he held himself always with dignity, even while resting. There was never any remissness, not the slightest casualness, never a trivial gesture, so much so that his company could prove trying to those unaccustomed to such wakefulness. At the same time, Schuon's concentrated alertness was perfectly supple and natural, never artificial given that he manifested at the same time a childlike gratefulness for being in the presence of God. In Islamic terms, one would say that Schuon was devoid of *ghaflah* (negligence). . . .
>
> To live close to Schuon required at all times an alertness of response. First, impeccable discipline and, as a gentle complement, gratitude: discipline with respect to the sloth of inertia as well as to the dissipation of temptation—"I would rather die of effort than yield to carelessness", he once told us—and gratitude with respect to the qualities of existence which everywhere testify to the Divine and thus are gifts to be treasured. With women, Schuon was not only chivalrously courteous, but was, for obvious reasons, gentler in general than with men. . . .
>
> What impressed one always in Schuon was the intensity of his attention and the electrifying instantaneousness of his reflexes. Of course, there is also a gentle aspect to contemplation which is the blissful repose of faith in the Divine Presence; Schuon manifested this through the grace of his inner serenity. "*Hari Om*", he would sigh from time to time in a spontaneous evocation of a classic Hindu name of God.[3] Never mind the world's turbulence and senselessness.[4]

For the benefit of his disciples, Schuon wrote a short statement entitled "Our Perspective in a Few Words".[5] This outline serves also to indicate principles and qualities that the sage himself manifested in his daily life:

> Spirituality: No distractions, passions, worldly ambitions. The spiritual first of all. To live for the spiritual.
>
> Aristocracy: Nothing democratic. It is necessary to be correct in everything. No casualness tending toward vulgarity. No misplaced, inappropriate, familiarity. Proper language, without laxness, from the point of view of elocution as well as of grammar.
>
> Childlikeness: To retain alongside metaphysical science a childlike faith. Not to be exclusively adult; to retain a childlike heart capable of delighting in little things.
>
> Aestheticism: Sober beauty in the forms and colors surrounding us. Colors that are natural, happy, calm. Berber, Japanese, Red Indian.
>
> Virtue: Effacement. Generosity. No pettiness. No pretension.

In using these key terms to describe Schuon's personal life, the relevance of "spirituality" and "virtue" are self-evident, these two principles forming, in a sense, the *leitmotif* of his life's story. His use of the terms "aristocracy" and "nothing democratic" remind us to avoid blind obedience to the superficial conventionalism of the majority, for we must base our actions on what pleases God, not on what pleases men. "Be ye therefore perfect, even as your Father which is in heaven is perfect",[6] Christ said, an injunction that is independent of outward, social circumstances. It should, indeed, be "hardly necessary to recall here that believing peasants and artisans are often of an aristocratic nature, and that they are so through religion; without forgetting that aristocracy in itself, namely nobility of sentiment and comportment and the tendency to control and transcend oneself, derives from spirituality and draws its principles from it, consciously or unconsciously."[7] Schuon expresses himself similarly in his poem "On Nobility":

> Noble airs that are merely outward
> Are far removed from true nobility.
> Certainly, the noble man always manifests refinement;
> The churl who merely feigns it is without nobility.
>
> A noble disposition you can find everywhere:
> With the lord in the castle, with the servant in the stable.
> Nobility of soul is a profound being;
> Inflated pretense is despicable.
>
> The core of true nobility is not worldly;
> It is in the spirit — it is a ray from the Lord.[8]

It may surprise some readers to see the metaphysician's reference to and description of "childlikeness"—what he also refers to as "holy childlikeness". "What is good about the state of childhood", Schuon explains in a letter,

> is precisely that the soul is still fresh and unspent: there is gratitude for the humblest gift of the world and of life; what is more, there is an unconscious and yet wholly real trust in God. The aging man tends to see everything in connection with a whole universe; the child, on the other hand, when he takes joy over a flower, the flower is the only thing there. Both kinds of experiences—for each has its justification—are united in the spiritual man's sense of the sacred, for the celestially divine archetypes.[9]

Of Schuon, Whitall Perry has observed that "children manifested a complete spontaneity and naturalness in his presence: on occasion they came to him with their ball or balloon inviting him to share in their game and he graciously accepted."[10] According to Perry, "this highlights yet another aspect of his nature, which was that alongside the metaphysician there existed the child, with a readiness for the innocent and naïve."[11] Schuon's love of noble animals—most notably his affection for his cat, Tigerli, the "little tiger"—was likewise characteristic:[12]

> A year after we moved into our house in Pully . . . it happened that a very small tiger-kitten ran after us; when we went faster and then looked round, we saw that he too had gone faster and was not at all pleased that we had tried to elude him. He ended by following us into our garden and played with us while we were raking up the hay. After some hesitation, we decided to keep the kitten; I suddenly had a distinct feeling that he had to stay with us.
>
> We called the cat Tigerli and had him for ten years; that is a whole life cycle. On the one hand he was a prankster and a ruffian, but on the other he had, like most or indeed all cats, something contemplative about him, in fact a pronounced sense for the sacred, and he always wanted to be present when we sat still and, in whatever manner, thought of God. He loved to lie on my lap as often and as long as possible, while I silently prayed; often he would get up and look into my eyes, performing a kind of dance with his front paws.

Schuon would also, from time to time, capture in simple line drawings the essence of a situation or event of his daily life. In many cases these "*petits dessins*" (little drawings) were sent to his close friends as a memento of a recent visit with them or to describe for them a journey he had undertaken or some other recent event. "The *petits dessins* are very charming", remarks Barbara Perry; "they have a kind of innocence that reflects the nature of the situations—a holy childlikeness."[13] In their unassuming way, these small, rounded figures can remind us of what children have not yet forgotten—that there is merit in "all things great and small".[14]

> Is it not strange how the smallest of things
> Can give us delight, even in our later years,
> When we are wise and full of experience —
> And more detached than ever before.
>
> This is because we never outlive the child within us,
> And rightly so, for it bears witness to Heaven.
> What is great can shimmer through what is small,
> For God ceaselessly shows us His Goodness.
>
> Life brings us much, the path is long —
> God appreciates in us simple gratitude.[15]

Some additional remarks may provide a fuller appreciation of the importance he placed on aesthetics. "Our formal ambience must be in conformity with our inner life, whence the rules of sacred art and traditional art—or craftsmanship—in general; no material object escapes these disciplines:

With Tigerli—the "little tiger", 1956

In Venice at San Marco

symbolism and beauty; mathematical and musical qualities. 'God is beautiful, and He loveth beauty.'"[16] Without the qualities of morality and aesthetics, he writes in a letter, "I cannot conceive any metaphysical wisdom or operative science. . . . It goes without saying that I speak of intrinsic and not merely social morality, and of integral and not merely profane aesthetics. In a word, one cannot be a metaphysician with impunity without being at the same time a moralist and an aesthete in the deepest meaning of these terms, something that is proven by all traditional civilizations, the climate of which is compounded of virtue and beauty."[17]

The fact that beauty is an objective reality does not prevent individuals from having personal preferences for particular expressions of natural, traditional, or sacred beauty. There is a common misconception that a goal of the spiritual life is the annihilation of one's individuality. Schuon has refuted this error at length in various articles,[18] and also quite succinctly in saying, "The sage is not without form, but he is without prejudice."[19] One of Schuon's later poems provides a synthetic summary of his preferences for his own personal ambience:

> When I decorate a house or an apartment,
> I keep in mind three artistic summits:
> The Maghrib, Japan, and the South Seas. Simple and beautiful,
> These are three formal languages, and three spiritual worlds.
>
> For the ambience that is the framework
> Of our everyday life is not indifferent;
> It should not be dull or heavy,
> But close to nature, simple and free.
>
> The peasant's wooden house can also be a model;
> A primordial dwelling — even in our time.[20]

Schuon performed all actions with a full awareness of their purpose and meaning, and this included his enjoyment of music. He counseled against filling oneself up with things that usurp the place of the invocation. Thus, for example, he did not follow the common practice of turning on music as background for another activity, such as work, conversation, or reading.[21] Schuon rarely attended a public performance of traditional music or dance. He did, however, visit the home of one or another of his disciples from time to time for such performances. Although he had a deep respect for sacred music such as Hindu ragas, Gregorian chants, and Islamic liturgies, he rarely listened to these forms on such musical occasions. He explained that this music was created to induce a spiritual state, often as part of the methodic spiritual practice of the religion from which the music originated. Because his spiritual practices already included specific forms of meditation, he did not look for this quality when he listened to music. He was most attracted to music containing strong contrasting melodies, pieces expressing grandeur and nobility of soul, often combined with an element of melancholy.[22] Within the receptive listener, these stimulate what Schuon called a nostalgia or "a noble longing" for God and paradise.[23]

In his poems, Schuon indicates certain musical affinities:

Although I am indebted to Shankara,
I take pleasure in the music of Spain,
Russia, the Gypsies, and the Red Indians —
What is the profound meaning of this contrast?

Extremes meet; and not only as regards forms —
The dance-song is the vehicle of deep insight.[24]

— ·:· —

Gypsy, thy violin wept a long time —
It was a love-song without name
That faded away unheard, at the brink of night.

Because thy soul avoided thine own heart,
Thou knewst not whither thou wouldst wander,
And stoodst lonesome as the day took leave.

Until the singing of thy violin told thee
That thou shouldst turn towards thine own depth,
Where all is made complete in the love of God.[25]

Catherine Schuon provides another description of the music her husband favored:

> [W]e possessed only a few records, but they were well chosen for the interiorizing and uplifting power of the melodies. In addition to records of Hindu, Japanese, or Balinese music, we had some classical pieces of which the Shaykh said they were true inspirations and like doors opening upon Paradise; for example, the "Lullaby" of Sibelius, the Moonlight Sonata, the second movement of Beethoven's Seventh Symphony, the second movement of the Concerto of Aranjuez by Rodrigo, "Goyescas" by Granados, "In the Steppes of Central Asia" by Borodine. And Gypsy music! We never tired of listening to it. The Shaykh's father was a violinist and had given concerts in Russia and Scandinavia; he had specialized in the Eastern European composers and he himself could play like a Gypsy.[26]

A view of Schuon's daily life must include an appreciation of the recurring annual celebrations in his life.[27] Each December throughout their marriage the Schuons decorated a Christmas tree as part of their annual holiday celebration, which included a simple exchange of gifts. Throughout his life the philosopher remembered the "intimate, radiant Christmas celebrations" of his youth. He often recalled the symbolism of the Christmas tree and wrote a number of poems concerning the universal meaning of the Christmas celebration and its connection with holy childlikeness:[28]

> It is strange how the celebration of Christmas — and with it
> The Christmas tree — has spread everywhere;
> Even to the Muslims, for whom this feast
> Provides a wonderful image of Paradise.
> The reason is that one likes to see something
> That is apart from the everyday world —
> One likes to return to childhood,
> With its innocence and joy.[29]

c. 1980

Schuon's attention to aesthetics included the art of dress: "Prior to dress there was the naked body; and prior to habitation there was virgin nature. Thus dress must express or prolong the sacred character, the nobleness, and the beauty of the body, as habitation must express or prolong the sacred character, the nobleness, and the beauty of virgin nature. . . . In no case ought the elements that are part of our ambience—according to the meaning we have given to this word—be contrary to the theophanic dignity of our body and of surrounding nature; and nothing in our bodily appearance ought to be rendered contrary to the creative intention of God." (text, "Specifications on the Question of the Ambience", partially quoted in James Cutsinger, *Advice to the Serious Seeker*, 134-135)

14. Travels

Immediately following their marriage, Schuon's wife took him to Graubünden National Park in the Swiss Alps. "Thus began a new period of my life. . . . For years I had lived almost exclusively as a city dweller and had encountered God's free nature only in parks or in the frequently wooded regions around the cities; this could be no more than a foreshadowing of the powerful, soul-expanding encounter with the immeasurable, Heaven-touching solitude of the mountains."[1] Soon thereafter, between 1950 and 1955, a beautiful small chalet at Verbier in the Swiss Alps was placed at the Schuons' disposal, where this "first and unforgettable encounter with God's free and virgin Nature . . . was often repeated."

> [T]he days we frequently spent there were altogether close to nature and almost medieval, with sunny hours on the high mountain meadows where only the murmuring of a stream and distant cowbells broke the infinite silence. Sometimes we climbed to the remotest of the flower carpets where there were scarcely any more trees; and sometimes too there was everywhere deep snow, whose shining purity joined with the blissful silence of the silver or deep-blue sky.

Schuon later wrote of a journey to the American West where he once again experienced nature as sanctuary and as theophany. "The Bighorn Mountains are amongst the most beautiful sights that we have ever seen; they remind us of the paradisal high valleys of the Alps, only everything is much more spacious and untouched; the whole of this blissful expanse is strewn with flowers. Here one would gladly live and die. I said to Yellowtail [an Indian friend] that I was no longer abroad, but at home; should I someday disappear, one should look for me in the Bighorn Mountains."[2] Following Schuon's return from this voyage he first wrote of the characteristic of "polysynthesism", a term which he defined as the "consciousness of the profound homogeneity of the created world and the sense of universal solidarity which results therefrom." From within such a point of view, "All creatures, including plants and even minerals—and likewise things in Nature, such as stars or wind—are brothers; everything is animate, and each thing depends in a certain manner on all the others. Man, while mediator in a determinate respect, is not opposed, in another respect, to the rest of creation."[3]

"For Schuon", explains Barbara Perry, "virgin nature carries a message of eternal truth and primordial reality, and to plunge oneself therein is to rediscover a dimension of the soul which in modern man has become atrophied."[4] Schuon describes this liberating and purifying quality of God's free and virgin nature as follows:

At the Matterhorn

The chalet at Verbier used by the Schuons

> Virgin Nature is at one with holy poverty and also with spiritual childlikeness; she is an open book containing an inexhaustible teaching of truth and beauty. It is in the midst of his own artifices that man most easily becomes corrupted, it is they that make him covetous and impious; close to virgin Nature, who knows neither agitation nor falsehood, he has the hope of remaining contemplative like Nature herself. And it is Nature—quasi-divine in her totality—who, beyond all the erring ways of human beings, will have the final word.[5]

As Harry Oldmeadow has noted, Schuon's love of nature "runs through his work like a haunting melody."[6] One could say the same for his love of prayer—a fact which is no mere coincidence, since at its deepest level all of nature is a prayer. It is for us to join in her praises of the Most High.

> Man prays and prayer fashions man. The saint has himself become prayer, the meeting place of earth and Heaven; he thereby contains the universe, and the universe prays with him. He is everywhere where nature prays, and he prays with her and in her: in the peaks, which touch the void and eternity; in a flower, which scatters its scent; in the carefree song of a bird.
>
> He who lives in prayer has not lived in vain.[7]

Between 1954 and 1980 the Schuons made a series of trips to traditional places, often accompanied by their friends Whitall and Barbara Perry. Whitall Perry writes that "Schuon taught that travel in someone spiritually inclined, when done for legitimate purposes, can sharpen the faculties of the soul through the contact one has with unfamiliar scenes and the challenges of situations not met with at home.[8] He himself on these occasions was always alert, punctual, disciplined, and keenly observant. He had ever present a small notebook for recording ideas or sketching faces of marked interest, or for composing diagrams delineating metaphysical and cosmological conceptions."[9]

Morocco was one of their most frequent destinations of travel. For many years, "Nearly every spring one of these journeys took place, and they were always an occasion of much grace." "The center is everywhere", Schuon writes, "but in holy places—as, for example in Chaouen or in Fez [in Morocco]—one experiences the center also in the outward; it comes to meet us and takes us in. In such places the remembrance of God is as it were in the air."[10] Whenever possible, Schuon would visit the aged Shaykh Hassan at Chaouen, discussing all aspects of the spiritual path. When the venerable Shaykh Hassan predicted, in the late 1960s, that Schuon would end his life in the "Extrême-Occident" ("Far West"), no one at that time could foresee the import of the prophecy.

On their way to Morocco, the Schuons often traveled through Spain, receiving the flavor of both its Christian and Islamic heritage. They first visited Greece in 1957, where Schuon was deeply moved by the encounter with Orthodox Christianity, for "everything here", he writes "reminds one of Christ, the Apostles, the Early Church." In 1968, after stopping in Venice, "the incomparable city", and again in Greece, the Schuons traveled to Turkey where they visited Istanbul and, most significantly for Schuon, the house of the Holy Virgin at Ephesus. Other travel destinations within Europe included France, Germany, Belgium, Holland, and England,[11] journeys which gave Schuon the opportunity to visit places of religious and cultural significance, as well as to meet with members of his spiritual community.[12]

Excerpts from Schuon's journal offer a taste of his experiences and thoughts while traveling:

> From the spiritual point of view a journey is always something of a two-edged sword, because of the dispersion which results from the contact with so much that is new. One cannot simply shut oneself off from this newness or one might just as well stay at home, for if one is going to travel one naturally wishes to learn something; and this dispersion has as its consequent reaction an accentuation of the ego, from whose smallness one then suffers until one has mastered this unavoidable situation. . . . In this way we realize that God is everywhere, that He is everywhere the same Bestower and Liberator, and that we are happy and secure, indeed we are born, only where we encounter God. I might almost add that we are with God wherever we breathe with the remembrance of God, and since we are always breathing, we are always with God, in the Center, in the golden Now. (Athens, April 5, 1957)

> The Alhambra is like a reddish flower in the desert. Its dreamlike surfaces, filled with arabesques, transpose the green profusion of the gardens into the realm of the spirit; indeed, as our Spanish guide said, the Muslim contemplates the beauty of nature thereby the better to know the beauty of God. . . .
>
> Contemplating the Alhambra for hours, I understood better than ever how contemplative Islamic art is, in contrast with Gothic art, which is volitive, not to speak of Renaissance art, in which the volitive element becomes worldly, hypocritical, sensual, and arrogant. (Granada, August 15, 1954)

> Yesterday evening, in the narrow streets of Seville, we heard an archaic trumpet music, then heavy, powerful drumming. We followed the sounds and came upon a procession that, slow and dreamlike, made its way along the street; a statue of the Madonna—tall, rigid, resplendent with gold and silver, and surrounded by many candles—was being borne along through the dark, half Arab city. . . . After the bullfight,

which we had seen earlier, this was another aspect of Spain—its death drunken mysticism; in the one as in the other, the Spanish soul reveals its sense of grandeur, death, austerity, magnificence. A huge silver triangle, surrounded by many heavy candelabra, which appeared to be pushed along on a heavy, silver and gold ornamented float—in reality, there were men beneath this metal pedestal to carry it—thus did the divine image move slowly forward through the night, to the accompaniment of a now shrill, now melancholic funeral music. Sometimes the procession would make a long halt, until a jolt and a shudder would go through the Madonna, and the statue, laden with its power of blessing, would move further along the street, scraping against the houses on its way. At length we stood still and watched as the glittering and resounding enchantment slowly passed out of sight. (Seville, August 15, 1954)

Kaisariani is a deserted monastery in the neighborhood of Athens; picture it to yourself: walls of which it would be hard to say whether they are made of stone or of earth, and on top of them roofs that look like clods of earth; everything yellowish or reddish, with pink-flowering trees, then pines and cypresses and a dry landscape all reds and olive greens bathed in an intensely clear, crystalline light. The building is early Christian and the church painted inside; and there are icons and lighted candles. Then a wild garden with the monks' dwellings around it, very small cells such as there must be on Sinai and Athos. This place has something paradisal and one-with-Nature about it, something spring-like and blissful. (Athens, April 7, 1957)

Venice is one of the few places I always like to come back to, for I experience it as spiritual Center; here this center is San Marco, the incomparable city being simply its outward radiation. San Marco is a direct expression of the sacred which manifests God; here the golden sacred presents itself to us in a most beautiful display, but people do not see it, nor do they understand it; for them it is a "period" or a "psychology"; and this psycho-spiritual decay is unforgivable. In San Marco one finds oneself beyond time, in the eternal, golden Now and the inwardly infinite Center. And the Holy Virgin looks down upon us from the mosaics; San Marco is obviously a shrine of the Virgin, and throughout the whole city one feels the imprint of this destiny and of this presence.

What I wish to say is this: Venice is one of the few places where I feel that I am really altogether in the center, in the sense that the surroundings are like a direct expression of myself; not that elsewhere I do not feel myself to be in the center. If I am center, then whatever I see of God's creation becomes also in a certain way center; but this is a general truth, and I am thinking now, in connection with Venice, of a particular truth, one that is conditioned rather from without. (on board the "San Giorgio", May 4, 1968)

The Hagia Sophia is a San Marco enlarged into gigantic dimensions and blended with Islam. One of the mosaics representing the Madonna is over the prayer niche in the apse and the other farther forward, just inside the entrance. Over the prayer niche, and then on one of the windows above it, I read the Koranic verse that speaks of Mary in the prayer niche.

A complement in terms of spirit and soul to the shining, golden Hagia Sophia is to be found in the Blue Mosque; in both sanctuaries one is as it were drawn upward into the splendid, arabesque-ornamented dome, only in one case the *barakah* is golden and in the other it is blue as the sky.

What makes San Marco so familiar to me is its Oriental, timeless, and all-embracing quality. Now that I have seen the Hagia Sophia I can say that I had an intimation of its wonder in San Marco—not indeed of its exclusively Christian wonder, but rather of the one that is Islamic or Gnostic-Platonic. . . .

In another respect these two sanctuaries are incomparable, without any question of a "more" or a "less", and there is no temptation to think of the one in terms of the other. (on board the "San Giorgio", May 8, 1968)

There is a special wisdom connected with traveling. The world seeks to distract us and thus to harden the ego—one observes that not only unpleasant things try us but pleasant things as well; the latter of course in a more esoteric sense. But the world is all the more easily seen through—I mean because of the continually changing outward scene—and it is the world which loses the wager. I can understand how perpetual wandering can be a spiritual vocation, as with pilgrims and *sannyāsins*. (Sparta, Greece April 9, 1957)

15. Noteworthy Encounters

Frithjof Schuon's penetrating insights into the heart of the different spiritual traditions came from his inner vision of divine Reality and how It manifests Itself in the world of forms. His gift for seeing the revealed religions as different "languages" of the sole sacred Essence found a corollary in his innate knowledge of humanity in all its diversity. Hans Küry, Schuon's longtime friend, wrote, "As a youth he differed from us friends in that he had not come to the Orient through the books of Guénon in the first instance, however valuable the doctrine they expounded may have been to him; rather, he had, because of a remarkable gift which pointed to human polarity and centrality, an extremely vivid and entirely realistic idea of the races of the whole world, including an understanding of their thinking and attitudes. The enthusiasm with which boys often admire foreign peoples . . . was in his case allied with an exceedingly precise understanding of their nature. He experienced on the long journeys he undertook during his life, in his encounters with numerous cultures, the principial corroboration of this early dream; . . . one can scarcely overestimate the richness of points of comparison or contact acquired in this way."[1]

"Man is 'made in the image of God'", Schuon writes to Marco Pallis,

> hence I have always been interested in man, in races, in castes, in human types—astrological and other, in costumes, in the arts; in religions and in the wisdom traditions, of course, but this pertains to the Divine Order as much as to the human; the knowledge of Heaven does not *a priori* depend on the knowledge of earth, it is rather the other way round. I have taken interest in man, but not first and foremost; there is a universal phenomenology of which man is indeed the center, but not necessarily the key.[2]

While Schuon wrote prolifically between the years of 1954 and 1980, he nevertheless found time to meet with practitioners and representatives of diverse religions. Many of these meetings, which took place at his home and abroad, were a result of someone's asking to see him after reading his books or articles. The present scope of this book allows reference to only some of the meetings with individuals whose names may be recognized in the English-speaking world.[3]

His first close contacts with members of an authentic spiritual tradition took place within Western Christianity in the time of his youth. Of Catholicism and Protestantism, he recalls: "I experienced both forms of faith inwardly, and consequently I experienced, beyond all theology, their respective relationship to God. . . . In both camps I met precious people."[4]

His first contact within the Eastern Orthodox Church was with Russian Archimandrite, Fr. Anthony Bloom,[5] who twice came to see Schuon in Switzerland and whom Schuon visited in London. Besides his own brother, a Trappist monk, his numerous other relations with eminent Christians included the Athonite *staretz* Sophrony,[6] a noted disciple of Saint Silouan of the Holy Mountain, and the well-known Roman Catholic monk and writer Thomas Merton, who in the latter part of his life grew to admire Schuon.[7] And, Schuon, of course, met with his Christian admirers, some of whom were prominent in their own right, including Rama Coomaraswamy[8] and, later, James Cutsinger[9] in the United States.[10]

Buddhist leaders who came to visit Schuon at his home included the venerable Shojun Bando,[11] a leading priest of the Japanese *Jōdo Shinshū* school, the Zen masters Sohaku Ogata[12] and Shinichi Hisamatsu,[13] and the Tibetan Buddhist Lobsang Lhalungpa.[14] Marco Pallis was one of the early Western writers on Tibetan Buddhism. His encounters with the Buddhist tradition, its people, and their lands during his trips to Tibet and its neighboring countries in the 1930s and 1940s resulted in several books. As both a disciple of Schuon and a practicing Buddhist, Pallis translated several of Schuon's books and acted as his emissary during his extensive travels.

Frithjof Schuon also had numerous encounters with Hinduism, including his war-shortened stay in Bombay in 1939. In London, Schuon met the venerable Hari Prasad Shastri, a translator and interpreter of Hindu texts and the founder of the Shanti Sadan *āshram*.[15] Schuon also met twice in London with Swami Ramdas, the famed Hindu saint and author of *In Quest of God*.[16] One of Swami Ramdas' subsequent books contains a chapter that chronicles this meeting entitled, "Visit to a Sufi Saint": "His face was bright with the light of inner illumination", Ramdas says of Schuon. "He possessed a regal bearing . . . but he was at heart so humble, simple, and loving. . . . The love in his heart was manifest on his face. . . . The tall and stately figure of the Sufi saint stood out in great prominence above us all—a very prince among saints."[17] In his memoirs, Schuon makes mention of this occasion, which included not only Swami Ramdas, but his large entourage among whom was "Krishna Bai, the famous brahman woman". Also present were "our Christian friends, and naturally the two Buddhists were there;"[18] thus, four faiths were represented: Hinduism, Islam, Christianity, and Buddhism.

One of Schuon's poems describes his first meeting with Ramdas:

Ramdas

Ramdas came with his disciples
They were singing "*Jai Ram, Jai Jai Ram.*"
It sounded like the Ganges' waves —
This was how they came wandering.

A holy evening, till late at night,
We spent with him and his small circle.
We could give to each other spiritually —
In God-remembrance we were one.[19]

Of the second meeting with Swami Ramdas, Schuon writes:

> The Hindus behaved towards me as if I were a Swami. . . . When we left, the Hindus accompanied us out into the street and continued to wave after us as we drove away. The picture of the orange-clad Swami as he stood there in the garden with Krishna Bai and the other Hindus, waving after us, is unforgettable. It took place in a rose garden in an agreeable London suburb, with few people around; [a disciple of Swami Ramdas] had picked two roses, one for the Swami and one for me, and so we took leave of one another with the yellow roses in our hands.

Given Schuon's deep-seated affinity for Shankara's crystalline exposition of Vedantin metaphysics, it is hardly surprising that he had a special relationship with the 68th Jagadguru of Kanchipuram. The Jagadguru is Shankara's living representative, and his *āshram* traces its history back sixty-nine generations to its founding by the Hindu sage. Although Schuon and the Jagadguru never met in person, there was communication between the two spiritual leaders through the intermediation of their followers. Mudumbaï Ramachandran, one of Schuon's Hindu admirers, regularly visited him both in Lausanne and in Bloomington. He related: "Every time before I came to meet the Shaykh, I would go to the Jagadguru. He would ask me, 'Are you meeting Schuon?' I would tell him, 'Yes, I'm going to meet him.' He said to send his greetings of peace to the Shaykh. And, whenever I met the Shaykh he would ask me to convey his greetings to the Jagadguru. It was a great opportunity for me to think of both of them."[20]

In 1959 Schuon published *Language of the Self* in India, which he dedicated to the Jagadguru.[21] In his Foreword to this edition, Professor V. Raghavan, of the University of Madras introduces Schuon and "Traditionalism" to an Indian audience:

> [T]his book, the first publication in India of a class of writings which, if not so well known in this country, has nevertheless contributed in a unique way to the true understanding of Hinduism in the West. . . . To this elite of authentic exponents in the West of Eastern wisdom belongs Frithjof Schuon whom it is the privilege of the present writer to introduce to our readers here [in India]. . . . Nothing is perhaps more significant or has climaxed this effort in a more befitting manner than the fact that His Holiness Śrī Śankarācārya, Jagadguru of the Kānchī Kāmakoti Pītha, has been pleased to accept the dedication of this book to him; the orthodoxy and authenticity of Schuon's exposition stand in need of no further testimony. . . .

HH the 68th Jagadguru of Kanchipuram

Krishnabai and Swami Ramdas

> The service that this group of writers in the West has done is both to the East and the West. The integration they have achieved on the basis of a traditional and spiritual outlook is not exactly Oriental, for as they have shown, this outlook is common to the mediaeval and scholastic West. "What we have in mind for the Christian", says Schuon . . . , "is a return to his own sources and not an orientalisation of the West.". . .
>
> To many modern Indians and their leaders who are intensely allergic to the words *Tradition*, and *Orthodoxy*, this growing school of Western thinkers should act as a shock-absorber. Their re-affirmation of the value of this ancient, in fact timeless, wisdom should lead to a reawakening in the East, and to an arrest of the spreading decay of its tradition. . . . For awakening us with their true and revealing exposition of this knowledge, these *vivekins* of the West are entitled to our gratitude and respect.

Jean-Claude Petitpierre[22] also acted as an intermediary between the Jagadguru and Schuon. Petitpierre has written: "In 1963 I went to see the Jagadguru from Ceylon, where I lived at that time, in order to offer to him a copy of *Understanding Islam*; the English translation had just been published. His Holiness accepted the gift. Sometime later someone in his entourage informed me that the Guru had read the book and selected passages which he had asked chosen disciples to read and study."[23]

One of Schuon's poems is entitled "The Jagadguru":

I never saw him. But we greeted
Each other through friends who went to India;
He knew of my work, and I knew him
Through Hindus who reverently surrounded him.

As heir of the great Shankara, he was
The wise bearer of the Vedanta-light;
A man of God, who kindly thought of me —
The greeting of my heart reached him from afar.[24]

Schuon's intimate understanding of Sufism and Islam is well recognized in large part based upon his 1961 book *Understanding Islam*, which has now been translated into twelve languages and is one of the world's best known books on Islam written in a Western language.[25] His writings on Islamic spirituality are also known through the work of several authors who acknowledge Schuon's guidance as the decisive factor in their spiritual and intellectual formation, including Titus Burckhardt, Martin Lings, Seyyed Hossein Nasr,[26] Yusuf Ibish,[27] Jean-Louis Michon,[28] and Victor Danner,[29] all respected authorities on Sufism and on other aspects of traditional spirituality. The fact that they all lived for many years in various countries throughout the Islamic world and are fluent in multiple languages has added to the dissemination of Schuon's influence.

Schuon's standing in the Oriental world brought him into personal contact with many eminent members of Sufi orders who either wrote to him or came to visit him in Switzerland or America. After the death of the Shaykh al-'Alawī, the leadership of his center in Algeria went to Shaykh Adda Ben Tounes, who in 1935, as noted earlier, had authorized Schuon to confer initiation into the 'Alawī Sufi brotherhood. In 1951, Shaykh Adda sent Schuon a very cordial letter. "One of our friends", Schuon wrote, "showed our themes of meditation to Shaykh Adda, in Mostaghanem, who found them to be perfectly orthodox."[30] Shaykh Adda died the following year.

In 1954, the son and successor to Shaykh Adda, Shaykh Mahdi Ben Tounes (1928-1975), came to visit Schuon in Switzerland. Whitall Perry was present at this meeting and recorded the comments made by Shaykh Mahdi: "'You [addressing Schuon's disciples] live in a desert and this desert is the profane world about you. But in the middle of the desert is an oasis with a never-failing fountain. It is for you to refresh yourselves spiritually at this fountain, which is Shaykh 'Īsā.' And he extended his hand towards Schuon."[31] In subsequent years, however, the young Shaykh Mahdi had ambitions to expand his influence and prestige over larger parts of the Islamic world and Europe, establishing a journal called *Les Amis de l'Islam*, whose propagandist content supported this aim. Schuon and Titus Burckhardt both refused to contribute to the journal, which meant that relations with Mostaghanem became distant and to a certain extent strained.[32]

Another notable encounter provides us with a further appreciation of Schuon's relationship with Shaykh Ahmad al-'Alawī. While visiting Morocco in 1967, Schuon twice met Shaykh Hassan, a Sufi master who lived in Chaouen. A few days later he wrote about the meetings to Titus Burckhardt, who also knew Shaykh Hassan: "When I greeted the old shaykh for the first time, he sat down for a while beside me and tears ran down his cheeks; he was happy like a child."[33] In the same letter Schuon confides to his close friend what Shaykh Hassan had learned from an aged Sufi who was a direct disciple of Shaykh Ahmad al-'Alawī. "The old disciple, moreover, remembered me and said the Shaykh al-'Alawī had loved me very much. I am writing this to you simply because it was said. What I knew before was that Shaykh Ahmad [al-'Alawī] had awaited my coming."

16. The American Indian Spirit

There are three spiritual worlds to which I belong:
The primordial world of the *Veda*, then Sufism,
And then, in the West, the world of the Indians;
Each branch of humanity has something to teach,
For every cosmos shines in its own way.
Metaphysics means the words of the *Vedas*;
The Name of God is the world of the Sufis;
And our harmony with surrounding creation
Is what pleases the heart of the Indian.[1]

From his youth, Schuon felt a profound connection with the spiritual world of the North American Indians, in particular those of the Plains.[2] "Love of the Indians is a family tradition with us", Schuon wrote to Chief Medicine Robe of the Assiniboine people,

> and this is why: as a young girl, our paternal grandmother lived in Washington where she became acquainted with an Indian chief who loved her and made a marriage proposal to her. He was called "Singing Swan", and, with many other chiefs, he had come to Washington for a congress. Unfortunately, my grandmother had to go to Europe with her family and could not marry "Singing Swan". He sent her letters in which he called her "my little child"; he also sent her dried flowers from the prairie. The recollection of "Singing Swan" was so vividly impressed on my grandmother's mind that at the age of eighty she still remembered her friend as if she had seen him the day before, and shortly before she died she still spoke of him. When my brother and I were children, she used to talk to us about "Singing Swan"; she pictured to us his beautiful long hair and his buckskin dress of light blue tinge. Thus we were brought up with the love of the Indian peoples, and this was a providential disposition in the plan of the Great Spirit.[3]

One of Schuon's childhood friends recalled how, at age eleven, they "played as Indians, especially in the zoo and in the zoological gardens, where we gathered some friends. His [Schuon's] elder brother was there and took the Indian name of 'Reindeer'. Afterwards we gathered also in the forest in the neighborhood of Basle—that was very serious; we had to practice. Once we had a small battle in the forest."[4] The boys made Indian clothes, practiced Indian dancing, and also read books to learn about the traditional customs of the Plains Indians.[5]

Schuon's first encounter with members of an Indian tribe took place in Alsace when he was fifteen years old. "There was a big German circus with Sioux Indians; it was in 1923, so the Indians were still true old-timers. They were singing and riding on horseback with wonderful costumes. I already knew English and so I went every day to the circus to talk with these impressive people."[6]

In the winter of 1953, Schuon and his wife traveled to Paris in order to attend the performances of a visiting dance troupe of Crow Indians. Among the dancers was Thomas Yellowtail, who was to become one of Schuon's closest friends. Yellowtail himself describes their introduction:

> When we first met, I was a common man and not well known. Although I was a sun dancer, I was not yet selected to be a medicine man and the Sun Dance Chief of the Crow tribe.[7] Our friendship has always been based on the love we both have for all sacred things and prayer. This is the most important thing for both of us, prayer and the sacred. In this we are in the same boat.
>
> We first met in 1953. In that summer of 36 years ago, my wife[8] and I were members of a group of Crow Indian dancers who toured Europe, North Africa, and the Middle East performing traditional Indian dances. On that trip we performed in Paris for several weeks. One day the Schuons introduced themselves to my wife and me in the lobby of our hotel. They explained to us that they had watched our performance for several days and wanted to meet us. We spoke awhile and knew right away that we had much in common. During the next few days in Paris we saw them often and even held a Sun Dance prayer meeting with them in our hotel room. We arranged to meet them later and stay with them at the Schuon home in Switzerland. About a month later our opportunity came and my wife and I spent a week in the Schuon home.[9] That is how we met.[10]

Schuon later commented: "Yellowtail is a saintly man", adding that when they first met, they "immediately talked of spiritual things, about religion and prayer."[11] Catherine Schuon recalls that on the evening when she and her husband attended the Sun Dance prayer ceremony which Yellowtail held in his room, "Yellowtail asked my husband to offer a prayer for the Indians at every full moon, just as he himself would pray for our spiritual community at the same time."[12] With these two visits in Paris and Lausanne began a friendship between Yellowtail and Schuon that became even closer in future years.

Five years later, the Schuons traveled to Brussels, where a group of sixty Sioux had come to give Wild West performances as part of the World's Fair. The Schuons made the acquaintance of numerous individuals, and formed several friendships, including a particularly close relationship with a Lakota couple, Jackson and Elva One Feather. The Schuons' ties to members of both the Crow and Sioux tribes lead to their spending the summers of 1959 and 1963 in the American West, visiting the Sioux, Crow, and other tribes and meeting with tribal leaders.[13] A part of Schuon's journal, containing memories and impressions of events he experienced, was later published in *The Feathered Sun*, his anthology of writings on the American Indians. A few selections from this material give one a sense for the nature of their journey:

> The opening of the Sun Dance was one of the most powerful things I have ever witnessed. We stood near the entrance of the Sun Dance Lodge among many Indians. After a while came the sun dancers, men and a few women, and twice went round the Lodge in opposite directions; in single file, the ones went round from left to right and at the same time the others—crossing with the first—went round from right to left; then they all entered the Lodge. In the darkness an extraordinarily powerful, rapid drumming began, and at the same time a monotonous, wild, and thrilling singing; it was like a war cry, and yet was not of this world.
>
> After some time, a fire was lit inside the Lodge; the Sun Dance Tree, brightly illuminated and golden, stood out against the very clear, star-studded night sky; opposite us, on the eastern side, hung the aforementioned eagle with the outspread wings, and on the other side of the Tree, facing the west, hung an uncanny, shaggy buffalo head. The sacred Tree was forked; where the trunk divided, a large bundle of sacred willow shoots was fastened, and the twelve crossbeams forming the roof of the Lodge also met here. At the top of the Tree fluttered two ribbons, one yellow and one white—one for Heaven and one for Earth.
>
> . . . The consonance of all these impressions—the Sun Dance Tree under the starry sky, the flickering fire, the thunderous drumming, the wild, proud singing, whose melody cascaded from high to low, the wonderful and timeless figures and faces—resulted in a truly grand and majestic image, indeed as powerful a one as senses or imagination can grasp.

> In the evening we attended a dance festival at Wounded Knee; as at the Sun Dance, there was a large circular ground with a pole in the center and shades all the way round; nearby, three tipis, a painted shield, and a feathered lance had been set up; a painted buffalo skull was also there.
>
> Fools Crow was also there, in splendid dress adorned with long fringes and a war bonnet flowing to the ground—an apparition which combined eagle and sun, and at the same time had something of the powerful heaviness of the buffalo. He danced like a mountain in motion; coupled with this there was his grandiose, stone-like face. Seldom have I seen anything so unequivocal and powerful. The big drum thundered; the singing resounded, monotonous and yet with bold upward and downward movements; and all the while, there was lightning everywhere along the horizon. One was transported into a timeless past, when Heaven still touched Earth. And then that crowd of swarthy people, often with faces of ravishing beauty; the impression is as fresh and amazing as it was on the first day.

Left to right: Catherine Schuon, Susie Yellowtail, Thomas Yellowtail, and Frithjof Schuon, Switzerland, 1953

Shoshone Sun Dance, c. 1950

Left to right: Jackson One Feather, Ben Black Elk, and Schuon, 1963

> It was an unforgettable evening: [Ben] Black Elk and One Feather sang incessantly, drumming all the while—sometimes the two women sang along with them—and finally the Sacred Pipe was placed on the ground and the Pipe Song was sung; for this all the lights were put out, as in a session of magic. Then the lights were lit again and the Pipe was passed round; prayers were said. Ben explained amongst other things, that the distinctive sign of the Indian religion was the circle with the cross within it.
>
> When One Feather speaks of spiritual things, he becomes a completely different man; he then speaks slowly and softly, becomes solemn, and emphasizes his words with impressive gestures. His tremendously angular and sharply chiseled face, with the triangular eyes, then becomes altogether spiritual.[14]

At Pine Ridge in 1959, the Schuons were adopted into the family of Chief James Red Cloud, a grandson of the great chief known to history:

> *Red Cloud*
> He was the grandson of Chief Red Cloud
> Of the Ogallala band. We met —
> The noble old man and I — and had a long talk
> In Pine Ridge, beneath the shade of a tree.
>
> He talked first about old times; then there was
> Silence, until I began to speak, and said:
> The world is but dream-stuff —
> The dream vanishes before Reality.
>
> The Chief adopted me into his clan,
> Gave me many good words, and then he died.
> Let the winds blow over the wide land —
> The heart will live forever in the Great Spirit.[15]

The old chief, in taking Schuon as his brother, gave him the name "Brave Eagle" (Wambali Ohítika). Later that summer, at the All-American Indian Days in Sheridan, Wyoming, the Schuons were escorted onto the main stage and officially received into the Sioux tribe by a delegation of tribal members; Ben Chief, a Sun Dance chief whom Schuon had first met in Pine Ridge, acted as the spokesman. Schuon was given the Lakota name Wicáhpi Wíyakpa—"Bright Star"—along with a painted shield.[16] The master of ceremonies, Joseph Medicine Crow, told Schuon "Your name is Bright Star; each time we see the Morning Star we shall remember you."[17] When Schuon was later asked about the significance of his adoption by American Indians, he explained:

> These adoptions have always existed among the Indians; there have always been Whites—or sometimes men of other races—that have been adopted into an Indian tribe, or into a family, which amounts to the same thing practically speaking. From the point of view of the Indians, this means that they consider you henceforth as one of theirs; and this implies, for the person who is adopted, a sufficient understanding of the mentality and spirituality of the Indians. In my personal case, this has even more meaning, given my spiritual function; this indicates a certain bond with a form—late as it may be but nonetheless real—of the primordial Tradition; and it is also like a marriage with virgin nature.[18]

Whenever Schuon met with representatives of different religious traditions the conversation inevitably turned to the underlying Truth within each religion. During his travels to the American West, he carried photographs of leaders from other religious traditions, which he would show to the people he was visiting. Schuon wrote an article that describes his meeting in 1959 with Last Bull, the Keeper of the Sacred Arrows of the Cheyenne tribe, including the reaction of the American Indian holy man when he saw a photograph of the Jagadguru of Kanchipuram.[19] In his article, which is dedicated to the Jagadguru,[20] he notes that "A spiritual encounter between His Holiness the Jagadguru and a Red Indian holy man has taken place, through the medium of a picture of His Holiness and a prayer of the Red Indian." Schuon concludes his article by commenting:

> All this may give the impression of a rather singular contribution in honor of His Holiness the Jagadguru; but it is in reality not so unrelated, and this for three main reasons: firstly, it is certainly a great event that, for the first time in history, a Red Indian holy man manifests his love for a Hindu holy man; secondly, this apparently small incident reminds us of the unity of the Primordial *Sanātana Dharma*, which is more or less hidden beneath the many forms of intrinsically orthodox Traditions; and this unity is especially represented by the very function of the Jagadguru, who incarnates the Universal Truth. Thirdly, this little incident marking a symbolical encounter between a Red Indian priest and a Hindu priest was in fact an act of prayer; and it shows us that in prayer all earthly differences such as space and time are transcended, and that in prayer we are all united in one state of purity and in one perfume of Deliverance.

Finally, mention should be made of Schuon's relationship—through letters and intermediaries—with Black Elk (1863-1950), the famed Lakota medicine man. In 1946, when virtually no westerners were interested in Plains Indian spirituality and only a few serious scholars were studying shamanistic sacred traditions, Schuon suggested to Joseph Epes Brown,[21] one of his first American disciples, that he attempt to find Black Elk, the holy man who was the subject of John Neihardt's 1932 book, *Black Elk Speaks.* Schuon hoped Brown would be able to record and preserve the wisdom of some of the nomadic old timers still living at that time, including Black Elk. In later life, Schuon explained in a film interview: "I see that the American Indians have been crushed and their culture has been destroyed. I am a European, so I feel a debt towards the red race; I want to help revive Indian culture."[22]

Joseph Brown was successful in his search and lived with Black Elk and his family near Manderson, South Dakota for extended periods over the course of two years. The book that resulted was *The Sacred Pipe: Black Elk's Account of the Seven Sacred Rites of the Ogallala Sioux*, first published in 1953. While Neihardt's *Black Elk Speaks* remains an invaluable biographical work, Schuon noted that "for the doctrine one has to refer to *The Sacred Pipe*, all the more as this book is strictly faithful, word for word, to the account given by the Indian author".[23] Schuon himself wrote the Introduction to the original edition of this landmark work—the only such contribution that he ever made to another's work. According to Brown, who was present at the time, Black Elk was extremely pleased when parts of Schuon's Introduction were read to him.[24]

While living with Black Elk, there was an ongoing correspondence between Brown and Schuon, including two letters Schuon sent to the venerable Lakota holy man that were translated by his son, Benjamin Black Elk.[25] One of Brown's letters to Lausanne recounts:

> He [Black Elk] said that he had told as yet no one [about the sacred rites of the Lakota], but was telling me because he believed it was connected with my being there and with the Holy Man who had sent me. . . . The letter from the Shaykh has had a tremendous impact on him. His son translated the whole letter to him; he is excellent at this, and you should also know that he is responding . . . extremely well.[26]

Brown later wrote, "I might first mention, for I do not think that I have done so before, that one of the reasons why Old Black Elk has been so receptive to us is the fact that some time ago he had a vision in which he saw that Holy Men—or representatives of them—would come to him and his people from the East and would help him in his work. A few days ago he told me that he was very happy, for should he die soon, he now knows that his work shall be continued by the Shaykh and others."[27]

When Brown spoke with Black Elk about Schuon's impending marriage, the venerable holy man gave his betrothed a Lakota name.

> In the year before my marriage, our American friend Joseph Brown was living with the Lakota Sioux and there frequented Black Elk, the old sage of whom the book *Black Elk Speaks* gives a moving testimonial.

> I was in close correspondence with Joseph Brown and received news of Black Elk regularly, so that in a sense I myself frequented him from a distance. Through Joseph Brown he learned much about me and my community—and hence about my bride as well—and he took a keen interest in everything that concerned me; and one day it came about that Black Elk gave her the Lakota name Wámbli Oyáte Win, which means Eagle People Woman; the Eagle People is my community.[28]

Brown's letters also speak to the close relationship between Black Elk and Schuon's elder brother, Father Gall, whom Black Elk accepted as his adopted son and to whom he gave the name Lakota Ishnala ("Solitary Lakota").[29]

> Black Elk has taken a great interest in his son, Father Gall; he talks of him often, and is having several things of buckskin made for him. He is also sending him his necklace made of sacred deer hoofs, and we are sending him a pipe and sacred tobacco.[30] It of course means much to Black Elk to have the support of a Christian Father, for the priests here have been continually after Black Elk to give up his "heathen practices", and "works of the devil", and to participate fully and only in Catholicism.[31]

For the rest of his life, Joseph Brown remained in contact with Black Elk's family and other Indian leaders, while maintaining correspondence with and periodically visiting Schuon, first in Switzerland and later in Indiana. When Joseph Brown returned to visit Black Elk's family in 1954, Lucy Looks Twice, Black Elk's daughter, told Brown of her father's recurring dream visions during the final weeks of his life in 1951. Brown wrote to Schuon:

> Finally she explained that before his death they had been worried about Black Elk. Every afternoon at about the same time he would go into something of a trance as if he were talking with some unseen person. Once he scolded his daughter-in-law for entering the house at that time, for he said that she had made the man leave. When they asked him who it was who came to talk with him, (more precisely this person came to pray for Black Elk, saying that he knew that he was soon to die, and he wished to help him in his suffering), he said that it was "a holy man from Europe". His relatives were frightened by these experiences so Mrs. Looks Twice noticed a large wooden rosary which always hung over his bed—a Moroccan one that I had given him because of his fondness for its *barakah*—and took this away from him. According to her after this he did not talk anymore with the "strange man". At Black Elk's death, possibly thinking that it had not been right to do this, she saw that this rosary was buried in the coffin with him.[32]

With Chief James Red Cloud, 1959

Below:
Inscription on the back of the photograph at right, given by Black Elk to Schuon, which reads, "Mita Kola, Hehaka Sapa" ("[To] my friend, [from] Hehaka Sapa [Black Elk]")

Black Elk

During Black Elk's final illness, Joseph Brown had informed Schuon that the aged Lakota holy man was suffering intensely and approaching death. For the last month of Black Elk's life, the Schuons recited special prayers of divine Mercy for him on their Moroccan rosaries. Schuon and his wife followed this practice every evening in their home in Lausanne, corresponding to the mid-afternoon in South Dakota. Thus it was that Black Elk's visions of a visiting holy man came at the same moment that Schuon was reciting prayers for the venerable Lakota sage.

"The work of Black Elk is alive, it lives on", Schuon affirms, "but the Indians, true to their nature, keep it more or less secret."[33] As a "belated witness of the Primordial Tradition",[34] the Indian world "represents on this earth a value that is irreplaceable; it possesses something unique and enchanting . . . which it expresses with profound originality."[35] He once wrote: "What one can give to the Indians is strengthening light and what one can receive from them is luminous strength."[36] If, through his writings, Schuon helped to cast the strengthening light of the perennial religion on the Indian civilization, he also acknowledged that he "received from the Indians a special kind of spiritual blessing."

17. A Spiritual Patroness

In the Spring of 1965 Schuon made a journey to Morocco, a country he had first visited in 1935. While on a ship docked at Port Vendres,[1] Schuon had a visionary experience of the Virgin Mary that was to change the remainder of his life. In later poems he speaks of this event:

Port Vendres, where the ship lay at anchor —
I will never forget that golden day.
I was alone in my room: the others
Wanted to walk for a while along the shore.
They had given me a bunch of flowers —
I gazed into their bright splendor
And thought, like a child, of Paradise;
Then came — a waking dream — the Virgin sweet,
And stayed with me, hidden deep within me,
With her grace, which never disappeared —
Holy presence and luminous remembrance.
An image come from Heaven; I like to call it
The *Stella Maris* — my morning star.[2]

— ·:· —

Stella Maris

My soul was once weary and sad —
On a ship, in the Mediterranean.
The Holy Virgin came to me, in waking dream,
So that I might not be consumed by bitter grief,
And that my joy and strength might not be paralyzed —
I felt as if the end of life were near.

O *Stella Maris*, miracle upon the sea —
I wished the journey would forever last.
Thy heavenly fragrance remained with me —
and thy Grace
Is like the morning star upon my path.[3]

Not only in Christianity but also in Islam, the Blessed Virgin is honored above all other women. According to Schuon, she is unique and exalted "inasmuch as she is in fact the only feminine *Avatāra* in the Semitic cosmos; hers is the only feminine name in the Koran, and not only is this name mentioned more than thirty times, but it is even the title of a *sūra*." One reads in the Koran (3:42), "O Maryam, verily God hath chosen thee and purified thee, and hath chosen thee above all women".[4]

Schuon saw the Holy Virgin as a symbol of supra-formal Wisdom—the *Sophia Perennis*—and of primordial sanctity, combining Purity and saving Grace. He also described her as the feminine aspect of the Logos and the archetypal personification of spiritual poverty, of submission to God, and of quintessential prayer.[5] The Virgin Mary, therefore, "is not merely the embodiment of a particular mode of sanctity; she embodies sanctity as such. She is not one particular color or one particular perfume; she is colorless light and pure air. In her essence she is identified with merciful Infinitude, which—preceding all forms—overflows upon them all, embraces them all, and reintegrates them all."[6]

His veneration for the Holy Virgin existed long before this mystical contact and heavenly adoption.

> My first encounter with the Holy Virgin was through my father's poem, "Of Wine-Gold-Red Roses". Then I recall how my father once became angry because someone had scoffed at Marian devotion. When after my father's death I became a Catholic in Mulhouse, I met Mary in two ways: first, in the monastery chapel in Riedisheim where I attended Mass; there was the large and beautiful image of Our Lady of Perpetual Help, the famous Byzantine icon on a gold background. And secondly, I said my rosary in that same little monastery church and thus spoke to Mary, which I had never done before.[7]

Catherine Schuon recalls that at the time of their first meeting in 1947 a statue of the Holy Virgin was a feature of her future husband's small one-room apartment:

> He . . . sat down on a low divan covered with a Turkmen blanket. . . . On the wall behind him hung a beautiful Indonesian fabric. The room was divided in two by a golden curtain . . . the larger part, which looked out on a balcony, was furnished with the divan and a Gothic chest on which stood a Romanesque statuette of the Virgin Mary in majesty. The whole room was covered with nomadic Afghan rugs. Next to the divan, near the window, a ficus tree and two azaleas added a welcoming note to the sober and peaceful beauty that reigned in this place.[8]

Schuon describes how, in the early 1940s, he came to purchase this image of the Madonna:

> When, after my war experiences, I had fled to Switzerland and at last could rent an apartment in Lausanne, I wished to furnish this small home as beautifully as possible. One day I passed a shop displaying costly draperies and the like, and in the center of the show-window stood a particularly beautiful Romanesque Madonna, of chased metal over wood, and I could not resist it. Partly because I wished to own it and partly in order to rescue it from the show-window, I purchased this little statue at a high price. . . .[9]

Schuon's Romanesque statuette of the Virgin and Child

Darshan

I read in an old prayerbook:
In Heaven Jesus shows his wounds
To Mary, so that his salvation's work
Might shine, at consecrated hours, in her soul;

The Holy Virgin then shows him her body,
To remind him of what she gave him
With this sacrament, prepared by God:
His flesh and blood, his sacred heart, his life.

Darshan: the contemplation of sacred signs,
So that we may reach their deepest meaning,
And feel that Heaven is rewarding us —
That the belovèd Other dwells within.

Understand: first comes seeing, and then becoming —
There is on earth no better loving glance.

(*Autumn Leaves & The Ring*, 93)

A year and a half after the experience on the ship at Port Vendres, Schuon's heavenly benefactress returned to him in a visionary dream—"not an ordinary dream, but a dream-experience in a mode that was visionary and real." He recorded the fact that the event took place but did not describe the dream-experience: "All at once she was there—a tall apparition, like snow and sun. But to say more would not become me."[10]

When speaking of Schuon's mystical experiences we must recognize that he repeatedly warned of the danger inherent in misinterpreting such experiences and the risk of putting too much emphasis on them, even if they are genuine and properly interpreted.[11] "The master . . . has realized 'sober drunkenness', his human substance being adapted to his spiritual state, for mastery is precisely 'keeping a cool head'—but without the least pretension—within the beatific experience."[12] Elsewhere he informs us, "When a spiritual experience is authentic and profound, it leaves a trace in us; now one must be faithful to this trace. He who has benefited from such a grace . . . must not seek to do extraordinary things; from the point of view of the spiritual method and social comportment, nothing changes, unless there was in this comportment something abusive. What Heaven wants of us is our soul; it invites us therefore to inwardness. 'The kingdom of God is within you.'"[13] At all events, as Schuon emphasizes:

> our spiritual life should not depend on any sensible grace; it is fine to feel a celestial presence, but this has nothing to do with our path; our path is active, not passive, and it is based on ideas and practices, not on experiences. We should not be overly interested in whether our states of soul are agreeable or not; we can certainly accept sensible graces with respect and gratitude, but what matters in the eyes of God is what we do and not what we experience.[14]

At the request of his close friends, he wrote about some of the visions and tangible graces that he received throughout his life. Nonetheless, he did not write a great deal—in most instances no more than a one or two sentence description of the actual experience and in several instances he recorded the fact that an event took place without describing the experience.[15] In 1973, for example, the mystery of the Holy Virgin returned to Schuon, and while he noted the event, he left no description. He did, however, explain that "Since those graces which I received on the ship and in Morocco, I could no longer lose myself in books, reviews, and theatrical performances; after that which I was permitted to behold inwardly, I could no longer read or look at just anything; I was as if marked by Heaven. It was as though I lived in a special protective aura belonging already to Heaven, which at the same time carried with it an obligation. . .".[16]

In the wake of his first Marial graces, Schuon wrote several poems in Arabic that express his veneration for his spiritual protectress. In 1968 he traveled to Turkey, and especially to Ephesus, where he visited Maryamana Evi, the house of the Virgin Mary where both Christians and Muslims come to pray.

> Every day we visit the house of the Holy Virgin on the mountain—the "Maryamana Evi"—and let ourselves be penetrated by this *barakah*; there is also a spring here which was flowing in the time of the Virgin. It had been blocked up for hundreds of years; only in the last century when the house was discovered did it gush forth again. . . .
>
> In the house of the Blessed Virgin there are two adjoining rooms; one of them, the larger of the two, faces East; the other, smaller room faces South. In the larger one, through which one has to go first, Mass is said facing East; the second room is empty, but there are prayer rugs for Muslims. In the larger room hang Christian *ex voto* offerings—testimonies to miraculous cures or other graces—and there are also many lighted candles. In the smaller room hang the colored silk ribbons of the Turks, with the same *ex voto* meaning. In the smaller room, in the place where the prayer niche would be—that is, against the south wall—the Holy Virgin had her couch; before this place we stood and sat for a while today and inwardly invoked the Supreme Name.[17]

In honor of his spiritual patroness, Schuon added the title *Maryamiyyah*—of Mary—to the name of his *Ṭarīqah* in the summer of 1969.[18] "Our *Ṭarīqah* is *Maryamiyyah*", Martin Lings reports Schuon as having said. Lings also recalls that "he told us that more than once she had made it clear to him that she had chosen us for herself and that she was our protective patroness. He went so far as to say: 'It is not we who have chosen her; it is she who has chosen us.'"[19] When asked, "Why did she choose us?", Lings recounts Schuon's response: "A possible answer is this, she herself is a Jewish princess of the house of David; she is also the mother of the founder of Christianity; and she stands, in relation to Islam, at the summit of the hierarchy of women. She loves all three of these religions, and religion in general, as we do . . . and like her, we are much more interested in what these three religions have in common than we are in what separates them one from another. So in a sense we stand on her territory."[20] Schuon himself wrote concerning the significance of his community's Marial designation: "It is our insistence upon the nature of things . . . that explains and justifies our connection with Sayyidatnā Maryam; it is because our perspective is *a priori* metaphysical, esoteric, primordial, and universal that our *Ṭarīqah* has the right to be named *Ṭarīqah Maryamiyyah*, in perfect accordance with the teachings of Sufi Tradition."[21] Later, Schuon also used the Latin term *Ordo*

Mariana—"Order of Mary"—to refer to the spiritual way for his Christian disciples.[22]

Following the Sufi custom, the new name of Schuon's *Tarīqah* was added to his personal name. Schuon's complete traditional name thus became Shaykh 'Īsā Nūr ad-Dīn Ahmad ash-Shādhilī ad-Darqāwī al-'Alawī al-Maryamī. The term Shaykh refers to his spiritual function; the name 'Īsā (Jesus) was received when he entered Islam in Mostaghanem; the name Nūr ad-Dīn ("light of the religion") when he was initiated into Sufism; and the name Ahmad during his second trip to Mostaghanem in 1935; next follow the names of the three major figures in the history of his spiritual lineage; and finally the name of his *Tarīqah*—the *Maryamiyyah.*

These first and decisive encounters with celestial femininity took place at the very center of his spiritual life: thirty-three years after being received by the venerable Ahmad al-'Alawī and thirty-three years before his crossing to the other shore. The profound consequences of this event made themselves evident, among other ways, in the expanded subject matter of his paintings.

At the house of the Blessed Virgin, outside Ephesus, 1968

18. An Artistic Dimension

> Man lives by Truth and Beauty; Schuon writes books and paints pictures. His books express the metaphysical doctrine in which all the religious systems and all the spiritual methods have their origin; he thus takes his stand in the perspective of the *philosophia perennis*. In his paintings, Schuon's intention is to express inward truths, and he does this in a manner that is quite simple, spontaneous, and natural, and without any affectation of didactic symbolism. Fundamentally, what he portrays are higher realities as lived though the medium of his own soul. . . .[1]

As a child Schuon took pleasure in drawing and painting, but he never received any formal training in the arts. Prior to 1949 he produced several sketches and simple canvases, but it was only shortly after his marriage that he began to realize his mature style and thematic focus. Schuon considered this to be the beginning of his authentic period of painting. "Soon after my marriage I began to paint; it is true I had done so before, when I was working as a textile designer in Mulhouse and later in Thann, but in my opinion the pictures that came into being at that time—most of them with an Oriental influence—had not as yet anything essential in them."

The subject of Schuon's art is, broadly speaking, "on the one hand the Plains Indian world and on the other hand the mystery of cosmic and human femininity—Goethe's 'Eternal Feminine' (*das Ewig-Weibliche*) or the Hindu *Shakti*." While there is no strict line of demarcation between the two, the first subject "has its roots in his affinity with the fascinating world of Red Indian heroism and mysticism", while the second "has its roots in metaphysics and cosmology . . . [and], in a more relative sense, in Schuon's affinity with Hinduism."[2] Between 1950 and 1965 Schuon's artistic vision was focused on the world of the Plains Indians.

> My first painting portrayed two Red Indian women, one clothed and the other naked; since then I have more than once repeated this theme, as it signifies the antithesis between sacred form and sacred content, or between the veiling and the unveiling of the holy. Besides purely narrative Indian pictures I often painted the sage—or the masculine nature of wisdom—in the form of an old Indian chief; I often represented him as the center of a council. My paintings of women represented the complement to this, namely beauty, with all the virtues that go with it; my starting point here—in these as in other pictures—was not a deliberate symbolism, but simply a reality that flowed forth from my nature; the meaning was prefigured in my inward being, and did not lie in my conscious intention.[3]

During this period, Schuon also created many painted leather hides depicting the sacred image of the Indian Feathered Sun.

> The [Feathered] Sun is composed of concentric circles formed of stylized eagle feathers; the resulting impression is particularly evocative in that the symbol simultaneously suggests center, radiation, power, and majesty. This symbiosis between the sun and the eagle, which is to be found again in the celebrated headdress of feathers formerly worn by chiefs and great warriors, brings us back to the symbolism of the Sun Dance: here man is spiritually transformed into an eagle soaring towards Heaven and becoming identified with the rays of the Divine Sun.[4]

The Feathered Sun, Schuon writes in a letter, "has become a symbol of our spiritual message, without my having had this deliberate intention".[5]

Leather hide painted with the Feathered Sun, c. 1970

As a painter, Schuon's affinity with the message of femininity is evident from his earliest canvases. One is reminded that many spiritual traditions throughout the ages have considered woman not only as the highest expression of terrestrial beauty but also as a symbol of divine wisdom, love, goodness, and mercy. Following his spiritual encounter with the Holy Virgin in 1965, the majority of Schuon's paintings represented the Virgin-Mother and the Eternal Feminine. For some time after that experience, he acknowledges that in fact he "could scarcely paint anything other than the Holy Virgin".

"If I were asked why I paint images of the Holy Virgin", Schuon writes, "I should answer: to transmit, thus to make accessible to others, an inward vision, and to make possible a participation in this vision."[6] He depicted her, according to Barbara Perry, "not in the style of Christian icons, but in the form of the Biblical Shulamite or the Hindu *Shakti*."[7] His representations "are not intended to be Christian icons; they universalize the celestial Virgin in a manner which makes one think of Hindu and possibly Mahayanic art."[8]

"I painted her, not as she is portrayed in Christian religious art, but as I had inwardly experienced her, that is as virginal Mother or as motherly Virgin and beyond all theological forms; as the embodiment of the Divine Mercy and at the same time of the *Religio Perennis*, somehow uniting in her person Christianity, Islam, and Hinduism, in conformity with my own nature. . .". A point which he makes again in one of his poems:

> When I painted the Virgin, I never thought
> That my paintings should merely reflect Mary's features;
> I thought of femininity as such,
> Not of Jesus' Mother alone.
> And likewise the Child: thou see'st him pray inwardly —
> It is the devotion of all the world's Prophets.[9]

There has been only one public display of Schuon's original artwork, due, on the one hand, to his insistence that his message is to be found primarily in his published writings and, on the other hand, to his lack of interest in public acclaim. In 1981, however, shortly after his move to America, his paintings were the subject of an exhibition entitled, "Scenes of Plains Indian Life" at the Taylor Museum in the Colorado Springs Fine Arts Center.[10] Barbara Perry explains in her catalogue notes that "As a writer, Schuon is recognized as a master of thought. As a painter, he makes no claims for his art, and he does not even desire to be publicly known. Springing as they do from his rich and unique personality, Schuon's paintings nonetheless have a rare value, not only as regards artistic merit but above all because of their gift for manifesting the human soul at its noblest and most beautiful—hence, as a vehicle for Truth—and it is for this reason that we wish to present them to the public."[11] In 1990, reproductions of many of the canvases exhibited were included as illustrations to *The Feathered Sun*, a collection of his various writings on the Indians of North America.

Two years later, a book containing reproductions of his paintings was published under the title *Images of Primordial and Mystic Beauty*.[12] "When the question was broached of publishing Schuon's paintings", the work's editor, Michael Pollack, explains, "he at first was rather reluctant because he was concerned that such an art book might detract from the image of his intellectual and spiritual identity; for, let us repeat, the main accent of his message is spiritual and not artistic. However, because Schuon's art also contains in its way a spiritual message—since his doctrinal message finds a spiritually transparent expression in his art—he has granted permission for this publication."[13]

Pollack offers this further insight into Schuon's artistic message and style:

Maharaja, c. 1928

Samurai, c. 1928

Murid, 1934

Mandarin, 1935

Published in *Images of Primordial and Mystic Beauty* (clockwise, from top left), 198, 201, 200, 185

American Indian sketch
Published in *Images of Primordial and Mystic Beauty*, 163

The Two Sisters, 1966
Published in *The Feathered Sun*, 27

Pow Wow, 1953

The Descent of the Sacred Pipe, 1986
Published in *The Feathered Sun*, 131

"A typical personification of the *Shakti* is the White Buffalo Cow Woman who brought the Calumet to the tribe of the Lakota Indians. In her celestial substance, she is the goddess Wohpé, who is the equivalent of Lakshmī." (*Roots of the Human Condition*, "*Mahāshakti*", 43)

> It is essential to understand that Schuon as a painter is not interested in originality and innovation; he is fascinated by the subject matter alone, its origin being what he observed among the Indians or an inner vision of spiritual realities. As for style, Schuon applies the general rules of traditional pictorial art, the first principle being that a painting must take into account the flatness and immobility of the surface; it should not represent three-dimensional space nor a too accidental and hence fragmentary movement. Schuon has an affinity with Hindu art and Christian icons, and also, in a more secondary way, he accepts—at least partially—the techniques of a Van Gogh, a Gauguin, a Hodler, or a Covarrubias. We should also mention that Schuon likes to repeat his subjects, which fact derives from his interest or fascination with them; it would be superficial and pedantic to reproach the painter for this kind of monotony, all the more so in that traditional art always has the tendency to repeat the same motifs, thus to unfold their potentialities.[14]

Schuon's natural talent for painting is interconnected with his extraordinary aesthetic intuition. "It suffices for him to see—in a museum, for example—an object from a traditional civilization, to be able to perceive, through a sort of 'chain reaction', a whole ensemble of intellectual, spiritual, and psychological principles which operate in that world."[15] His lifelong friend, Titus Burckhardt, commented similarly that at the moment of sanctity a saint is given a special gift and that "In the case of Schuon, this gift was the discernment of forms." Schuon has the ability, Burckhardt noted, "to look at a piece of clothing or an artifact from a culture and know everything about that culture. He sees the archetypes inherent in all things and immediately understands the essence of the form and the entire culture from which it came."[16]

Schuon's paintings of the sacred White Buffalo Calf Woman (Pté San Win), the celestial messenger who brought to the Lakota people their original Sacred Pipe, provide a striking example of his discernment of forms. During the 1960s and 1970s he painted several canvases of the Buffalo Calf Woman bringing the Sacred Pipe; in some she is clothed in white robes and in some she is naked.[17] Until 1980, every published account of the story of the bringing of the Buffalo Calf Pipe described the Pté San Win as wearing a white buckskin dress. In 1980 a book appeared containing English translations of the recordings James R. Walker collected from Lakota holy men during the last years of the nineteenth century.[18] Two of these accounts describe the Buffalo Calf Woman as completely naked. When the metaphysician and artist was asked how he had known to paint the Pté San Win in this manner, he responded that the Pté San Win is a goddess of the Lakota and that the celestial messenger of this primordial religion had to have been naked when she brought the revelation of the Sacred Pipe.[19] He went on to compare her with other manifestations of celestial femininity in Hinduism, Buddhism, and Shintōism, who are often traditionally depicted in a primordial state without clothing. He noted also that the hostile attitude of the early Christian missionaries toward nudity explains why the Lakota would change their original account—in order not to give offense or draw censure.[20]

In her catalogue notes for the 1981 exhibition of Frithjof Schuon's paintings, Barbara Perry explains the presence of nudity in many of his paintings:

> A remark is necessary here regarding the symbolism of nudity. It is common knowledge that in Hinduism, as in most other ancient religions—and notably also with the American Indians—nudity has a sacred connotation. It manifests both the primordial and the universal, and it is not without reason that one speaks of the "paradisal innocence" which was before the Fall. Again, there is in hieratic nudity a moral meaning as well as an intellectual one: under the first aspect, nudity—of the Hindu goddesses, in particular—expresses the generosity that welcomes and provides, likewise exemplified in the mystical *lactatio* of the Blessed Virgin; and under the second aspect, nudity indicates the esoteric "unveilings", and it is in this sense that one speaks of the "naked truth". And lastly, let us remember that, according to St. Paul: "Unto the pure, all things are pure."[21]

While remaining foremost a metaphysician and philosopher, Schuon also manifested his philosophy through his art. As Michael Pollack declares, "[H]is fundamental vocation is the *philosophia perennis* as it is expressed in his written works, whereas his art appears rather as an expression of the aesthetic, psychological, or moral dimension of this primordial and universal philosophy. In other words, Schuon is interested not only in metaphysical principles, but also in their cosmic and human radiation. . .". Schuon's own description of his fundamental intention as an artist is quoted in the Introduction to his *Images of Primordial and Mystic Beauty*: "What I seek to express in my paintings—and indeed I cannot express anything other—is the Sacred combined with Beauty; thus, spiritual attitudes and virtues of soul. And the vibration that emanates from the paintings must lead inward."[22]

Celestial Virgin and Child, c. 1970
Published in *Frithjof Schuon: Connaissance et Voie d'Intériorité, Biographie études et témoignages*, 78

"In the outward world we first of all find the God-given sanctuary: this is the place of prayer, which must resemble prayer itself; just as man must enter into prayer and live in it, so must men enter into the sanctuary and find their spiritual abode in it. This is indeed the meaning of sacred art: to immobilize in the Center the human being who strays, or is tossed about, in the world; to hold him fast by means of beauty, but beauty of the holy, which is beauty of the Inward, the beauty of Paradise, of prayer; the beauty of God. And this is also represented in human form by the Holy Virgin: she is 'exteriorization with a view to interiorization', visibleness of the Invisible; she is the merciful Inward in the outward, and hence the merciful way to the Inward; she is prayer become man, and thus also Paradise become man."

19. Expanding Readership

Frithjof Schuon's circle of readers spread first within the French-speaking world, where his books were initially published and where they were widely available. The 1970s and '80s, however, marked a significant expansion of his readership in the English-speaking world, in particular within North America.

In the summer of 1973 an international colloquium took place in Houston, Texas, at which twenty-five distinguished scholars and spiritual leaders from around the world presented papers on the theme, "Traditional Modes of Contemplation and Action". The event was sponsored by the Rothko Chapel, Houston, while the primary organizer of the event was Yusuf Ibish.[1] The deliberations of the conference began with the reading of Frithjof Schuon's keynote, "Message to the Colloquium". Ileana Marculescu, one of the participants who also served as a co-editor of the condensed edition of the colloquium, provided this overview of the proceedings:

> While each colloquist's contribution to this book stands by itself, taken in its entirety the volume properly inaugurates a genre which is more than, say, the learned illustration of pragmatic ecumenism: it is the fruit of an exceptional encounter of world religions at the esoteric level. It not only brings into focus a huge amount of first-hand information otherwise scattered throughout scholarly periodicals, but also carries the ecumenical dialogue to a level of depth and essentiality, of sympathetic communication, and of tolerance unprecedented in events and writings of this kind.
>
> Nobody chose to ignore the deep-seated differences between traditions; on the contrary, all the authors seemed acutely aware of the irreducible originality of each tradition. But while the main endeavor of the representatives of various religions was to situate each mystical discipline within its traditional ground and also to exhibit the "flowers of action" that stem from this rerooting, they all became aware of the sacredness presiding over this enterprise, a result that far transcended what could be expected from the well-worn philosophical principle of "unity in diversity".
>
> Frithjof Schuon's idea of the "transcendent unity of religions at the esoteric level" functions naturally as Ariadne's thread for many articles included in this volume. . . .[2]

The following year, Jacob Needleman, the editor for the "The Penguin Metaphysical Library" series,[3] described the impression made upon him by essentially the same group of writers:

> One of the most interesting intellectual developments of the 1960s was the publication in England of a periodical called *Studies in Comparative Religion.*[4] When it first came across my desk, it had seemed to me merely another gray scholarly journal—an impression that was only strengthened by its stated purpose of presenting essays concerning "traditional studies". Like many Americans, I was put off by the very word "tradition". But I pressed on because I had heard that this journal contained some of the most serious thinking of the twentieth century. And in fact I quickly saw that its contributors were not interested in the hypothesizing and the marshaling of piecemeal evidence that characterizes the work of most academicians. On close reading, I felt an extraordinary intellectual force radiating through their intricate prose. These men were out for the kill. For them, the study of spiritual traditions was a sword with which to destroy the illusions of contemporary man. . . .
>
> All I could have said definitely was that they seemed to take metaphysical ideas more seriously than one might have thought possible. It was as though for them such ideas were the most real things in the world. They conformed their thought to these ideas in the way the rest of us tend to conform our thought to material things. Perhaps it was this aspect that gave their essays a flavor that was both slightly archaic and astonishingly fresh at the same time. . . .
>
> That these writings bring something that has been entirely lacking in Western religious thought is therefore not open to question. But that is not the court at which their work deserves to be judged, nor would they wish it so. Something much more serious is at stake than merely renewing the comparative study of religion throughout the land. . . .[5]

Concerning the implications of Schuon's work in particular, Needleman writes: "Readers of this volume [*Sword of Gnosis*] will certainly find in the writings of Schuon and those he has influenced completely new perspectives in every aspect of religious thought. . . . Very probably, it will seem to the reader that until now he has ignored an entire dimension in his thinking about tradition."[6]

Most of Schuon's French works written before 1970 were translated into English and published in Great Britain, where they found a not inconsiderable audience. During this time only one of his books, *The Transcendent Unity of Religions* (Pantheon, 1953), appeared in an American edition. In the 1970s, however, three of his books were published in paperback editions by two of the largest United States publishing houses: *Understanding Islam* (Penguin, 1972), *The Transcendent Unity of Religion* (Harper & Row, 1974), and *Logic and Transcendence* (Harper & Row, 1975). A fourth book, *Sword of Gnosis* (Penguin, 1974), is an anthology edited by Jacob Needleman that contains six of Schuon's essays. These four books made Schuon's writings widely available for the first time throughout North America.

The publication of these and other books drew attention to what has come to be called the Perennialist (or Traditionalist) school of writers[7] and thrust Schuon into the position of its preeminent spokesperson. As a result, in the late 1970s, scholars affiliated with the American Academy of Religion (AAR)[8] began to debate the merits of the perennial philosophy in various publications. The debate emerged at the AAR's Annual Meeting in 1982 and gained force during the remainder of the 1980s, with several sessions at Annual Meetings devoted to considering Perennialism as a methodology for understanding the phenomenon of religion.[9] Parallel to this was an increase in the discussion of the perennial philosophy in various publications, which continues to take place inside and outside of academia, including several intellectual journals that are more or less dedicated to the discussion of tradition and its relationship with modernity.[10] One scholar recently offered this general observation: "One rarely encounters academic specialists in the spiritual dimensions of religious studies who have not in fact read several of the works of Schuon, but this wide-ranging influence is rarely mentioned publicly because of the peculiar processes of academic 'canonization'"[11]

While it is appropriate that Frithjof Schuon's message has been and continues to be considered within academia, it is undeniable that this message goes far beyond the confines of the academic order. Individual readers who understand and accept his message are obliged to live up to the responsibility of the human vocation described in his works; they must be serious about their relationship to God, to religion, and to their neighbors.[12] Schuon is interested in the "integral understanding—the rediscovery—of . . . tradition", and not, as Needleman observed, in "the marshaling of piecemeal evidence that characterizes the work of most academicians".[13] By definition, such an understanding could never depend exclusively upon "historical researches" but must base itself "on the constants of the tradition on the one hand, and on the other hand, on the metaphysical and mystical knowledge of the person seeking to rediscover its spirit".[14] We are here far from contemporary scholarly standards and much closer to the spirit and approach of the great saints and sages of history. As Needleman concludes:

> The highest praise that I can offer concerning the writings of Frithjof Schuon is that they are worthy of their subject matter—the teachings of the great spiritual traditions. Whether one's views are supported or challenged by these writings, any serious person will feel grateful to be confronted by such a generously discerning intellect and to witness the emergence of authentic contemplative thought in this darkening time.[15]

20. The Move to America

They built for me a beautiful wooden house
In a forest where deer live —
And spiritual friends dwell all around;
A few Indian tents are pitched nearby.

It is a little earthly paradise,
Made so that, undisturbed, one may strive upwards,
Towards the archetype, about which the soul knows full well.[1]

In September, 1980 the seventy-three year philosopher and his wife left their home overlooking Lake Geneva and the Alps for the hills and forests of southern Indiana.[2] Catherine Schuon later wrote about the reason for the move, the immigration process, and their new circumstance in Bloomington, Indiana, where a number of Schuon's followers lived:

> [O]ne day the Shaykh received an absolutely certain sign from Heaven to emigrate to America. This sign was so imperious that when I told him, after a visit to the American Consulate, that there was no possibility for us to immigrate, he had a crisis of asthma and said in that case we should try Canada or Mexico. Fortunately, thanks to the help of an American friend who was a lawyer, the obstacles could be removed and it is thus that we left for the forests of Indiana. . . .[3]

Three months before his move to Bloomington, Schuon wrote to Martin Lings about his decision to leave Europe for America:

> We have taken a very serious resolution, and I must say that I had a premonition of this for quite some time already. We have the intention of settling in Bloomington. . . .
>
> There are for this—that is to say for this project—inward as well as outward reasons. . . . [N]ow I feel that there is a dimension that is missing in my life, and that Bloomington could be its framework. I long for a vast and quiet ambience away from the pressures and dispersions of the world. . . . I am well aware of the incredible momentousness of this change.[4]

We recall the much earlier prediction made by the venerable Moroccan Shaykh Hassan that Schuon would end his life in the "*Extrême-Occident*" ("Far West"). As Schuon observed in the same letter to Lings, "Destiny did not want for me to retire in the Maghreb, which is the Farthermost West for the Muslim world; now America is the Farthermost West as such." Later he added, "A thought that came to mind is the following: the fact that we were solemnly adopted by the tribe of the Lakota indicates a certain destiny; the

Indians are America, and they are at the same time virgin nature, primordiality, the *religio perennis*. I carried this dimension in myself since my childhood, and my work bears its imprint." In one of his first letters written in Bloomington, Schuon explains that his move signified "a moving away from the *Religio formalis* by virtue of a moving toward the *Religio perennis*. . .".[5]

In October 1980 Thomas and Susie Yellowtail came to Bloomington, where they became the first of the Schuons' friends to visit them in their new home.[6] Schuon pointed out to the Yellowtails that they were also the first visitors to stay in his new home in Lausanne in 1954. On several evenings during the Yellowtails' stay, Schuon relates,

> rites of healing, with long prayers, took place, in the course of which Yellowtail touched and stroked [those] who were being healed with his eagle fan. I was the first he treated in this manner, and this contact with the *Barakah* of his eagle feathers had a special meaning for me: it was a meeting, through the medium of the Indian world, with the *Religio perennis*, and this at the beginning of my stay on this continent. When we showed the Indians our new house, Yellowtail said a long prayer in our prayer room and so to speak consecrated it, and this again had a meaning similar to that of the above-mentioned event. [7]

When the Schuons were living in Lausanne, and after their formal adoption into the Lakota tribe, there occurred a simple event which, during the Bloomington years, Schuon would call an Indian Day. Originally, the four adopted Lakota, Frithjof and Catherine Schuon and Whitall and Barbara Perry, put on their Indian clothing, sang a Lakota song and prayed for the Indians by the tipi in the Schuons' backyard. The first Indian Day in Bloomington in 1981 was a similar event. Then in October 1983 Thomas Yellowtail brought his traditional Indian clothing when he came for his annual visit. "Yellow Tail was recently here", Schuon wrote to Titus Burckhardt.

> [W]e organized an "Indian Day" in which many friends, both men and women, participated in Indian dress; Yellow Tail too wore Indian dress, even the feathered headdress. He showed the women how they should dance; after the midday meal—outside on our lawn near the forest—the women did a round dance, according to his instructions, while he drummed along and sang. I too wore, very exceptionally,[8] my headdress for this occasion, but stayed only for a short while at the celebration. . . . At the end the friends, both men and women, sat around Yellow Tail and listened reverentially as he explained to them many things. . . . "It was like in the old times", he told us afterwards and he was very happy.[9]

Left to right: Frithjof Schuon, Catherine Schuon, Barbara Perry, and Whitall Perry, Lausanne, c. 1964

"To wear a traditional garment to which one has a sufficient right . . . is to be clothed with an archetype, a spirit." (*The Play of Masks*, back cover)

With Yellowtail beside the tipi in the Schuons' garden, autumn 1983

This was the first time that a number of Schuon's followers, encouraged by Yellowtail, performed traditional Indian dancing behind Schuon's home near his tipi.[10]

Yellowtail continued to attend such celebrations each year until his death in 1993.[11] On one memorable occasion, in the Fall of 1987, the venerable Crow Sun Dance Chief adopted all of those present into his family.[12] Later that day Yellowtail said of Schuon: "He is my brother, we are in the same boat together in all things." He added: "My spiritual family is in Bloomington."[13] One of Schuon's poems, written after Yellowtail's passing, recalls his friend's enjoyment of these occasions of shared participation in Indian life:

> At the forest fringe of my garden is a place
> That pleased our friend Yellowtail;
> Here he loved to stay in the sunshine
> With us, his brethren, taking part in our Indian celebration.
> He is no longer of this world;
> But the soul of the Red people is in the air —
> And with it the Great Spirit, that never fades away.[14]

During his years in Lausanne, Schuon had enjoyed periodic retreats in the mountains so as to be surrounded by virgin nature, whereas the Bloomington years were, in a sense, a permanent retreat within virgin nature. Thus, during the remaining eighteen years of his life he made only four journeys outside southern Indiana. In many other respects, however, his daily life continued to follow the pattern established in Switzerland, including writing, receiving visitors, and often sharing a midday meal in the home of friends.[15] Weather permitting, he took daily walks in the surrounding woods, and in 1993 a long veranda was added to the back of his house, which allowed him to walk outside even in inclement weather.[16]

The move to Bloomington marked in a certain way the beginning of a new phase in Schuon's life. In two letters written to his longtime friend Leo Schaya[17] in 1980 and 1981, the sage looked back on his life as a spiritual guide and identified four broad phases, the first beginning in 1936 with the descent of his function as spiritual guide; the second beginning in 1942 with the gift of the Themes of Meditation; the third beginning in 1965 with the visitation by the Holy Virgin; and the fourth beginning in 1980 with the move to Bloomington. "The first phase is characterized by the fact that we, as young travelers on the spiritual path, without any experience, were necessarily under the spell of Guénon and also the psychic atmosphere of exoteric Islam." The characteristics of the second phase, he continues, "are, on the contrary, that this spell was broken and that the emphasis was now placed on the Themes and the Invocation, which in principle includes everything and that there was also a certain *barakah* stemming from Hinduism and the American Indians, or rather: there were two different radiations which affected us spiritually and psychically."[18]

Of the third phase, Schuon writes, "The outward characteristic of this phase is above all, it seems to me, the fact that, proceeding from an inner vision, I painted the Virgin and wrote Arabic poems, or rather prayers, to her; whereas what was new for my inner life was that I suddenly felt separated from my surroundings and their godless din, and that I was as it were enclosed in a golden aura, which I could also compare to a little heavenly garden." He concludes by adding that, "in the third phase it became a certitude to me that the Holy Virgin is the living and heavenly link between Islam and Christianity, and that she also links us to Judaism and even to all religions. . .".[19]

The fourth phase, inaugurated by the move to Bloomington, was marked by his life in a forest abode—a return to nature—and by the synthetic nature of his writings, which included the radiation of his gift as a poet. Notwithstanding the constant stream of visitors that came from all quarters of the world to seek an audience with him, Schuon's forest home provided a refuge from the bustling technological world, as well as an ideal setting for his writing and his life of prayer.

Home
Rolling forest. In its deep center,
A clear brook; above, the wooden house
With the veranda, that winds westward
And links my abode with the trees.

A wild meadow around my house;
An Indian tent, some tall pines too;
A carpet of flowers; the deer come here.
I could not imagine a better home

Upon this earth, and in the realm of time.
My timeless heart dwells in Eternity.[20]

The entryway of the Schuons' home, Bloomington

"The houses of the friends here . . . have a marked touch of Japan that already results from the fact that the sliding doors (*shoji*) and certain lamps are made by a Japanese carpenter; this touch has for me a deep significance, the Japanese art of building and furnishing bearing witness, in its fashion, to the Primordial Tradition—through Shintō, which has always been close to me—just as does the Indian tradition." (letter to Hans Küry, September 21, 1980)

The living room of the Schuons' home, Bloomington

Sunrise over the Schuons' home, autumn 1981

"Here the woods are lit up with glowing autumn colors, from the most delicate yellow to the most fiery red, and when a light wind blows, the leaves glide to earth as if it were raining gold, as in a fairy-tale. A few days ago it rained, and afterward, at sunset, the whole landscape was plunged in a rosy and golden light; there was a sweet inebriation in the air as if all had turned into singing wine; rarely in my life have I seen something of such fairy-tale-like beauty." (letter to Leo Schaya, October 1980)

In front of his home, c. 1990

21. Reflections

Following his move to America in 1980, Schuon looked back on his life and work in what are an important series of letters to some of his oldest and closest followers in Europe. At the beginning of his eightieth year, he wrote of the phenomenon of old age in a letter to Marco Pallis, who had just reached ninety-three years of age:

> The more I age, the more I see that there is something mysterious in the condition of old age; I have in mind him for whom life has a meaning. Most persons are passive in regard to phenomena and events, they let themselves be corroded, so to speak, by duration; time has the power to change them; from this stems the characteristic psychology of the average old person, who is someone tired and "disillusioned". Altogether different is the position of the man—whatever his age—who by his spiritual attitude keeps himself outside time: duration does not corrode him, he does not abandon himself to the powers of the world, he learns not to be the dupe of his own soul; he abides in the changeless freshness of the "Eternal Present". What is curious in the average old man, is that certain of his youthful "illusions" were worth more than the "disillusion" of his old age; for there are experiences and evaluations that, not being wisdom, merely prove the smallness of the individual; the man who knows how to age soundly, on the contrary, always keeps some of the happiness of childhood. The key to his happiness, to a large extent, is gratitude.
>
> It could be said that space disperses us whereas time enslaves us; the worldly man, in the first respect, is someone agitated; in the second respect, he is someone passive. To know the meaning of life and to take it seriously, is to keep one's freedom; it is to rest at the Center and in the Present. Obviously there is a certain fatigue in old age, but it need not determine our personality; and alongside it there is a perfume of holy childlikeness and second youth.[1]

The following 1989 letter was written to one of his early classmates from Basle and represents a summary of Schuon's life and teachings:

> We are now quite old, and this prompts us to look back on our past. I often think how miraculous it is that with God's help and despite all opposition from the environment, I succeeded in making my real nature and my Message prevail—in remaining true to myself and in giving to the world what I have to give. In my childhood I had four ideals which in fact constitute my personality: the Essential or the Truth; the Sacred; Beauty; Greatness. And this in a world of error, the meaningless, the profane, ugliness, and pettiness; these contrasts nearly destroyed me, not only through the absurdity of the bad, but also on account of the

tremendous and unremitting strain of my inner resistance; you yourself must necessarily have experienced something similar.

On the basis of those four ideals, I from my childhood bore within me the certainty that I had a spiritual mission; and as is apparent from the earliest pages of my diary and from many letters, I was awaiting an "inner rebirth" and already very early had the plan to emigrate to a "holy land"; from this break with the West and this contact with the East I expected everything. And it was fulfilled: the great journey was my flight to Algeria; the inner rebirth was the descent of the Supreme Name. Afterwards, my mission was fulfilled through my spiritual function, and later I received my particular Message, the Themes.

Already as a child I read the *Bhagavad Gītā* and was deeply moved by Hindu and Buddhist art; therein I found on the one hand the whole Truth and on the other hand the most direct expression of the Sacred. In Hinduism I felt completely at home, it was for me the native land of pure metaphysics as well as of the primordial spiritual world and thus also of sacred nudity; it contains indeed every spiritual possibility, from the simplest to the most complex and the most extensive.

And in addition to this I had from childhood a special relationship with the Red Indian world: boundless virgin nature; Eagle and Sun; metaphysics of the Directions of Space; the all-transcending and at the same time all-pervading Great Spirit. Then the ideal of self-domination, of transcending oneself, of dignity; the Eagle soaring to the Sun, relived in the Sun Dance.

My relationship with Islam results from the fact that Islam is founded on the confession of Unity; then, from the circumstance that everyone is his own priest, and also that Islam could offer me an initiation and a spiritual method; and finally from my providential encounter with an Islamic saint.

The most important—and therefore altogether decisive—thought in life is the consciousness that God is the Sovereign Good, of which all earthly goods give evidence. Then come two fundamental attitudes: surrender to the Will of God and trust in God's Goodness; one must resign oneself to the unavoidable, and this without ever doubting God's Mercy, which indeed for us has the last word, and which is contained in the Supreme Name.

Our right relationship with the world results from our right relationship with God; from this second relationship, which in reality is the first, come also the essential virtues; and these are at the same time a condition of that relationship.

The primordial thought that God is the Sovereign Good silences—by its very nature—all the mental din of the world; its pre-eminence in the soul constitutes the spiritual nobility of man, and thus also the right relationship to the world around him.

Wherever we are conscious of God, there always is the Center, and there also is the essence of our happiness.[2]

Many of the poems Schuon wrote in the last years of his life also reflect on his life and work:

The German ambience — this was my earliest world;
Very soon France was added to it.

I also became an Arab and a Red Indian —
True to myself, and according to the way of wise men.

In the present age I felt homeless —
Driven around as on a raft.

The Eternal-Feminine saw me from afar;
The Holy Virgin became my morning star.[3]

— ·:· —

Early in my life there came the Psalms, the *Bhagavad Gītā*,
The *Upanishads*, and Shankara's *Vedānta*;
Sacred books, my first nourishment —
Then came the free revelation of the Spirit.
A holy shaykh spoke to me about the prayer of the heart —
The profound meaning was the same as *Vedānta*.
Later life taught me many things —
But everything was given me by the One God.

Stern is the spirit that fights for the True;
But holy wrath is accompanied by music.
Be grateful, pay thy debt to the Most High —
With devotion, humility, generosity, and patience.[4]

— ·:· —

Life's Work

The work, a lifelong struggle — first
Youthful dreams: the True, the Beautiful,
The Sacred, and the Great. Then dreams
Come true, that the Word might be heard.

All this amid the shadows — will it shine or not?
Does destiny wish that the Word grow weary
And weaker throughout life? *Fiat Lux* —
God willed that it should flourish and remain.

In the book of my message you have read
And ask: from whence resounds the Master's voice?
His substance is part Shankara, part Krishna —
Singing gnosis is his primordial essence.[5]

During these years several of Schuon's oldest friends passed into the next world—among them Hans Küry, Leo Schaya, Lucy von Dechend, Marco Pallis, Johann Jakob Jenny, Thomas Yellowtail, Titus Burckhardt, and his brother, Father Gall.[6] "One certainly does not have the right to complain about living on this earth, but when one learns that a friend has left this station of the *samsāra*, one cannot help feeling happiness for him. . . . *Gate gate paragate parsamgate bodhi svaha*! ['Gone, gone, gone to the other shore, attained the other shore, O Enlightenment, be blessed!']"[7] Schuon rarely wrote descriptively of those who were close to him, even in his private papers, but multiple references to and descriptions of both Titus Burckhardt and Thomas Yellowtail are exceptions to the rule:

> Now that he [Titus Burckhardt] is in the next world, I feel that he is even closer to me than before. . . . I have known S. Ibrāhīm [Burckhardt] since I was twelve years old; at school we competed with one another in drawing pictures of the Greek myths. Actually, our friendship began in Riehen, at the home of Frau von Dechend; there we had a long conversation about Guénon, Islam, and the Maghrib. What was precious in him, humanly speaking, was the conjunction of an unusually acute and profound intelligence with high artistic gifts; since he could not become a creative artist—and it is fortunate that he was prevented from so doing—his talents went wholly into the spiritual life, and all the more so as he was to a high degree mystically inclined. . . .
>
> There was something eternally young and liberating about Titus Burckhardt; in his presence, one never felt constricted. He was certainly not lacking in humor, and he also had a sense of adventure and was enterprising and adaptable; moreover, he was kind-hearted and of a childlike guilelessness and purity.
>
> To this I would add that he was an excellent writer, as we all know. . . . I mention all this because I feel the need to say it here in memory of my friend.[8]

—·:·—

> With Yellowtail I have a quite special relationship; between him and me there is a kind of unspoken friendship that is rooted in our natures. He belongs to those people of whom one knows they will go to Heaven, because the contrary would be quite unimaginable. Yellowtail is a combination of a kind of childlike earth-heaviness and simplicity with an undertone of saintliness; he has in his being . . . something contemplative, sacerdotal, serene, profoundly good and God-centered. When he speaks, he strings image upon image, the flow of speech is mild, slow, and endless, free of all self-mirroring and hypocrisy; withal he is a rock, not out of hardness, but out of strength and patience, and something recollected and profound permeates his whole being. He always accompanies his words with Indian gestures, thereby adding

a picturesque and solemn quality to his monotonous and meditative speech. . . . This infinitely mild, yet tough man seems to live outside time, as if time flowed more slowly for him.

Schuon also wrote in verse of both of these close friends:

"Feather from the Tail of the Yellow Hawk" was
My friend, the sun dance priest of the Crow;
From his eagle fan one could feel
The healing power of his good spirits.
He was a man of a childlike disposition,
And deeply penetrated by a sense of Being and of life.
Everything for him was prayer; and he faithfully sang
His song to the Great Spirit until the end.[9]

—— ·:· ——

God often gives us in our earthly life
A brother-soul, who embellishes the Path,
And who, in this or that respect,
Reconciles us with the ups and downs of life.

The wise Titus Burckhardt was a friend
As there can be no better in life;
A brother, given me in far off days,
From earliest youth until the grave. . . .[10]

With Titus Burckhardt in the Swiss Alps, c. 1970

Lucy von Dechend

Johann Jakob Jenny

Four of Schuon's long-time friends

Leo Schaya

Hans Küry

22. The Close of Two Cycles

In his function as a spiritual guide, Frithjof Schuon recognized and accommodated the wide, legitimate divergences in what he called "the human margin",[1] while always insisting on the uniformity of essential principles, namely metaphysical doctrine, prayer in the framework of an orthodox religion, intrinsic virtue, and the importance of natural and traditional beauty.[2] Although his followers represented a variety of backgrounds, tendencies, and characters, the comments of Mudumbaï Ramachandran, one of Schuon's Hindu admirers, point to Schuon's unifying influence.

> Knowing Schuon created for many of us all over the world a fraternity. We often met for the first time in his name and became fast friends. Humanly he created a cosmopolitan international fraternity, which reaches far beyond the circles that any one of us individually knows. In a very important sense, he has been a presence as well as a felt absence at our encounters with one another. For this enrichment of our lives at so many levels, from the practical to the social, the intellectual and above all, the spiritual, thousands of people all over the world will remain truly grateful.[3]

In the late 1980s and early 1990s there was a certain amount of speculation among his disciples regarding the possibility of a successor for such a humanly diverse group of seekers. All speculation was put to rest on July 15, 1992 when Schuon wrote a short statement announcing that he had "decided to retire and . . . since it is practically speaking impossible to choose a successor, each representative will be independent. . .".[4] During the previous years, as the need had arisen, Schuon had authorized more than a dozen representatives in different parts of the world, in much the same way as he had been authorized in 1935 to represent the 'Alawī Sufi brotherhood.[5] This declaration granted autonomy to each of his representatives and thus created more than a dozen independent branches of his followers.[6] "[T]he transmission of the spiritual influence or *barakah* in Islamic initiatic organizations", René Guénon explains, ". . . permits a *khalīfah* [representative] to take the place of the Shaykh and legitimately fulfill his function without actually having attained to the Shaykh's own spiritual state."[7] In the subsequent period of his retirement, Schuon continued to receive visitors regularly from around the world, providing important counsel to individual followers as well as to his designated representatives.

Three years later, at the age of eighty-seven, Schuon completed his final metaphysical book, *The Transfiguration of Man*,[8] thus bringing to an end a cycle of writing that began more than sixty years earlier.[9] Looking back on Schuon's completed *oeuvre*, Harry Oldmeadow has observed that

> Schuon's works are governed by an unchanging set of metaphysical principles. They exhibit nothing of a "development" or "evolution" but are, rather, re-statements of the same principles from different vantage points and brought to bear on divergent phenomena. Schuon's vision was complete from the outset. The recent translation and publication of Schuon's first book, which he commenced in 1927 and which was published in German in 1935, makes this perfectly evident. . . . When considering Schuon's writings one is immensely impressed by his learning but there is something here far beyond "erudition": Schuon not only knows "about" an encyclopedic range of religious manifestations and sapiential traditions, but understands them "from the inside", in a way which, for want of a better word, we can only call intuitive.[10]

Schuon's last metaphysical work ends with a collection of short texts on the spiritual life.[11] The last of these is entitled "The Two Great Moments" and constitutes, in a sense, his parting council:

> There are two moments in life which are everything, and these are the present moment, when we are free to choose what we wish to be, and the moment of death, when we have no longer any choice and when the decision belongs to God.
>
> If the present moment is good, death will be good; if we are now with God—in this present which ceaselessly renews itself but which remains always this one and only moment of actuality—God will be with us at the moment of our death.
>
> The remembrance of God is a death in life; it will be a life in death.
>
> Analogously: if we enter into God, God will enter into us.
>
> If we dwell in that center which is His Name, God will dwell in that center which is our heart. In the whole extent of the world, there is nothing else than this reciprocity: for the center is everywhere, just as the present is always.
>
> Between the present moment, when we remember God, and death, when God will remember us—and this reciprocity is to be found already in each Invocation—there is the rest of life, the duration which extends from the present moment to the last moment; but duration is merely a succession of present moments, for we live always "now"; it is thus, concretely and operatively speaking, always the same blessed instant in which we are free to remember God and to find our happiness in this Remembrance.
>
> We are not free to escape from death, but we are free to choose God, in this present moment which sums up every possible moment. It is true that God alone is absolutely free; but our freedom is nonetheless real at its own level—otherwise the word would not exist—since it

> manifests the Freedom of God and therefore participates in it. In God, we are as free as we can be, and to the extent that God reintegrates us into His Infinite Freedom.[12]

Foundational ideas for this text were included in a letter that he wrote more than sixty-five years earlier: "Death is one of the great facts of Being, or a face of Reality; the present moment is another. This present moment is everything; may we win it! Even when we die, we survey the world from the point of view of one unique Present, which recompenses all our existence and absorbs it into one Inevitability."[13]

The completion of this cycle of metaphysical writing coincided with the beginning of the final cycle of his poetry.

23. A Profusion of Songs

My parents wanted me to be a painter;
But I read poets and wished to be like them,
And lived until my twelfth summer
In romanticism's somber melody.

Then came India, early enough; the poet
Still had his say, but never in the foreground;
Then he kept silent for many years.
In old age
The poet awoke again — not in order to dream —
But to sing new songs sprung from the Spirit.[1]

"Since from childhood I had delighted in drawing and painting . . . my father cherished the wish that I should become an artist". However, contrary to the wish of his parents—in particular his father—Schuon found that he wanted to be a poet, not a painter. "What spurred me towards poetry was my discovery in my father's bookcase of all the German lyricists, and I eagerly read in them; the melancholic folksong style specially appealed to me." A poem written at the age of ninety incorporates one of the first poems to flow from his pen:

Late summer has now kissed the land;
With weary rustling in the woods;
The little flowers on the hill
Bow their heads towards autumn.
The rose glows in the evening light,
And fades away — spring is long past;
A man stands there and, quite alone,
Harkens to the Creator's song.

This poem — not the last two lines —
I wrote as a child almost eighty years ago.
When I was a child, I wanted to be a poet —
God can also reveal Himself in little flowers.[2]

Schuon's poetic gift continued to manifest itself at various points throughout his life, and he acknowledged that some of his poems were written "in the ecstasy of an inspiration". In 1947 he published two small volumes of poetry written between the years 1932 and 1942.[3] "I was a poet, then, during a long and unhappy period of my life. . . . When it happens that, looking back, I read these poems, I meet in them on the one hand a person who no longer exists, and on the other the music of my immutable soul, depending upon which poems, passages, or words I read."[4]

After some twenty years of silence, there suddenly came the series of Arabic poems mentioned previously, written by Schuon in the wake of the graces he received from the Holy Virgin. Then for many years the poet again remained silent, until at the age of 86, he wrote a small series of poems in English, which were subsequently published in the collection called *Road to the Heart*. The following year, returning to his native German, he began his last, unimaginably rich, and unforeseen poetic cycle. During the next three years, Schuon wrote more than three thousand "teaching poems" (*Lehrgedichte*), their inspiration coming in such abundance that it was not unusual for him to complete several poems in a day.[5] William Stoddart, in his Introduction to a bilingual (German-English) volume of Schuon's poetry entitled *Adastra & Stella Maris*, speaks of the inexhaustible wealth of these "last songs":[6]

> A blessing lies not only in the quality of the poems, but also in the quantity—they constitute an all-inclusive totality. . . . The poems cover every possible aspect of metaphysical doctrine, spiritual method, spiritual virtue, and the role and function of beauty. They express every conceivable subtlety of spiritual and moral counsel—and this not merely in general terms, but with uncanny intimacy, detail, and precision. They exhibit incredible sharpness, profundity, comprehensiveness, and compassion.
>
> Some of the poems are autobiographical, with reminiscences of places experienced: Basle and Paris, the fairy tale-streets of old German towns, Morocco and Andalusia, Turkey and Greece, the American West. Others evoke the genius of certain peoples, such as the Hindus, the Japanese, the Arabs, the American Indians, and also the Cossacks and the Gypsies. Yet other poems elucidate the role of music, dance, and poetry itself. In one or two poems, the godless modern world comes in for biting, and sometimes fiercely humorous, comment.[7]

In her Foreword to the same work, Annemarie Schimmel,[8] herself a native German speaker, describes the way in which "the great mystics all over the world used the language of poetry when trying to beckon to a mystery that lies beyond normal human experience. . . . Taking this fact into consideration", Schimmel continues, "we are not surprised that Frithjof Schuon too felt compelled to write poetry. . .". After comparing the ideas, images, and sound of Schuon's German verses to those of Rilke, Schimmel notes:

> This sound [of the German] could not be maintained in the English translations of his poetry. Yet, as he himself explains, what really matters is the content, and here we listen to the thinker who, far from the intricate and complex scholarly sentences of his learned prose works

> sings the simple prayers of the longing soul: God is the center, the primordial ground which comprehends everything, manifesting Himself through the colorful play of His creations. And it is the human heart which alone can reflect the incomprehensible Being, for humanity's central quality is divinely inspired love, which is the axis of our life.
>
> I hope that Schuon's mystical verse will be read not only by English speaking readers but even more by those who understand German. They will enjoy many of these tender lyrics which show the famous thinker in a very different light and from an unexpected side.[9]

Echoing Schimmel's view, the editors of a collection of his poems affirm that "The poetic expressions in this volume offer an insight into the mind and heart of a sage, and one is able to enter more closely into contact with the personality and soul of the author. His poems derive, he says, not from mental effort, but from an interior vision: 'I have Paradise written in the ground of my being — I have only to go there to see it.' And the creative process, he tells us in several poems, is like stepping into a river—a river of song, whose irresistible current is the love that flows, beyond name and time, from God to God."[10]

This final poetical opus is in many ways a synthesis of his life's written work and provides a complement to the sage's articles. "Why did Schuon write poetry", one might ask, "when he had already expounded his message in his metaphysical books?" To which question, "One can only reply that a simple reading of these poems will furnish their own answer, for as with any great artistic production, theirs is a language at once direct and synthetic, which speaks straight to the heart. Readers familiar with Schuon's many books and articles will find here the same elements that characterize the rest of his vast corpus: universality, essentiality, primordiality; yet in a form that makes his message more easily accessible, and they speak to the heart, the mind, the soul with compelling immediacy."[11]

Frithjof Schuon's last poem was written on March 12, 1998, fewer than two months before his death:

> I have for long wished to end this book —
> I could not do so; I had to write more poems.
> But this time my pen lies down of itself,
> For there are other preoccupations, other duties;
> Be that as it may, whatever we may wish to do:
> Let us follow the call of the Most High —
>
> Let us repose in God's deep Peace.[12]

During the last two years of the philosopher's life, he had several times predicted that the flow of poems would soon stop, but inspiration constantly returned. When, however, the ninety year old poet wrote his last poem, few doubted that Heaven had "other preoccupations" in store and that this cycle of his poetic inspiration had come to a close; for Schuon, as always, remained obedient to the call of the Most High. The last seven weeks of his life were a peaceful period spent in the remembrance of God, his vital forces gradually withdrawing.

In April he wrote his final spiritual text, entitled "Hope and Faith":

> How can the spiritual man conquer the natural tendency to sadness that old age entails? It will be said: by the hope of a better hereafter; but this is not enough, for the elderly person must find already in the here-below a reason to be happy, and it is Faith. Faith is our relationship with God; if this relationship is living, then the possibility of dominating our purely natural tendencies is already there.
>
> Man lives in time; God is the Eternal. In prayer, the human and the Divine meet—when we say Yes to God in the depths of our heart.

At his desk, c. 1995

Excerpt from the final lines written by Frithjof Schuon, days before his death: "The essentially qualitative phenomenon that is Intelligence can arise everywhere; likewise, the no less qualitative phenomenon that is Goodness, and the same is true for the quantitative, and thus neutral, phenomenon that is genius—supersaturation. The supremely qualitative phenomena of Sanctity and Wisdom can appear everywhere, otherwise Man would not be Man." (*Sophia*, Vol. 4, No. 2, Winter 1998, 14)

24. Departure

On Tuesday May 5, 1998, Frithjof Schuon arose just before dawn to say his morning prayers. A short time later he died in his armchair, gazing toward the heavens while immersed in the consciousness of God. His funeral was delayed for four days until Saturday, May 9 in order to accommodate the large number of friends and admirers who came from many parts of the world to render homage to him. During this time his body lay in state in the middle of his living room, allowing his followers to sit around him in prayer. The entire four days before his funeral was a time of great blessing; when coming into his presence, grief was replaced by serenity and immense gratitude.

In accordance with his prior request, his funeral included elements reflecting different aspects of his life, beginning with recitations from the Koran and personal prayer. This was followed by the recitation of three of Schuon's poems from his English-language collection *Road to the Heart*. The final couplet of the final poem, entitled "Treasures", produced a profound and indescribable silence, broken only by the singing of the birds:

> Because I made my heart a holy shrine,
> My soul belongs to God, and God is mine.[1]

After six men had lowered his coffin into the grave with ropes, the women came forward and placed flowers on top of the coffin. Each man then placed at least one shovelful of earth into the grave until a mound was formed. Then each woman came again, placing flowers on top of the covered grave. The ceremony ended with a Crow Sun Dance chief[2] saying a prayer with a sacred pipe, accompanied by an American Indian song in honor of Schuon. A prolonged period of individual prayer followed the ceremony. Today, Schuon's body rests in a private wooded cemetery not far from his home.

Afterword

While words and photographs can provide a partial portrait of Frithjof Schuon, they are unable to convey the lived experience of being in his presence. Mark Perry has called to mind the image of Schuon as "a priest carrying a sacred object and who therefore advances slowly but firmly while holding himself erect".[1] It will not surprise most readers to learn that many who met him recognized a tangible charisma.[2] To recall the formulation of Swami Ramdas: "[Schuon's] face was bright with the light of inner illumination".[3] This spiritual radiation corresponds to similar accounts in the biographies of venerable saints and sages in the world's religions.[4]

Huston Smith, who met many of the most respected spiritual leaders of our time, concluded that Frithjof Schuon is perhaps the only person he has known "who invariably made me feel, on leaving him, that I had been in the presence of a different order of human being".[5] This biographer would say that each encounter with him reinforced the awareness that the spiritual life is an ever-present reality—that each moment and every human interaction is an opportunity to practice virtue and to remember God. But without having had the opportunity to encounter such a person, this is difficult to imagine fully. The dearth of spiritual paragons—those who connect heaven with earth—is among the most grievous realities of our day in that it leaves us without the ineffable teaching conveyed by their presence.

An interview comment by Martin Lings presents his immediate impression of Schuon when he met him for the first time in 1938:

> I knew when I was in his [Schuon's] presence that I was in the presence of a true saint and also the spiritual master that I was seeking. When I say "true saint", I don't mean just a saintly man but a true saint of the first magnitude, such as one cannot expect to meet in the twentieth century. I mean a saint of the magnitude of St. Bernard, St. Francis, or St. Augustine in Christianity; of Ibn 'Arabī or Rūmī in Sufism, of Shankara in Hinduism, and of Milarepa in Buddhism. I knew this with a certainty.[6]

His friend of fifty years, Whitall Perry, writes:

> Schuon always rejected efforts made to label his intellectual or spiritual role in the world. "I do not know who or what I am", he insisted; "it is Heaven that knows."[7] The closest he came to definitions was to say that he represented the compendium or seal of wisdom for our moment in the cosmic cycle.[8] And yet if someone claimed for him a wisdom greater than what a Shankara or a Plato possessed, his rejoinder was that he benefited from a hindsight available at this point in history which those coming earlier did not have at their disposal.[9]

"Everything has already been said, and even well said", Schuon informs us, "but it is always necessary to recall it anew, and in so doing, do what has always been done: to actualize in thought the certitudes contained, not in the thinking ego, but in the transpersonal substance of the human intelligence."[10] Such was Frithjof Schuon's task to fulfill—to be in this modern world a messenger of the Perennial Philosophy. It was a message that he bore within, as he himself concedes in his penultimate poem, penned in March of 1998:

> Do not think that what I say here of myself
> Lacks modesty or is exaggerated:
> All that one finds in good old books
> Regarding Being, and the question of the universe,
> God has inscribed in the substance of my heart.[11]

Schuon's teachings live on through his written works: situated within the protective framework of an intrinsically orthodox religion, they provide the keys for each individual first to comprehend the nature of the Real; then to concentrate on the Real through prayer; and finally to conform to the Real through intrinsic virtue in an ambience of sacred and traditional beauty. At the same time, it might be said that his most enduring legacy will be invisible in the world, owing to the hidden nature of prayer. Thomas Merton succinctly describes the redemptive power of those solitary men and women of prayer who,

> out of pity for the universe, out of loyalty to mankind, and without a spirit of bitterness or resentment, withdraw into the healing silence of the wilderness, or of poverty, or of obscurity, not in order to preach to others but to heal in themselves the wounds of the whole world.[12]

Lord Northbourne[13] describes this as "the inward-looking way", which, in its purest form, "is the way of the saint, whose goal is the unseizable Spirit and whose inward state it is beyond the power of words to convey. . . . The withdrawal of the saint from the world, in his search for that which is within himself, is sometimes criticized as being selfish. . . . The truth is the exact opposite. He is seeking a truth that can only be found by inner experience and not by observation, and it is the very truth without which humanity is lost. . .".[14] Schuon expresses a similar view: "[T]he world needs hermits as much as preachers. In Islam it is said that the equilibrium of the world depends largely on the existence—sometimes hidden—of the saints, or also on the Invocation of God's Name. If man is not holy, nonetheless, the Name is holy, and man is made holy by the invocation."[15] And elsewhere he affirms that, "to give oneself to God—though it were hidden from all—is to give oneself to man, for this gift of self has a sacrificial value of an incalculable radiance".[16] Such a legacy, at its deepest level, is subtle, sacred, and invisible.

Others may judge the worth of his life's work according to various criteria, but it was by a simple—yet humanly crucial—standard that Schuon measured his own accomplishment: "Even if our writings had on the average no other result than the restitution, for some, of the saving barque that is prayer, we would owe it to God to consider ourselves profoundly satisfied."[17]

We can think of no more fitting close to this biography than these words of Frithjof Schuon, written to his older brother, Father Gall, during what proved to be his brother's final illness before death:

> When all is said and done, life is simple: one is standing before God from birth until death; everything lies in being aware of this and in drawing the consequences from it. The consciousness of the Sovereign Good is the greatest of consolations; it should keep us in equilibrium always. What results from this consciousness is first of all the quality of resignation, the constant acceptance of God's will; this virtue is difficult to the extent that we wish to force the world to be other than it is, to be logical for example. The complement of resignation is trust; God is good, and everything is in His hands. There is also gratitude, for every man has reasons to be thankful; one must remember frequently the good things we enjoy and not forget them because we lack something else. Finally, one must do something in life, for man is an acting being; and the best of acts is the one having God as its object, and this is prayer.[18]

On his veranda, 1995

APPENDIX I

Sophia Perennis[1]

"*Philosophia perennis*" is generally understood as referring to that metaphysical truth which has no beginning, and which remains the same in all expressions of wisdom. Perhaps it would here be better or more prudent to speak of a "*Sophia perennis*", since it is not a question of artificial mental constructions, as is all too often the case in philosophy; or again, the primordial wisdom that always remains true to itself could be called "*Religio perennis*", given that by its nature it in a sense involves worship and spiritual realization. Fundamentally we have nothing against the word "philosophy", for the ancients understood by it all manner of wisdom; in fact, however, rationalism, which has absolutely nothing to do with true spiritual contemplation, has given the word "philosophy" a limitative coloring, so that with this word one can never know what is really being referred to. If Kant is a "philosopher", then Plotinus is not, and vice versa.

With *Sophia perennis*, it is a question of the following: there are truths innate in the human Spirit, which nevertheless in a sense lie buried in the depth of the "Heart"—in the pure Intellect—and are accessible only to the one who is spiritually contemplative; and these are the fundamental metaphysical truths. Access to them is possessed by the "gnostic", "pneumatic", or "theosopher"—in the original and not the sectarian meaning of these terms—and access to them was also possessed by the "philosophers" in the real and still innocent sense of the word: for example, Pythagoras, Plato, and to a large extent also Aristotle.

If there were no Intellect, no contemplative and directly knowing Spirit, no "Heart-Knowledge", there would also be no reason capable of logic; animals have no reason, for they are incapable of knowledge of God; in other words, man possesses reason or understanding—and also language—only because he is fundamentally capable of suprarational vision, and thus of certain metaphysical truth.

—— ·:· ——

The fundamental content of the Truth is the Unconditioned, the Metaphysical Absolute; the Ultimate One, which is also the Absolutely Good, the Platonic *Agathón.* But it lies in the nature of the Absolute to be Infinity and All-Possibility, and in this sense St. Augustine said that it is in the nature of the Good to communicate itself; if there is a sun, then there is also radiation; and therein lies the necessity of the cosmos which proclaims God.

However, to say radiation is also to say separation from the source of light. Since God is the absolute and infinite Good, whatever is not God—that is to say, the world as such—cannot be absolutely good: the non-divinity of the cosmos brings with it, in its limitations, the phenomenon of evil or wickedness which, because it is a contrast, emphasizes all the more the nature of the Good. "The more he blasphemes", as Eckhart said, "the more he praises God."

The essential here is discrimination between *Ātmā* and *Māyā*, between Reality seen as "Self", and relativity seen as "cosmic play": since the Absolute is infinite—failing which it would not be the Absolute—it must give rise to *Māyā*, a "lesser reality" and in a sense an "illusion". *Ātmā* is the Principle—the Primordial Principle, one might say—and *Māyā* is manifestation or effect; strictly speaking *Māyā* is in a sense also *Ātmā*, since in the last analysis there is only *Ātmā*; both poles therefore must impinge on one another and must be bound up with one another, in the sense that, in *Ātmā*, *Māyā* is in a way prefigured, whereas, contrariwise, *Māyā* in its own fashion represents or reflects *Ātmā*. In *Ātmā*, *Māyā* is Being, the Creator of the world, the Personal God, who reveals Himself to the world in all His possibilities of Manifestation; in *Māyā*, *Ātmā* is any reflection of the Divine, such as the *Avatāra*, the Holy Scriptures, the God-transmitting symbol.

In the domain of *Māyā* or relativity, there is not only "space", there is also "time", to speak comparatively or metaphorically: there are not only simultaneity and gradation, but also change and succession; there are not only worlds, but also "ages" or "cycles". All this belongs to the "play" of *Māyā*, to the well-nigh "magical" unfolding of the possibilities hidden in the Primordial One.

— ·:· —

But in the Universal All there is not only "that which is known", there is also "that which knows"; in *Ātmā* the two are undivided, the one is inseparably present in the other, whereas in *Māyā* this One is split into two poles, namely object and subject. *Ātmā* is the "Self"; but one can also call it "Being"—not in the restrictive sense—depending on the point of view or relationship in question: it is knowable as Reality, but it is also the Knowledge, dwelling within us, of all that is real.

From this it follows that the knowledge of the One or the All calls, in accordance with its nature, for a unifying and total knowledge; it calls, over and above our thinking, for our being. And herein is defined the goal of all spiritual life: whoever knows the Absolute—or whoever "believes in God"—cannot remain stationary with this mental knowledge or with this mental faith, he must go further and involve his whole being in this knowledge or in this faith; not in so far as knowledge and faith are purely mental, but in so far as, in accordance with their true nature and through their content, they demand more and give more than mere thinking. Man must "become what he is", precisely by "becoming that what is". This immediate spiritual necessity applies both to the simplest religion and to the profoundest metaphysics, each in its own way.

And all this proceeds from the fact that man not only knows, he also wills; to the capacity of knowing the Absolute, belongs also the capacity of willing it; to the Totality of the Spirit pertains the freedom of the will. Freedom of the will would be meaningless without a goal prefigured in the Absolute; without knowledge of God, it would be neither possible nor of any use.

Man consists of thinking, willing, and loving: he can think the true or the false, he can will the good or the bad, he can love the beautiful or the ugly. It should be emphasized here that one loves the good that is ugly for its inner beauty, and this is immortal, whereas outward ugliness is ephemeral; on the other hand, one must not forget that outward beauty, in spite of any inward ugliness, bears witness to beauty as such, which is of a celestial nature and may not be despised in any of its manifestations.

Thinking the true—or knowing the real—demands on the one hand the willing of the good and on the other the loving of the beautiful, and thus of virtue, for this is nothing else than beauty of soul; it was not for nothing that, for the Greeks, virtue pertained to true philosophy. Without beauty of soul all willing is barren, it is trivial, selfish, vain, and hypocritical; and similarly: without spiritual work, that is, without the co-operation of the will, all thinking remains, in the last analysis, superficial and of no avail. The essence of virtue is that one's sentiments or feelings should correspond to the highest truth: hence in the sage his rising above things and above himself; hence his selflessness, his greatness of soul, his nobility, and his generosity; metaphysical truth as content of one's consciousness does not go hand in hand with triviality, pretentiousness, ambition, and the like. "Be ye therefore perfect, even as your Father in Heaven is perfect."

Furthermore: one could not love earthly values, if these were not rooted in the Divine; in earthly things one is unconsciously loving God. The spiritual man does this consciously, the earthly good always leads him back to the Divine: on the one hand he loves nothing more than God—or loves nothing so much as God—and on the other hand he loves everything that is lovable in God.

There is something that man must know or think; something that he must will or do; and something that he must love or be. He must know that God is necessary, self-sufficient Being, that He is That which cannot not be; and he must know that the world is only the possible, namely that which may either be or not be; all other discriminations and value judgments are derived from this metaphysical *distinguo*. Furthermore, man must will whatever directly or indirectly leads him to God, and thus abstain from whatever removes him from God; the main content of this willing is prayer, the response to God, and therein is included all spiritual activity, including metaphysical reflection. And then, as already mentioned, man must love whatever corresponds to God; he must love the Good, and since the Good necessarily transcends his own selfhood, he must make an effort to overcome this narrow and weak selfhood. One must love the Good in itself more than one's ego, and this self-knowledge and selfless love constitute the whole nobility of the soul.

— ·:· —

The Divine is Absoluteness, Infinitude, and Perfection. *Māyā* is not only the radiation which manifests God and which, through this manifestation, necessarily distances itself from God, it is also the principle—or the instrument—of refraction and multiplication: it manifests the Divine not only through unique existence, but also through the innumerable forms and qualities that shimmer in existence. And since we perceive these values and recognize them as values, we know that it is not enough to call the Divinity the Absolute and the Infinite; we know that, in its Absoluteness and Infinity, it is also the Perfect, from which all cosmic perfections derive, and to which in a thousand tongues they bear witness.

— ·:· —

Pure "dogmatism" and mere "speculation", many may say. This in fact is the problem: a metaphysical exposition appears as a purely mental phenomenon when one does not know that its origin is not a mental elaboration or an attitude of soul, but a vision which is completely independent of opinions, conclusions, and creeds, and which is realized in the pure Intellect—through the "Eye of the Heart". A metaphysical exposition is true not because it is logical—in its form it could also not be so—but it is in itself logical, that is to say, well-founded and consequential, because it is true. The thought-process of metaphysics is not an artificial support for an opinion that has to be proved, it is simply description that has been adapted to the rules of human thinking; its proofs are aids, not ends in themselves.

St. Thomas Aquinas said that it was impossible to prove the Divine Being, not because it was unclear, but, on the contrary, because of its "excess of clarity". Nothing is more foolish than the question as to whether the suprasensory can be proved: for, on the one hand, one can prove everything to the one who is spiritually gifted, and, on the other, the one who is not so gifted is blind to the best of proofs. Thought is not there in order to exhaust reality in words—if it could do this, it would itself be reality, a self-contradictory supposition—but its role can only consist in providing keys to Reality; the key is not Reality, nor can it wish to be so, but it is a way to it for those that can and will tread that way; and in the way there is already something of the end, just as in the effect there is something of the cause.

That modern thought, still wrongly called "philosophical", distances itself more and more from a logic which is deemed to be "scholastic", and more and more seeks to be "psychologically" and even "biologically" determined, does not escape our notice, but this cannot in any way prevent us from thinking or from being in the manner that the theomorphic nature of man, and hence the sufficient reason of the human state, demands. One speaks much today of the "man of our time" and one claims for him the right to determine the truth of this "time", as if man were a "time", and as if truth were not valid for man as such; what in man is mutable does not belong to man as such; what constitutes the miracle of "man" is not subject to change, for, in the image of God, there can be neither decrease nor increase. And that man is this image follows from the simple fact that he possesses the concept of the Absolute. In this one primordial concept lies the whole essence of man and therefore also his whole vocation.

APPENDIX II

The Basis of Religion and Metaphysics
An Interview with Frithjof Schuon[1]

I. Spirituality

Question: You have written more than twenty books on religion and spirituality. Your first book has the title *The Transcendent Unity of Religions.* May I ask you how one should understand this unity?

Frithjof Schuon: Our starting point is the acknowledgment of the fact that there are diverse religions which exclude each other. This could mean that one religion is right and that all the others are false; it could mean also that all are false. In reality, it means that all are right, not in their dogmatic exclusivism, but in their unanimous inner signification, which coincides with pure metaphysics, or in other terms, with the *philosophia perennis.*

Q.: How can we know that this metaphysical meaning is the truth?

F.S.: The metaphysical perspective is based on intellectual intuition, which by its very nature is infallible because it is a vision by the pure Intellect, whereas profane philosophy operates only with reason, hence with logical assumptions and conclusions.

Q.: This being so, what is the basis of religion?

F.S.: The religious, dogmatic, or theological perspective is based on revelation; its main purpose is, not to explain the nature of things or the universal principles, but to save man from sin and damnation, and also, to establish a realistic social equilibrium.

Q.: If we have religion, which saves us, why do we also need metaphysics?

F.S.: It is because metaphysics satisfies the needs of intellectually gifted men. Metaphysical truth concerns not only our thinking, but it penetrates also our whole being; therefore it is far above philosophy in the ordinary sense of the word.

Q.: On the spiritual level, what does every human being need?

F.S.: Three things: truth, spiritual practice, morals. Pure and unveiled truth coincides with metaphysics; the religious dogmas are symbols of metaphysical truths; the deep understanding of religious symbolism is esoterism. Pure metaphysics is hidden in every religion.

Q.: And what about spiritual practice?

F.S.: Spiritual practice is essentially prayer. There are three forms of prayer: first, canonical prayer, for instance the Lord's Prayer; second, personal prayer, whose best model is given by the Psalms; third, the contemplative prayer of the heart; this is mystical spirituality, which requires certain conditions. The story of the "Russian Pilgrim" offers an image of it; also Hindu texts about *japa-yoga*, methodical invocation.

Q.: And what about morals?

F.S.: This is, after truth and spiritual practice, the third dimension of spiritual life. On the one hand, morals mean a reasonable, healthy, and generous behavior; on the other hand, it means beauty of the soul, hence intrinsic nobility. Without this quality, doctrine and spiritual practice would be fruitless.

Q.: You mentioned before intellectual intuition. Doesn't every man possess this faculty?

F.S.: Yes and no. In principle, every man is capable of intellection, for the simple reason that man is man; but in fact, intellectual intuition—the "eye of the heart"—is hidden under a sheet of ice, so to speak, because of the degeneration of the human species. So we may say that pure intellection is a gift and not a generally human faculty.

Q.: Is it possible to develop this higher intuition?

F.S.: There is no need to develop it. Man can be saved by faith alone. But it is evident that a very pious or contemplative person has more intuition than a worldly person.

II. Art

Q.: May I ask you what the role of art is in the spiritual existence of man?

F.S.: We could say that after morals, art—in the broadest sense of the word—is a natural and necessary dimension of the human condition. Plato said: "Beauty is the splendor of the True." So let us say that art—including crafts—is a projection of truth and beauty in the world of forms; it is *ipso facto* a projection of archetypes. And it is essentially an exteriorization in view of an interiorization; art does not mean dispersion, it means concentration, a way back to God. Every traditional civilization has created a framework of beauty: a natural, ecologically necessary surrounding for spiritual life.

Q.: What are the criteria for knowing the worth of a work of art, its level of inspiration?

F.S.: The archetypes of sacred art are celestial inspirations; all other artworks draw their inspiration from the spiritual personality of the artist. The criteria for knowing the worth of a work of art are: the content of the work, its mode of expression, and its technique, its style.

Q.: Are the criteria different for various types of art: painting, sculpture, dance, music, poetry, architecture?

F.S.: No, the criteria are not different for various types of art.

Q.: With beauty, there is what one might call an ambiguous element, since it can be conducive to a worldly self-inflatedness or on the contrary to a remembrance of the Divine. What is it about certain arts—music, poetry, and dance, for example—that makes the ambiguous element more pronounced in them?

F.S.: Painting and sculpture are in a way more cerebral and objective than poetry, music, and dance, which are more psychic and subjective; therefore the ambiguous element is more pronounced in these three arts.

Q.: Could one say that the Hindu notion of *darshan* has an application in experiencing art and beauty?

F.S.: Of course, the Hindu notion of *darshan* applies to any aesthetic or artistic experience; but in this case it also involves mental and auditive perceptions, not only vision.

Q.: Could one say that there is a natural link between beauty in the broadest sense and esoterism?

F.S.: Yes, there is a link between beauty and esoterism, because "Beauty is the splendor of the True". Traditional art is esoteric, not exoteric. Exoterism is interested in morals, not in beauty; it even happens that exoterism can be opposed to beauty because of a moralistic prejudice.

Q.: Would it be legitimate to say that esoterism has certain rights in regard to art and beauty which transcend the limits and prohibitions laid down by the various exoterisms?

F.S.: In principle, esoterism has certain rights which transcend the prohibitions of exoterism, but in fact, esoterism can rarely make use of these rights.

Nonetheless, it has occurred, for example, in the case of dervish dances or of apparently shameless Tibetan paintings.

Q.: Besides the "fine arts", there are—in Japan, for example—the art of flower arranging, the tea ceremony, even the martial arts, which are (or were originally) recognized as manifestations of a spiritual nature. How does it come about that an activity as "everyday" as preparing tea can become the vehicle of a spiritual *barakah* (grace)?

F.S.: The Zen arts—like the Tea Ceremony—crystallize certain manners of acting of the Buddha, or let us say: of Primordial Man; now the Buddha never handled a sword, but if he had, he would have done so like a Zen Master. Acting like the Buddha—even at such a level as preparing tea—means: to assimilate something of the Buddha-Nature; it is an open door to Enlightenment.

Q.: Modern art is not traditional. Does this mean that a modern artwork is necessarily bad?

F.S.: No, because a modern artwork—modern in the broadest sense—may manifest different qualities, in regard to the content as well as in regard to the treatment and also to the artist. Some traditional productions are bad, and some nontraditional productions are good.

Q.: What does art mean for the artist himself?

F.S.: By creating a noble work of art, the artist works on his own soul; in a way, he creates his own archetype. Therefore the practice of every art is a way of self-realization, in principle or also in fact. With unimportant or even negative subjects, the artist may remain intentionally unaffected, but with noble and profound subjects, he works with his very heart.

III. Primordiality

Q.: Your book *The Feathered Sun* reveals your interest in the American Indians. May I ask you what the stimulus of this interest or affinity is?

F.S.: The Red Indians—and especially the Indians of the Plains—have much in common with the Japanese samurai, who very often practiced Zen spirituality; morally and aesthetically speaking, the Plains Indians were one of the most fascinating peoples of the world. It was the great mistake of the nineteenth century to distinguish only between "civilized people" and "savages"; there are distinctions which are far more real and important, for it is obvious that "civilization" in the ordinary sense is not the highest value of mankind, and also that the term "savage" is not suitable to the Indians. What makes the value of a man is neither his mundane culture nor his practical or inventive intelligence, but his attitude in the face of the Absolute; and he who has the sense of the Absolute never forgets the relationship between man and virgin Nature, because Nature is our origin, our natural homeland and a most transparent Message of God. For the Arab historian Ibn Khaldun, the very condition of a realistic civilization is the equilibrium between Bedouins and city dwellers, which means between nomads and sedentaries; between the healthy children of Nature and the representatives of elaborated cultural values.

Q.: Your art books *The Feathered Sun* and especially *Images of Primordial and Mystic Beauty* deal with the mystery of sacred nudity. Could you explain in a few words the meaning of this perspective?

F.S.: Sacred nudity—which plays an important role not only with the Hindus but also with the Red Indians—is based on the analogical correspondence between the "outmost" and the "inmost": the body is then seen as the "heart exteriorized", and the heart for its part "absorbs" as it were the bodily projection; "extremes meet". It is said, in India, that nudity favors the irradiation of spiritual influences; and also that feminine nudity in particular manifests Lakshmī and consequently has a beneficial effect on the surroundings. In an altogether general way, nudity expresses—and virtually actualizes—a return to the essence, the origin, the archetype, thus to the celestial state: "And it is for this that, naked, I dance", as Lallā Yōgīshwarī, the great Kashmiri saint, said after having found the Divine Self in her heart. To be sure, in nudity there is a *de facto* ambiguity because of the passional nature of man; but there is not only the passional nature, there is also the gift of contemplativity which can neutralize it, as is precisely the case with "sacred nudity"; similarly, there is not only the seduction of appearances, there is also the metaphysical transparency of phenomena which permits one to perceive the archetypal essence through the sensory experience. St. Nonnos, when he beheld St. Pelagia entering the baptismal pool naked, praised God for having put into human beauty not only an occasion of fall, but also an occasion of rising towards God.

IV. Message

Q.: What would be your message for the average man?

F.S.: Prayer. To be a human being means to be connected with God. Life has no meaning without this. Prayer and beauty, of course; for we live among forms and not in a cloud. Beauty of soul first, and then beauty of symbols around us.

Q.: You have spoken of metaphysics. May I ask you what the main content of this perennial wisdom is?

F.S.: Metaphysics means essentially: discernment between the Real and the apparent, or the illusory; in Vedantic terms: *Ātmā* and *Māyā*; the Divine and the cosmic. Metaphysics is concerned also with the roots of *Māyā* in *Ātmā*—this is the Divine Personification, the creating and revealing God—and then with the projection of *Ātmā* into *Māyā*—this means everything that is positive or good in the world. And this is essential: metaphysical knowledge requires intellectual, psychic, and moral assimilation; discernment requires concentration, contemplation, and union. Therefore metaphysical theory is not a philosophy in the modern sense of the word; it is essentially sacred. The sense of the sacred is an indispensable qualification for metaphysical realization, as it is for every spiritual way. For the Red Indian, as also for the Hindu, everything in nature is sacred; this, modern man has to learn, because it is a question of ecology in the broadest sense of the word. What is needed first, is prayer; and then: back to Nature! One could object that it is too late; now, each person is responsible for what he or she does—not for what others do—because each one stands before God and can do what is requested for his immortal soul. The first step back to Nature is dignity; dignity of forms and of behavior; this creates the climate in which prayers feel at home, because dignity partakes of the immutable Truth.

APPENDIX III

Selected Texts on the Spiritual Life

Manifestation and Proof[1]

A proof presupposes: the absence of what is to be proven; the presence of an element that in some way is part of the thing to be proven; an epistemological axiom that renders a proof possible and therefore efficacious.

The proof prolongs the thing to be proven, either directly or indirectly: in the first case, the effect is of the same order as the cause; in the second case, the effect is of another order, which means that the causality is "vertical" and not "horizontal". Be that as it may, the proof is by definition a direct or indirect manifestation of the thing to be proven.

There are agnostics who deny even the necessity of a cause; now in the absence of this axiom, which pertains to the nature of the intelligence, no proof is possible.

It is an essential principle that the organ of knowledge must be proportioned to the thing to be known! For skeptics, this requirement is a *petitio principii*, since for them the question of epistemological qualification does not arise; and what transcends sensorial knowledge and the empirical order does not exist in their opinion.

To ask for a proof of the Absolute is absurd for two reasons, one objective and the other subjective: firstly, the Absolute cannot enter the phenomenal order, hence there is no common measure; secondly, if our intelligence is qualified for conceiving the Absolute, it will not require proofs on the plane of contingency or of relativity. However, these proofs necessarily exist because everything is a manifestation of the Absolute; but only sound intelligences, capable of intellectual intuition because inspired by the Absolute Itself, will perceive them. "The soul is not other than *Brahma*."

To say proof is to say direct or indirect manifestation; consequently, the existence of things proves the Absolute since existence manifests It.

To say Absolute is to say Infinite; and what manifests the Infinite, and therefore proves It, is the indefinite diversity of things and the illimitation of their containers, which are the existential categories, such as space, time, form, number, matter, energy.

And similarly: to say Absolute or Infinite, is to say radiating Good, Goodness, Beauty, Beatitude; and what manifests, and thereby proves, this hypostatic dimension is the whole of the positive qualities of things, including the faculties of creatures; and also, in an indirect and *a contrario* fashion, imperfections or flaws—through privation or through excess—which manifest the Good without wishing to, by denying and falsifying It. Now to deny the Good is to manifest It through contrast; the absolute Good is beyond all possible opposition.

This is not to say that the Real has need of any proof, nor that the Intellect has need of proof for its certitude; but the proof is there, and in its way it is a presence of God, with all that this demands of us, and with all that it offers us.

The Garden[2]

A man sees a beautiful garden, but he knows: he will not always see this garden, because one day he will die; and he also knows: the garden will not always be there, because this world will disappear one day. And he knows also: this kinship with the beautiful garden is the gift of destiny, because if a man were to find himself in the middle of a desert, he would not see the garden; he sees it only because destiny has put him, man, here and not elsewhere.

But in the innermost region of our soul lives the Spirit, and in it is contained the garden, as it were, like a seed; and if we love this garden—and how is it possible not to love it since it is of a heavenly beauty?—we would do well to look for it there where it has always been and always will be, that is to say in the Spirit; maintain yourself in the Spirit, in your own center, and you will have the garden and in addition all possible gardens. Similarly: in the Spirit there is no death, because here you are immortal; and in the Spirit the relationship between the contemplator and the contemplated is not only a fragile possibility; on the contrary, it is part of the very nature of the Spirit and, like it, it is eternal. . . .

Whatever you are in the Spirit now, you will remain so after death; and whatever is yours now in the Spirit, will be yours after death. Before God there is neither being nor ownership except in the Spirit; whatever was outward must become inward and whatever was inward will become outward: look for the garden in yourself, in your indestructible divine Substance; then this will give you a new and imperishable garden. Whatever you love outwardly is to be found in the Divine Name; therefore attach yourself to it, dwell in it, and live in it. The holy invocation is the seed of our eternity.

In the Supreme Name we are at the Center and at the Origin and we are already in a certain way in the place which by the Grace of God is destined for us in Paradise. This is why we must, already down here, be in our predestined place in Paradise and we must be so wholeheartedly and as much as we can and this ceaselessly; because we are made for Beatitude since knowledge of God and free will, that is to say Truth and Love, are our very nature.

On Virtue[3]

One must realize the virtues for their own sake, and not in order to make them "mine".

One may be sad because one displeases God, but not because one is not holy while others are.

To understand a virtue is to know how to realize it; to understand a fault is to know how to overcome it. To be sad because one does not know how to overcome a fault shows that one has not understood the nature of the corresponding virtue and that one's aspiration is motivated by egoism. Truth must be given precedence over self-interest.

To have a virtue is above all to be without the fault that is contrary to it, for God created us virtuous. He created us in His image; faults are superimposed. Moreover, it is not we who possess virtue, it is virtue which possesses us.

Vice, like every other privative and malefic phenomenon, is so to speak an irruption of nothingness into existence: it is a negation of Being, but it is ontologically condemned to imitate what it intends to deny, for this "existentialized" naught can do nothing of itself, precisely because it is nothing in itself.

Virtue, for its part, is a message from Being; it is like a reverberation of the Sovereign Good, in which we participate through our nature or through our will, easily or with difficulty, but always by the Grace of He who is.

Against Subtle Worldliness[4]

There is an outer man and an inner man; the first lives in the world and undergoes its influence, whereas the second looks towards God and lives in Prayer. Now it is necessary that the outer man not affirm himself to the detriment of the inner man; it is the inverse which must take place. Instead of inflating the outer man and allowing the inner man to die, it is necessary to allow the inner man to expand, and to entrust the cares of the outer to God. Prayer is there in order to re-establish the equilibrium.

Who says outer man says preoccupations of the world, or even worldliness: in effect there is in every man a tendency to attach himself too much to this or that element of passing life or to worry about it too much, and the adversary takes advantage of this in order to cause troubles for us. There is also the desire to be happier than one is, or the desire not to suffer any injustices, even harmless ones, or the desire always to understand everything, or the desire never to be disappointed; all of this is of the domain of subtle worldliness, which must be countered by serene detachment, by the principial and initial certainty of That which alone matters, then by patience and confidence. When no help comes from Heaven, this is because it is a question of a difficulty which we can and must resolve with the means which Heaven has placed at our disposal. In an absolute way, it is necessary to find our happiness in Prayer; that is to say that it is necessary to find therein sufficient happiness so as not to allow ourselves to be excessively troubled by the things of the world, seeing that dissonances cannot but exist, the world being what it is.

There is the desire not to suffer any injustices, or even simply not to be placed at a disadvantage. Now one of two things: either the injustices are the result of our past faults, and in this case our trials exhaust this causal mass; or the injustices result from our character, and in this case our trials bear witness to it; in both cases, we must thank God and pray to Him with all the more fervor, without preoccupying ourselves with worldly chaff. One must also say to oneself that the grace of the Remembrance of God compensates infinitely for every dissonance from which we can suffer, and that in relation to this grace, the inequality of terrestrial favors is a pure nothingness. Let us never forget that an infinite grace compels us to an infinite gratitude, and that the first stage of gratitude is the sense of proportions.

To Earn One's Salvation[5]

Being saved, and bringing others to be saved; there lies our whole vocation. It has been likewise said that the good tends by its nature to communicate itself.

For salvation, two things are needed before all else: Truth and Faith. Knowing something, and believing in something; that is to say: Knowledge of the Truth and union with the Truth.

And so also for Faith two things are needful, and they concern our will: namely, an activity and an abstention. Doing what is in conformity with Truth and what gives life and depth to Faith; abstaining from what is contrary to Truth and from what is harmful to Faith.

To be able to realize this throughout the whole of life, the soul has need of two virtues: Patience and Trust. Enduring for God, and rejoicing in God.

Everything is there. We cannot do anything better either for ourselves or for our fellow men; one would almost like to say: he who does not wish to be saved for his own sake, let him at least seek salvation for the love of others. For the good has a liberating radiance, whether we know it or not, and whether we have an outward vocation or not; not everyone has to teach, but everyone must be holy. In any case: the obtaining of salvation is accompanied by the consciousness that it benefits others also.

The symbolism of the lamp teaches us the relationship between Truth and Faith: the light is Truth, and the oil is Faith. Oil already somehow possesses luminosity in its own substance; this is inward Truth, inborn in us and inherent in our deepest nature. Or again: water is Truth, and wine is Faith.

The Open Door[6]

God has opened a door in the middle of creation, and this open door of the world towards God is man; this opening is God's invitation to look towards Him, to tend towards Him, to persevere with regard to Him, and to return to Him. And this enables us to understand why the door shuts at death when it has been scorned during life; for to be man means nothing other than to look beyond and to pass through the door. Unbelief and paganism are whatever turns its back on the door; on its threshold light and darkness separate. The notion of Hell becomes perfectly clear when we think how senseless it is—and what a waste and a suicide—to slip through the human state without being truly man, that is, to pass God by, and thus to pass our own souls by, as if we had any right to human faculties apart from the return to God, and as if there were any point in the miracle of the human state apart from the end which is prefigured in man himself; or again: as if God had had no motive in giving us an intelligence which discerns and a will which chooses.

Granted that this door is a center—and it must be one since it leads to God—it corresponds to a rare and precious possibility, one that is unique for its surroundings. And this explains why there is a damnation; for he who has refused to pass through the door will never afterwards be able to cross its threshold. Hence the representation of the afterlife as an implacable alternative: seen from the door—that is, from the human state—there is no choice other than between the inside and the outside.

What means everything for man is that the intelligence should become in fact, thanks to the content which corresponds to it, what it is in principle, and likewise, that the will should become really free thanks to the object which corresponds to it. In other terms: the intelligence is not truly intelligence except in so far as it discerns between the Real and the illusory, and the will is not truly free except in so far as it strives toward the Real.

Maintaining Oneself in Peace[7]

When we encounter evil—and we owe it to God and to ourselves to maintain ourselves in Peace—we may utilize the following arguments. First of all, no evil can affect the Sovereign Good, nor should it trouble our relationship with God; upon contact with the absurd, we should never lose sight of absolute values. Secondly, we must be aware of the metaphysical necessity of evil. Thirdly, let us not lose sight of the limits and the relativity of evil; for *vincit omnia Veritas.* Fourthly, it is obviously necessary to resign oneself to the will of God, that is, to our destiny; destiny, by definition, is what we cannot escape. Fifthly—and this follows from the preceding argument—God wishes to try our faith, hence also our sincerity, our trust, and our patience; and that is why one speaks of the "trials of life". Sixthly, God will not ask us to account for what others do, nor for what happens to us when we are not responsible for it; He asks us to account for what we ourselves have done. Seventhly, and finally, happiness is not for this life, but for the next; perfection is not of this world, and the last word belongs to Beatitude.

On the Holiness of the Name[8]

When we say that the Name of God is an effect of the divine Cause, this signifies: in the domain of language, to which all words and all names pertain. Now it goes without saying that, if the word "God" is an effect of the divine Cause, it is not so in a merely general sense as is the case for example with the words "stone" or "tree"; for we call the word "God" an effect of the divine Cause because, precisely, its content is God and nothing else, and because, in consequence, the fact of thinking or of uttering this word has an effect other than that of thinking or uttering the words "tree" or "stone". When I say "tree", nothing happens; when on the other hand I say "God", God listens to me, whether I invoke Him, whether I recognize His reality, or again, whether on the contrary I abuse His Name, and it is for this reason that it is said: "Hallowed be Thy Name". Moreover, writing belongs to the domain of language as well; and here also there is a quasi-magical difference between the inscription "God" and any other inscription; for God is not indifferent toward my manner of treating the inscription "God", while He is indifferent toward my manner of treating the inscription "tree", "stone", "house", or "mountain". This is so because God is the witness at once transcendent and immanent of all that happens, whether it be in the outer world or within the soul; to the degree that we understand this through direct knowledge, or that we apprehend it through faith,—the one does not exclude the other,—we are able to have the intimate experience of this connection between God and the word which expresses Him, therefore of His presence in His Name.

Certitudes[9]

I know with certitude that there are phenomena, and that I myself am one of them.

I know with certitude that underlying the phenomena, or beyond them, there is the one Essence, which the phenomena manifest in function of a quality of this Essence, that of Infinitude, hence of Radiation.

I know with certitude that the Essence is good and that all goodness or beauty in phenomena is a manifestation thereof.

I know with certitude that the phenomena will return to the Essence, from which they are not really separate, since at bottom It alone is; that they will return to the Essence because apart from It nothing is absolute nor in consequence eternal; that Manifestation is necessarily subject to a rhythm, as it is necessarily subject to a hierarchy.

I know with certitude that the soul is immortal, for its indestructibility results from the very nature of the intelligence.

I know with certitude that underlying the diverse consciousnesses there is but one sole Subject: the Self at once transcendent and immanent, accessible through the Intellect, seat or organ of the religion of the Heart; for the diverse consciousnesses exclude and contradict one another, whereas the Self includes all and is contradicted by none.

I know with certitude that the Essence, God, affirms Itself with regard to phenomena, the world, as Power of Attraction and Will of Equilibrium; that we are made in order to follow vertically this Attraction, and that we cannot do this unless we conform, horizontally, to the Equilibrium manifested by sacred and natural Laws.

NOTES

Foreword

[1] The first person known to have used the term "perennial philosophy" was the Vatican librarian Agostino Steuco in the sixteenth century. It was also adopted, in the seventeenth century, by Baron Gottfried von Leibnitz. The term was brought to Aldous Huxley's attention by Ananda Coomaraswamy who, in a letter to him dated August 10, 1944, spoke of the *philosophia perennis* or "perennial philosophy". It seems very probable that it was due to this that Huxley adopted it as the title of his anthology. The sacred texts quoted by Huxley are irreproachable, but unfortunately his commentary on them is lacking in depth.

[2] Two other writers (called by Schuon "continuators") who have contributed to the explication of this school are the Anglo-Indian Ananda Coomaraswamy (1877-1947) and the German Swiss Titus Burckhardt (1908-1984).

[3] We may note in passing that the "new-age" meanderings are a shallow and syncretistic hodgepodge. They are a parody of authentic, or esoteric, universalism. If I may paraphrase the words of Psalm 46: Instead of saying: "Be still and know that HE is God", the "new age" says: "Be still and know that YOU are God"! One doesn't know whether to laugh or cry.

Preface

[1] An exception to this practice has been made in the case of those oral statements attributed to Schuon whose precise accuracy cannot be confirmed. For the sake of simplicity, endnote citations to books, articles, and various private papers are uniformly presented in black lettering. On this last point, however, one should bear in mind Martin Lings' observation that, "It is indeed remarkable how many of the titles of [Schuon's] books can be said to sum up his whole literary output." (Martin Lings, *A Return to the Spirit*, 1)

[2] Later biographers and scholars may have an interest in knowing my vantage point and background. In 1971 the Crow Sun Dance Chief, Thomas Yellowtail, one of the most renowned and beloved American Indian spiritual leaders of the twentieth century, first advised me to seek out Frithjof Schuon for counsel. From 1972 onward, I maintained regular contact with Schuon; when he moved to America in 1980, I was to become his neighbor for the last eighteen years of his life.

[3] I often present writings by Schuon from the particular historical moment in his life that corresponds to the chronology; but the presentation also includes comments either by Schuon or by others that add context or insight, even though the comments were written or spoken much later. In order not to detract from the main narrative, the sources and dates of some comments are only identified in the endnotes. For this same reason, I have occasionally substituted English

language translations for foreign language terms and phrases.

[4] The film interviews with Schuon took place in 1991; interviews with more than twenty people who knew him well began in February 1992 in both Lausanne and Basle, and were collected during a period of over fifteen years in diverse settings. Some of the film is irreplaceable, including interviews with several of his old friends who are no longer living.

[5] The film is entitled *Interviews with Frithjof Schuon* and was co-directed and co-produced with Michael Pollack and Lynn Pollack. Michael Pollack (1947-2001) was also the editor of *Images of Primordial and Mystic Beauty: Paintings by Frithjof Schuon.*

[6] One of Schuon's biographers has clarified the meaning of the term "messenger" in a similar context: "Schuon has been . . . characterized as a 'messenger of the *Religio Perennis*', a term that obviously does not denote the idea of a 'message' as a formal and legal *risālah*, but [has] the more general meaning of an inspired legacy." (Patrick Laude, "Quintessential Esoterism and the Wisdom of Forms: Reflections on Frithjof Schuon's Intellectual and Spiritual Legacy", 160) See generally: "Build on God and do thy duty — / Then thou wilt also find joy. / For what the Lord has given thee in thy spirit — / Thou must willingly proclaim. / Fundamentally, every heart is a messenger — / This lies in the nature of man. Whether ye know it/ Or not, man's duty has this meaning: / That in everyone there is a message." (*World Wheel*, Fifth Collection, I, 47)

[7] From a letter to Leo Schaya, March 23, 1983. Schuon continues, "A relationship with God leads to a certain solitude, because God is not the world and the world is not God; in this solitude there is a sweetness from the next world, because God is the supreme Good. It is in this sense that an old proverb says: O *beata solitudo, o sola beatitudo.*" (quoted in Aymard & Laude, *Frithjof Schuon: Life and Teachings*, 45)

[8] Letter dated January 6, 1988.

[9] In the last three years of his life, after the completion of his metaphysical works, Schuon composed 23 collections of didactic poems in his native German, which constitute the final aspect of his written message (see chap. 23, "A Profusion of Songs"). Although their total number exceeds 3,200, each poem is essentially a message in itself, and, therefore, may be read and appreciated either together or individually: "Each poem is a world unto itself. / Some of them may bloom together — / Yet each one is for thee a single message, / And wants to flow through thy soul on its own. / The meaning of each is a unique gift, / There is neither a 'before' nor an 'after' — / Just as a song that nourishes thy love / Speaks to thy soul in its own way." (*Adastra* & *Stella Maris*, "Unto Itself", 233)

[10] *Songs without Names*, Second Collection, XLVI, 72. See also *World Wheel*, Second Collection, XXXV, 71 and *World Wheel*, Third Collection, LIII, 118.

[11] *Songs without Names*, Fifth Collection, XLI, 219. See also *Songs without Names*, Sixth Collection, XIII, 257.

Introduction

[1] *Understanding Islam*, "Preface", viii.

[2] Marco Pallis, *The Way and the Mountain,* 77. Antoine Faivre (b. 1934), Professor Emeritus at the Sorbonne, has said that Schuon "is not content with simply exhibiting a tolerant attitude toward various traditions or with finding similarities or commonalities between Christianity and other religions. For him it is more a matter of understanding and experiencing, out of his own soul and in his intellect, the inner core of what is Christianity-specific. . . . Some pages in this collection give the impression of having been written by a Christian who was desirous of putting forward arguments in favor of the truth of his faith." (*The Fullness of God: Frithjof Schuon on Christianity*, "Foreword", xii) Analogous comments could be made regarding Schuon's writings on each of the other great world religions.

[3] "In order to forestall the misunderstandings that sometimes result from such notions as 'school' or 'tendency'—and because we have had certain experiences—the reader ought to be warned that we do not necessarily subscribe to every assessment, conclusion, or theory formulated in the name of metaphysical, esoteric, or broadly traditional principles; in other words we do not espouse a theory simply because it belongs to a particular school, and we wish to be held responsible only for what we write ourself." (*Logic and Transcendence*, "Introduction", 5)

[4] "The word 'philosophy' ought to have its original meaning restored: philosophy—the 'love of wisdom'—is the science of all the fundamental principles." (*Transfiguration of Man*, "Thought: Light and Perversion", 3) See also *Sufism: Veil and Quintessence*, "Tracing the Notion of Philosophy", 89-100.

[5] "The Perennial Philosophy", 243. Different religions have recognized the existence of an eternal Truth that transcends the bounds of their own dogmas in varying degrees; the term "*philosophia perennis*" has cognates in different traditions that include *Sanātana Dharma* in Hinduism, *Lex Aeterna* in Greek philosophy, *Dīn al-Haqq* and *Hikmat al-Khālidah* in Islam (or *Jāvīdān Khirad* in Persian), and *Akālika Dhamma* in Buddhism.

[6] *Echoes of Perennial Wisdom*, "Foreword", iii-iv.

[7] From an unpublished document, September 1992, quoted in James Cutsinger, *Advice to the Serious Seeker*, 7.

[8] *Logic and Transcendence*, "Man and Certainty", 231.

[9] At other times Schuon further reduced the essential to the first two elements, referring to the "The two-fold definition of the *religio perennis*—discernment between the Real and the illusory, and a unifying and permanent concentration on the Real". (*Light on the Ancient Worlds*, "*Religio Perennis*", 121) See also *Songs without Names*, Twelfth Collection, CXXIX, 281 and *Songs without Names*, Fifth Collection, LI, 222.

[10] "*Sophia Perennis*", Appendix I, 144.

[11] *Road to the Heart*, "Synthesis", 88. And again: "Three things are sacred to me: firstly Truth; / Then, in its wake, primordial prayer; / And then virtue — nobility of soul which, / In God, walks all the paths of beauty." (*World Wheel*, Sixth Collection, LXXII, 111)

[12] *World Wheel*, Sixth Collection, CXXV, 127. And: "First the Truth, that saves the soul; / Then ceaseless thinking on the True. / Then our nobility of soul: arrayed / In beauty be the path of thy years. / These are the highest values which thy mind / Should always carry in its consciousness. / The rest is in the Hands of God. And what thou knowest, / Take to heart! Trust in God, and journey on." (*Adastra & Stella Maris*, "Values", 43)

[13] Text, "The Criteria of the Spiritual Man", and letter dated March 1, 1971, quoted in *Light on the Ancient Worlds,* "Appendix", 128, 131.

[14] "It is quite out of the question that a 'revelation', in the full sense of the word, should arise in our time, one comparable, that is to say, to the imparting of one of the great sutras or any other primary scripture; the day of revelations is past on this globe and was so already long ago. The inspirations of the saints are of another order, but these could in any case never falsify or invalidate tradition or intrinsic orthodoxy by claiming to improve on it or even to replace it, as some people have suggested." ("No Activity Without Truth", 10)

[15] Text, "The Elements of the *Religio Perennis*", quoted in *Light on the Ancient Worlds*, "Appendix", 130. "All the dogmas, all the prescriptions, and all the means of a religion have their sufficient reason in the three fundamental vocations of man: discernment, practice, and virtue. And all the gifts and means of a religion man bears within himself, but he no longer has access to them on account of the fall; whence precisely the necessity—in principle relative—of outward forms that awaken and actualize man's spiritual potentialities." (text, "The Criteria of the Spiritual Man", quoted in *Echoes of Perennial Wisdom*, 80-81) For more on Schuon's texts see chap. 22, "The Close of Two Cycles", 129, 219-220.

[16] Film interview, 2006. Jean-Claude Petitpierre speaks of how "Frithjof Schuon has written extensively about what it means to be a human being, what is our vocation, why are we on earth; and, he described the various paths through which, if we follow our vocation, we return to the Divine." (film interview, May 2005)

[17] Josep Prats & Esteve Serra, Prologue, *Frithjof Schuon (1907-1998): Notas biográficas, estudios, homenajes*, 19.

[18] See *Adastra & Stella Maris*, "The Choice", 35: "Thou hast chosen the path of Truth and Being, / The path found in Plato and Shankara. . .". See also *Songs without Names*, Seventh Collection, XLII, 18, *Songs without Names*, Tenth Collection, CXIX, 187, *Songs without Names*, Eleventh Collection, XXXII, 203, and *World Wheel*, Third Collection, XXVI, 110.

[19] *In the Face of the Absolute*, "Preface", 4. "*Pneumátikos*: Wisdom is his blood; / And yet: *Ex Oriente Lux* — which means: / Many a sacred word came from the East; / To it thou owest thy knowledge of *gnosis.* / But the source lies in the core

of our being, / Around which our thoughts are gathered; / Truth's lightning does not come from far away — / Before we were, it was within our heart." (*Adastra & Stella Maris*, "Portrait", 237)

[20] "The Perennial Philosophy", 243.

[21] "'*Brahma* is not the world' but 'all things are *Ātmā*'; '*Brahma* is true, the world is false' and 'He (the delivered one, the *mukta*) is *Brahma.*' In these statements the whole of gnosis is contained, just as it is also contained in the *Shahādah*, or in the two Testimonies, or again in the mysteries of Christ." (*Understanding Islam*, "The Path", 130-131)

[22] "I always like to return to Shankara, / For he is the deep happiness of my existence; / *Brahma satyam* — I cannot say anything better. / May God help me to carry life's burden." (*Songs without Names*, Twelfth Collection, CXVII, 277) See also *World Wheel*, Third Collection, CXIV, 138.

[23] Concerning the Absolute, Schuon writes: "God: the Absolute is real; that is, He is Reality (*Haqq*), Necessary Being (*al-Wujūd al-Mutlaq*), hence That which cannot not be, whereas things can either be or not be; being unique He excludes all that is not He; being total He includes all that is possible or existent; there is nothing 'alongside' Him and nothing 'outside' Him." (*Sufism: Veil and Quintessence*, "Preface", xv)

[24] *Roots of the Human Condition*, "Pillars of Wisdom", 85. For a further discussion of the transpersonal intellect, see chap. 5, "Beginning to Write", 21.

[25] "*Sophia Perennis*", Appendix I, 141-142.

[26] *Adastra & Stella Maris*, "*Advaita*", 235.

[27] *Christianity/Islam: Perspectives on Esoteric Ecumenism*, "The Question of Protestantism", 46. And also: "Knowledge saves only on condition that it engages all that we are: only when it constitutes a path that works and transforms and wounds our nature as the plough wounds the soil." (*Spiritual Perspectives and Human Facts*, "Knowledge and Love", 146)

[28] *Spiritual Perspectives and Human Facts*, "The Spiritual Virtues", 228.

[29] "I was asked how one should speak to God; / I said: canonical prayer / Is universal nourishment; then read the Psalms; /And invoke God, before whose Light ye stand — /All else is contained therein. / God Himself speaks in the deepest folds of thy heart." (*World Wheel*, Sixth Collection, LXIV, 108)

[30] *Stations of Wisdom*, "Modes of Prayer", 121.

[31] *Stations of Wisdom*, "Modes of Prayer", 121-122.

[32] *Stations of Wisdom*, "Modes of Prayer", 122.

[33] *Adastra & Stella Maris*, "Petition", 193.

[34] Text, "Reciting the *Fātihah*", discussed in *Frithjof Schuon: Life and Teachings*, 87, 170 (cited as *Book of Keys*, 194).

[35] *Stations of Wisdom*, "Modes of Prayer", 121.

[36] Text, "Canonical Prayer", quoted in *Prayer Fashions Man: Frithjof Schuon on*

the Spiritual Life, "Appendix", 197.

[37] *Songs without Names*, First Collection, XCI. And again: "Canonical prayer — it should come / From within; what thou must say — / What Heaven has prescribed for thee — / Thou must say it out of the joy of thy heart. / For this discourse is like Moses' rod; / So pray with the words God has given, / For He knows man's deepest needs. / Then open thy heart to God, committing to Him / The supplication that burns in thy soul." (*Songs without Names*, Fifth Collection, CII, 237)

[38] Schuon refers to the practice of the invocation of a Name of God by such other phrases as, perpetual prayer, God remembrance, quintessential prayer, and ejaculatory prayer.

[39] *Stations of Wisdom*, "Modes of Prayer", 125.

[40] In *Gnosis: Divine Wisdom*, "Some Observations", 108-109, 109n and "Christic and Virginal Mysteries", 119-124, Schuon discusses the recitation of the Latin Rosary, and in particular the Names of Jesus and Mary contained in the *Ave*, as a form of invocatory prayer. See also Jean Hani, "The Rosary as Spiritual Way". Rama Coomaraswamy, *The Invocation of the Name of Jesus: As Practiced in the Western Church* provides a summary of invocatory prayer in Western Christianity.

[41] The use of a *kōan* in Zen Buddhism has certain analogies to invocatory prayer, with the *kōan* being substituted for a divine Name or formula. "The *kōan* is a formula by intention absurd, destined to bring about a kind of liberating rupture in the mind of the person meditating on it, the mind in this instance being considered with regard to its hardness and blindness." (*Treasures of Buddhism*, "Remarks on the Enigma of the *Kōan*", 77)

[42] *Yellowtail: Crow Medicine Man and Sun Dance Chief*, 123-128 provides information on invocatory prayer within the Crow, Cheyenne, and Lakota tribes of North America. One is also reminded that the Kabbalists say that the entire *Torah* is included in the Tetragrammaton—the four Hebrew consonants of the ineffable supreme Name of God.

[43] *The Transcendent Unity of Religions*, "Universality and Particular Nature of the Christian Religion", 145.

[44] *Stations of Wisdom*, "Modes of Prayer", 125, 127.

[45] *Road to the Heart*, "The Name", 18. See also: "There is one Word, it is the saving key: / Dwell thou in God, and God will dwell in thee. / Out of compassion to our world He came; / His are two homes on earth: our heart, His Name." (*Road to the Heart*, "One Word", 28)

[46] "Virtue is the conformity of the soul to the divine Model and to the spiritual work; conformity or participation". (text, "The Six Fundamental Givens", quoted in *Echoes of Perennial Wisdom*, 15)

[47] *The Play of Masks*, "Prerogatives of the Human State", 10-11. "Truths make us understand virtues, giving them all their cosmic amplitude and their efficacy.

Virtues for their part lead us to truths and transform them for us into realities that are concrete, seen, and lived." (*Spiritual Perspectives and Human Facts*, "The Spiritual Virtues", 183) And also: "The intellective center of a being is not reached without involving his volitional circumference: he who wants the center must realize the whole; in other words, he who wants to know with the heart-intellect must 'know' with the whole soul, and this entails the purification of the soul and therefore the virtues." (*Spiritual Perspectives and Human Facts*, "The Spiritual Virtues", 196)

[48] Text, "There is Only One Religion", quoted in *Echoes of Perennial Wisdom*, 33. And: "The essence of the virtues is emptiness before God, which permits the divine Qualities to enter the heart and radiate in the soul. Virtue is the exteriorization of the pure heart." (text, "The Six Fundamental Givens", quoted in *Echoes of Perennial Wisdom*, 15)

[49] Text, "To Love Light and Air", quoted in *Echoes of Perennial Wisdom*, 32.

[50] *Spiritual Perspectives and Human Facts*, "The Spiritual Virtues", 185.

[51] *Language of the Self*, "A View of Yoga", 53-55.

[52] *Understanding Islam*, "The Path", 160.

[53] *Adastra & Stella Maris*, "Virtue", 215. See also: "One should not confuse true virtue / With morality — purely outward acts / That change with land and custom, / And do not transform the substance of the soul. / Virtue is inward — it resides in the nature / Of things; its values are the same / From people to people, and in every religion; / Humility, magnanimity, and devotion are the paths / That lead from the earthly world to Heaven." (*Songs without Names*, Sixth Collection, LXXX, 279)

[54] *Esoterism as Principle and as Way*, "Foundations of an Integral Aesthetics", 178-179.

[55] *Language of the Self*, "A View of Yoga", 56.

[56] *World Wheel*, Seventh Collection, XCVIII, 159. See also: "Truth and beauty go together: / What is divinely true, radiates beauty; / The beautiful and the noble bear witness to the truth; / The sacred is God's bouquet of flowers. / Only the fool sees nothing beautiful in the doctrine / And gives not to beauty the honor of wisdom. / One could exaggerate the rights of beauty — / But one should not call it an empty illusion." (*Songs without Names*, Seventh Collection, LX, 23)

[57] *World Wheel*, Fifth Collection, CXV, 80. See also: "Truth and virtue; beauty and love; / If these alone remained to me, / The world could sink into the waters — / Let me drink only from the beautiful and true." (*World Wheel*, Fifth Collection, IX, 49)

[58] *Road to the Heart*, "Truth", 25.

[59] Text, "Interiorizing Quality of Beauty", quoted in Michael Fitzgerald, "Beauty and the Sense of the Sacred: Schuon's Antidote to the Modern World", 133.

[60] Text, "The Three Dimensions of the Perennial Religion", quoted in *Light on the Ancient Worlds*, "Appendix", 133. Schuon explains why for a Shankara, the

question of congenial ambience did not arise: "Someone said to me that Shrī Shankara, the *jnānī*, / Was no esthete, that he remained within the strict realm / Of metaphysics, that questions of beauty were foreign / To him, that he was and remained the pure wise man. / Ye mathematicians, break not the rod / On him who speaks about the beautiful. / The wise men of the East did not preach beauty, / For in their world there was nothing else. / In the ancient worlds — and in every land — / Truth and the beautiful went hand in hand." (*Autumn Leaves & The Ring*, "Esthetics", 17). See also *Songs without Names*, Seventh Collection, LXXVI, 29.

61 *Esoterism as Principle and as Way*, "Foundations of an Integral Aesthetics", 182. Schuon further explains the sometimes restrictive and cautious attitude that religion takes towards beauty: "The Semitic exoterisms excluded the cult of nature for fear of idolatry, sacred dance for fear of worldliness, primordial nudity for fear of immorality, and, quite obviously, non-dogmatizing metaphysics for fear of heresy, and there are other scruples of this kind. We are not saying that exoterism should react differently, for it has the right and even the duty to be realistic in its own fashion and on its own plane; we say, rather, that we must take exoterism for what it is, and not for esoterism." (personal paper, 1994)

62 *From the Divine to the Human*, "The Sense of the Sacred", 105. And also: "The 'cerebral' should be balanced by the 'existential.'. . . Spirituality should never be something that accentuates the mathematical aspects of Truth to the detriment of its musical aspects. In India, home of the most rigorous metaphysic, one never sees such a hypertrophy; the atmosphere is suffused precisely with a sense of the sacred and with beauty, as is shown by its temples, its dances, music and other aspects." ("Notes on an Audience", Autumn, 1986)

63 *Adastra & Stella Maris*, "Paths", 49.

64 *World Wheel*, First Collection, XVII, 7.

65 *Adastra & Stella Maris*, "*Adastra*", 3.

66 *Adastra & Stella Maris*, "Paths", 49.

67 *Songs without Names*, Tenth Collection, V, 154. And also: "It might be asked whether we have a right / To the enjoyments that life offers — / Should one not make penance, is not sacrifice / Required in a world where folly rages? / Certainly, there must be renunciation and sobriety — / But also respect for the deep dignity / Of Beauty, for it bestows the wine of the Spirit. / In what is noble there is also pleasure, not merely burden; / There is also an opening towards the Above. / People are not / All alike, nor are the paths to the Kingdom of Heaven." (*Songs without Names*, Fourth Collection, LXXIX, 182) See also *Songs without Names*, Third Collection, XLV, 124 and *Songs without Names*, Eighth Collection, LXXXVII, 84, and CXVIII, 94.

68 *The Transcendent Unity of Religions*, "Preface", xxxiv. This 1953 publication was Schuon's first English-language book (his third book in print) and received wide acclaim. T.S. Eliot, a Nobel Prize Laureate in Literature, declared: "I have met with no more impressive work in the comparative study of Oriental and

Occidental religion." Some years later, Schuon freely retranslated the work into German as *Von der inneren Einheit der Religionen* (1981) using a more synthetic style and adding new material, including a chapter that is not in the original French. "The result", Schuon states, "is quite different in places from the French text; it is more concentrated, without losing anything of what is essential, quite on the contrary." (letter to Martin Lings, December 8, 1957)

69 Schuon's Preface to *The Transcendent Unity of Religions* continues: "If an example may be drawn from the sensory sphere to illustrate the difference between metaphysical and theological knowledge, it may be said that the former, which can be called 'esoteric' when it is manifested through a religious symbolism, is conscious of the uncolored essence of light and of its character of pure luminosity; a given religious belief, on the other hand, will assert that light is red and not green, whereas another belief will assert the opposite; both will be right in so far as they distinguish light from darkness but not in so far as they identify it with a particular color." He goes on to explain that light colored by the form of a religion, "will of necessity confuse the symbol or form with the naked and supra-formal Truth". (xxx-xxxi)

70 "If Revelations more or less exclude one another, this is so of necessity since God, when He speaks, expresses Himself in an absolute mode. . .". (*Gnosis: Divine Wisdom*, "Diversity of Revelation", 18)

71 *The Transcendent Unity of Religions*, "Limits of Religious Expansion", 79-80.

72 Schuon notes the problematical existence of a "fatuous universalism", insisting that it is "better to believe intelligently in one's own religion—while believing it to be the only true one—than to believe stupidly in the validity of the other doctrines and traditions; stupidly, that is to say on a sentimental basis devoid of any intellectual quality." (letter dated May 29, 1964)

73 Letter dated 29 May, 1964, quoted in *Gnosis: Divine Wisdom*, "Appendix", 133 (emphasis by Schuon). Schuon also notes: "The Divine Being contains all the spiritual possibilities and consequently all the religious and mystical archetypes; having projected them into existence, He looks upon each of them with a particular and appropriate Gaze; in an analogous sense, it is said that the angels speak to each person in the appropriate language. This 'Gaze' or 'Face' is a kind of new 'divine subjectivity', subordinated to that of God as such, and transmitting it to man in a particular mode; it is thus that colorless light, without ceasing to be light, projects the colors of the rainbow; and it is thus that water, transformed into ice, gives rise to crystallizations and consequently to differentiated and even opposed manifestations. If there is a conflict between religions, confessions, and ways, it is because there is competition between archetypes; these could never be fundamentally contradictory—the apparent opposition of the colors red and green is resolved precisely in their colorless origin—but they are nonetheless mutually exclusive, except at their centers, which by definition are non-formal and open onto pure light." (*Survey of Metaphysics and Esoterism*, "The Mystery of the Hypostatic Face", 92)

[74] Harry Oldmeadow, *Frithjof Schuon and the Perennial Philosophy*, 83-84, incorporating quotations from *Gnosis: Divine Wisdom*, "Diversity of Revelation", 20, 17.

[75] *Songs without Names*, Tenth Collection, XLIII, 165.

[76] *Survey of Metaphysics and Esoterism*, "Two Esoterisms", 115.

[77] *Transcendent Unity of Religions*, "Preface", xxxiv.

[78] *From the Divine to the Human*, "Structure and Universality of the Conditions of Existence", 60n.

[79] *Survey of Metaphysics and Esoterism*, "Creation as a Divine Quality", 55-56.

[80] *Eye of the Heart*, "Between East and West", 68.

[81] *The Feathered Sun*, "His Holiness and the Medicine Man", 113-114. Christianity does not have a precise parallel to the doctrine of the four ages, but the idea of a continual decline in spirituality over time is expressed by the fall from the Garden of Eden at the time of the Original Sin and the Biblical prophecies of Armageddon, the Apocalypse, the Last Days, and the Day of Judgment. The Islamic teachings contained in the Koran and the *hadīth* (sayings of the Prophet), are remarkably similar to the Christian teachings. See Martin Lings, *The Eleventh Hour*, for information on the Christian and Islamic teachings about the Last Days, Harry Oldmeadow, *Frithjof Schuon and the Perennial Philosophy*, chap. 12, "Cosmic Cycles and the *Kali-Yuga*", for an extensive discussion of this topic drawing on diverse sources and traditions, and, more generally, René Guénon, *The Crisis of the Modern World* and *The Reign of Quantity and the Signs of the Times*.

[82] Schuon's views on evolutionism and progress are summarized in Harry Oldmeadow, *Frithjof Schuon and the Perennial Philosophy,* chap. 13, "Scientism, Evolution, and Progress".

[83] *Of the Land and the Spirit: The Essential Lord Northbourne on Ecology and Religion*, 203.

[84] Schuon does not deny the startling results produced by modern science, nor does he condemn all aspects of modern scientific methodologies. However, "One must beware of sensory and mental illusions, / When making an objective investigation; / In such matters, the scientist is entirely right — / But he is not right when he thinks that the Intellect can be dispensed with, / As if the sage were but a dreamer; / Knowledge is deception, when the Intellect is not the center. / The truth is that pure objectivity is necessary — / And with it the whole Self, not merely the half; / The essential Self which sees all that is real — / The Light of Eternity." (*Songs without Names*, Third Collection, XCVIII, 142)

[85] *Language of the Self*, "The Meaning of Caste", 137, 137n.

[86] *Understanding Islam*, "Islam", 26.

[87] *Autumn Leaves* & *The Ring*, "Points of Rest", 29.

[88] *The Transcendent Unity of Religions*, "Preface", xxxiii.

[89] *Esoterism as Principle and as Way*, "Understanding Esoterism", 19.

[90] *The Transcendent Unity of Religions*, "Preface", xxxiii-xxxiv.

[91] Prior to the Renaissance, traditional societies were more or less closed in the sense that they did not mix with one another in most parts of the world. Each traditional civilization had its own way of life based on the spiritual genius of its primary religion and was unfamiliar with the beliefs of other cultures, except at the borders of their respective civilizations. A greater mixing of religions and societies began at the time of the Renaissance through more accessible modes of travel and the wider distribution of the printed word, a process that has accelerated into our day. This coming together and forced interaction of adherents to different religions is an unprecedented circumstance.

[92] *Transfiguration of Man*, "Thought: Light and Perversion", 10. See also: "We live in an age of confusion and thirst in which the advantages of communication are greater than those of secrecy; moreover, only esoteric theses can satisfy the imperious logical needs created by the philosophic and scientific positions of the modern world." (*Esoterism as Principle and as Way*, "Introduction", 7)

[93] *Esoterism as Principle and as Way*, "Introduction", 8.

[94] Oldmeadow (b. 1947) first contacted Schuon in 1980 when he was preparing his master's degree thesis at the University of Sydney, entitled "Frithjof Schuon and the Meaning of Tradition". He is now a professor at Latrobe University in Bendigo, Australia. Other sources to facilitate further study include: *The Essential Frithjof Schuon*, edited by Seyyed Hossein Nasr, *Frithjof Schuon: Life and Teachings*, by Jean-Baptiste Aymard and Patrick Laude, and *Advice to the Serious Seeker: Meditations on the Teaching of Frithjof Schuon*, by James Cutsinger.

[95] Letter dated 26 February, 1963, quoted in *Gnosis: Divine Wisdom*, "Appendix", 135.

Chapter 1: Childhood

[1] *Songs without Names*, Sixth Collection, LXIX, 275. See also *Songs without Names*, Second Collection, CXVI, 98.

[2] Frithjof Schuon, *Memories and Meditations*. Schuon kept notebooks during his life as an *aide mémoire* without any intention of having them published. However, in the early 1970s he collected and edited his notebooks and travel journals in response to repeated requests from his friends. He relates: "Regarding my memoirs, they contain above all personal reflections about my childhood and youth, then very short accounts, mostly about unforgettable meetings or impressions or important events. I have not at all made up my mind whether to burden you with the task of translating, however impatient some friends may be. I should probably have to make a selection, but have little time for this and, in my opinion, it is not a pressing matter." (letter to Leo Schaya, April 26, 1971) The resultant work, entitled *Erinnerungen und Betrachtungen* ("Memories and Meditations"), was privately circulated in 1974, and begins: "Not from any desire of my own, but in response to the oft-expressed wish of my friends, I shall

relate something of my past and of myself. . .". It should be noted that Schuon's memoirs do not provide a comprehensive autobiographical picture of his life and stop more than twenty-five years before his death. By his own wishes they remain unpublished to this day. Any uncited quotations in this biography are from his *Memories and Meditations*.

[3] "Margarete's mother later married the lawyer for whom she had been working. This man adopted little Margarete, who then received his family name, Benoit." (Catherine Schuon, private correspondence, 2007)

[4] "My father was a violinist; he traveled / To Norway and Russia, and he taught me / Many things; and there was many a song / That would not leave my mind / And wove itself into the veil of my soul. / For the wise spirit loves the aura / That points the way to the blissful land of Beauty." (*World Wheel*, First Collection, CXIII, 39)

[5] This event is discussed in *Frithjof Schuon: Life and Teachings*, 137-138, an authoritative account of Schuon's life. The book's co-authors, Jean-Baptiste Aymard (b. 1952) and Patrick Laude (b. 1958), personally interviewed people with direct knowledge of different events and reviewed various documents pertaining to Schuon's life. Jean-Baptiste Aymard is an independent scholar and author and has co-edited *Les Dossiers H: Frithjof Schuon*. Patrick Laude is a Professor at Georgetown University and the author and editor of several books, including *Pray without Ceasing: The Way of the Invocation in World Religions* and *Singing the Way: Insights in Poetry and Spiritual Transformation*.

[6] *Songs without Names*, Sixth Collection, XLIX, 270. See also *World Wheel*, Second Collection, LXXVI, 84 and *World Wheel*, Fifth Collection, XXXIX, 58.

[7] Martin Lings has remarked on the combination of Schuon's two names: "If you consider the meaning of these names. . . , what I have noticed over the years is the fact that he always disturbs false peace and he offers in its place true peace—that is noble peace." (film interview, 1993)

[8] See also *Frithjof Schuon: Life and Teachings*, 7. "Sound character and depth of soul, / Honesty, fidelity, and love of wisdom — hence / Also some dreaminess; all in all: / The German is energetic, but also heavy. / The German character contains much that is good; / But one does not wish to praise one's own house. / People are too unforgiving towards the Germans — / One only thinks of what they should have been." (*Songs without Names*, Seventh Collection, CXLII, 49) The autobiographical poems written by Schuon in the last years of his life refer to his Germanic heritage as one of the notable dimensions of his being: see *World Wheel*, Sixth Collection, LXXIX, 113 and *World Wheel*, Second Collection, XLIV, 74. See also *Songs without Names*, Second Collection, XV, 62, *Songs without Names*, Fifth Collection, CVIII, 239, and *World Wheel*, Seventh Collection, XXXII, 140.

[9] Letter to Hans Küry, June 7, 1983, quoted in *Frithjof Schuon: Life and Teachings*, 7. Schuon continues, "To be sure, many children of that time—it was the fading-

out of the Nineteenth Century—breathed in the same atmosphere, but soon there came a parting of the ways: a very few remained true to the world of fairy tales and saints—which was also the world of pious, warm-hearted folk art—while the majority were rapidly converted to the world of city streets, of noise and profanity, and thought that such was reality. I myself was never able—despite the pressure of my environment—to believe that Reality could be ugly and noisy, or that ugliness and din could be the Real."

[10] 'Abd al-Qādir al-Jazā'irī (1808-1883) was an Islamic scholar, Sufi, and military leader whose fierce struggle against French colonialism made him an Algerian national hero. After the French victory, he was exiled to Damascus where he and his household guard risked their lives to protect a large number of Christians from an angry Muslim mob. His chivalrous action—protecting the adherents of a different faith—earned him international acclaim.

[11] One of Frithjof Schuon's poems, "Heritage", incorporates some lines from a poem written by his father: "'Somewhere within my being / Must be a sacred land. / When I look inside me / I stand as by the sea.' / Almost a hundred years ago / My father wrote these words. / The sacred land he did not find — / He stood at *Janna*'s gate. / Yet not in vain: nostalgia drew / Him to a pious death. / His love for the sacred: / This remained in me — his heir. / Paradise is not so far: / 'God's Kingdom is within.' / My father sought. And this for him / Was righteousness. — / *Allāh karīm*." (*Autumn Leaves & The Ring*, 109) See also *World Wheel*, Third Collection, V, 104.

[12] See also *Songs without Names*, Fifth Collection, XXX, 215.

[13] Letter to Hans Küry, November 17, 1982, quoted in *Frithjof Schuon: Life and Teachings*, 7.

[14] *Autumn Leaves & The Ring*, "The Teacher", 109.

[15] Personal paper, "Concerning Our Perspective", quoted in *Light on the Ancient Worlds*, "Appendix", 134. See also: ". . . At school I lived among the Bible's palm trees — / With David's harp and his Psalms. / What I received there, I can hardly measure; / What I was given, I shall never forget." (*World Wheel*, First Collection, LXXXVIII, 31) and: "It is thus that David, in his Psalms, spreads out before us all the treasures of the dialogue between the creature and the Creator. Everything is manifested therein: distress, trust, resignation, certitude, gratitude; and all is combined and becomes a song of glory to the Sovereign Good." (*To Have a Center*, "David, Shankara, Hōnen", 131)

[16] Letter to Hans Küry, November 17, 1982, quoted in *Frithjof Schuon: Life and Teachings*, 7.

[17] Late in his life Schuon reflected on the city of his childhood in several poems, including one entitled "Rhineland": "Childhood by the Rhine. Fairy-tale land of old — / Home of songs and heroic sagas. / Dream-experience of a child's soul; / Its unconscious gaze wanted to ask: / Whither goest thou, O river, and whence dost thou come? / Myth of the source and of the sea: / The source, which proclaims the young I; / The sea — the Self — in which form disappears."

(*Autumn Leaves & The Ring*, 151)

[18] Film interview with Johann Jakob Jenny, 1992. Johann Jakob Jenny (1907-1997) was one of Frithjof Schuon's schoolmates in Basle, Switzerland and remained one of his closest and lifelong friends. Dr. Jenny's 1992 film interviews in Basle record many of his childhood recollections concerning Frithjof Schuon.

[19] *World Wheel*, Second Collection, LXXXIII, 86. See also *World Wheel*, Sixth Collection, LIX, 106.

[20] *Treasures of Buddhism*, "Treasures of Buddhism", 8. "It was in my early childhood — / The golden Buddha in the Japanese gallery / Was for me the image of the Great Transcendent, / The Holy One, that filled me with devotion. / Likewise, the great song of the *Gītā* / Was a grace that stilled my youthful longing." (*Songs without Names*, Tenth Collection, XCVII, 181)

[21] Letter to Marco Pallis, June 8, 1982, partially quoted in *Frithjof Schuon: Life and Teachings*, 7.

[22] Titus Burckhardt writes that it is not uncommon for Sufi masters to voice "general indications of the universality of the traditions", given that "Sufism has always recognized the principle according to which the Divine Revelation, transmitted by the great mediators, takes on different forms corresponding to the different aptitudes of the human groupings called on to receive them." (*Introduction to Sufi Doctrine*, xiv) In this connection Burckhardt cites the following two verses from the Koran in a footnote: "The Prophet believes what his Lord revealed unto him. The faithful also believe in God and his angels, His (revealed) books, and His messengers. They say: 'We make no distinction between the messengers of God'" (2:285); and "We have established for every nation rites which it practices" (22:67).

[23] *Adastra & Stella Maris*, "Symbolism", 189.

[24] Poem dated August 1, 1920, quoted in Catherine Schuon, "Frithjof Schuon: Memories and Anecdotes", 50. See also *Frithjof Schuon: Life and Teachings*, 10.

Chapter 2: A Time of Suffering

[1] "When my late father lay dying, / He looked unwaveringly / At a passage from holy Scripture / On the wall facing him; / 'The Lord is my shepherd' — David's psalm. / Painful is earthly death; / But celestial was my father's end — / He met his God." (*Songs without Names*, Seventh Collection, LXXXVII, 32)

[2] Quoted in Catherine Schuon, "Frithjof Schuon: Memories and Anecdotes", 50. This poem was written on December 21, 1920, shortly after his father's death.

[3] *World Wheel*, First Collection, CXII, 38. "It was in the time of my youth — / one wanted to make of me / A reasonable gentleman, / involved in everyday things; / But I dreamt of India, / of temples and dancing girls, / And brahmins / meditating on *Om*. / The clever ones failed completely — / But *Om* graciously thought of me." (*Songs without Names*, Twelfth Collection, LXVIII, 260)

[4] Letter to Leo Schaya, December 19, 1980.

[5] Previously unpublished.

[6] Letter to Leo Schaya, December 19, 1980.

[7] Film interview with Catherine Schuon, 2005.

[8] *Songs without Names*, Twelfth Collection, CXIX, 278.

Chapter 3: Entry into Manhood

[1] Film interview with Johann Jakob Jenny, 1992.

[2] In a 1991 film interview, a journalist said to Schuon, "I am continually struck by your success and the volumes that you've written without having very much formal education at all." Schuon responded, "I had formal education, but by myself."

[3] This is evidenced by Schuon's many didactic poems referencing the *Bhagavad Gītā*. These include: *Songs without Names*, Sixth Collection, LXXXIV, 280, *Songs without Names*, Sixth Collection, CLX, 306, *Songs without Names*, Ninth Collection, LIII, 123, *World Wheel*, First Collection, LII, 18, *World Wheel*, Third Collection, IX, 105, and *World Wheel*, Sixth Collection, LXVI, 109.

[4] As a general rule, it is not possible for non-Hindus to convert to a traditional form of Hinduism because each caste has a different *dharma*, thus different prescriptions and proscriptions.

[5] Letter to Leo Schaya, August 11, 1982, quoted in *Frithjof Schuon: Life and Teachings*, 10. Schuon later wrote: "My homeland is India — for already in my youth / I let myself be penetrated by the words of the *Veda*. / Only in the wake of Vedantic doctrine / Could I bring my own message to the world — / The Word of God, that I hear within me." (*World Wheel*, Fifth Collection, CIX, 78)

[6] Diary entry, 1925. Schuon's deep and lifelong appreciation for Shankara (788-820) and the doctrine of non-dualism (*advaita*) is frequently demonstrated in his metaphysical books as well as in the more than fifty didactic poems treating of the illustrious Hindu sage.

[7] Private correspondence, 2007. Stoddart (b. 1925) was for many years the assistant editor of *Studies in Comparative Religion*. His book, *Remembering in a World of Forgetting*, contains a chapter about Schuon's life and message, entitled "Frithjof Schuon and the Perennialist School".

[8] Diary entry, 1925.

[9] *Songs without Names*, Twelfth Collection, CVII, 274.

[10] *Songs without Names*, Twelfth Collection, XIX, 244. "What I am, I must be. I would gladly / Have been fashioned as simply as others, / But God gave me the heavy burden of my nature / Along with my duty, and said to me: now, go thy way. / And He wrote these words on the door of my heart: / Be without fear — the Most High is with thee." (*Songs without Names*, Eleventh Collection, XXXIII, 204)

Chapter 4: Introduction to René Guénon

[1] Lucy von Dechend (1899-1991) gave Schuon a review of Guénon's book *East and West*. The parents of Lucy von Dechend were close friends of the Schuon family. Catherine Schuon relates: "Lucy came to know Frithjof when he was four years old and she was twelve. From the beginning Lucy noticed that Frithjof was a very special child and became very fond of him. When growing up they never lost contact with each other. . . . She was his first female disciple and remained a faithful friend until the end of her life. She was also the recipient of many important letters which she copied and distributed on Frithjof's behest to their common friends and later did the same with his articles." (personal correspondence, 2007)

[2] Barbara Perry, "Introduction", in *Art from the Sacred to the Profane*, xiv.

[3] René Guénon's books continue to be widely read in France, where his ideas are often hotly debated.

[4] *René Guénon: Some Observations*, "René Guénon: Definitions", 1-3.

[5] *René Guénon: Some Observations*, "René Guénon: Definitions", 4-5.

[6] *René Guénon: Some Observations*, "Conclusion", 49.

Chapter 5: Beginning to Write

[1] *World Wheel*, Fifth Collection, LXXII, 67.

[2] By the age of eighteen, Schuon had already formed numerous ideas that he was to develop in his later writings. The "cult of genius", he noted, "is veritably pernicious, quite apart from the fact that it has no kind of knowledge as its background and is possible only in a life that is excessively sentimental; especially is this so in the case of unbridled and violent enthusiasts. . . . Belief in genius leads us into the discordant sphere of the earthly; it completely bypasses truth." (diary entry, 1925) This insight is the kernel of the article "To Have a Center", written more than sixty years later, which delves into diverse manifestations of the prevalent "cult of human genius" in artistic and literary society that grants celebrity without regard to the spiritual merit or human virtue of the so-called genius.

[3] Letter to Lucy von Dechend, July 1926.

[4] *Gnosis: Divine Wisdom*, "Vicissitudes of Spiritual Temperaments", 36.

[5] Letter dated November 14, 1927.

[6] Letter to Albert Oesch, January 2, 1928.

[7] Letter dated November 1927, quoted in *Sacred Web* 20, 2009, 2.

[8] Interview with Catherine Schuon, 2007.

[9] Interview with Catherine Schuon, 2007.

[10] Interview, September 7, 1988.

[11] Letter to Johann Jakob Jenny, October 1928.

[12] Letter to Johann Jakob Jenny, December 9, 1929.

[13] Letter to Johann Jakob Jenny, December 9, 1929, quoted in *Frithjof Schuon: Life and Teachings*, 57.

[14] One of Schuon's later poems recounts the use of a fabric he designed: "The *Virgen del Pilar* possesses a robe / That was designed by the poet of this book — / Heaven wills that from time to time / This grace-filled image shine according to our spirit." (*Songs without Names*, Third Collection, LXXXIX, 139)

[15] Schuon had a gift for languages. He wrote primarily in his native German and in French, but he also spoke and wrote in English and Arabic; he was conversant in Italian; he read Sanskrit and Latin; and he had a passing familiarity with Greek, Spanish, and Lakota. He studied, in addition, certain important scriptural texts in their original languages—for instance the *Tao Te Ching* in Chinese—in order to grasp their fundamental characteristics and deeper levels of meaning.

[16] Diary entry, 1931, quoted in *Frithjof Schuon: Life and Teachings*, 13.

Chapter 6: The Shaykh al-'Alawī

[1] *World Wheel*, Sixth Collection, CXIII, 124.

[2] "The most direct doctrinal expression of the *sophia perennis* is undoubtedly *Advaita Vedānta*, with its notions of *Ātmā*, of *Māyā*, and of *Tat tvam asi*; but this doctrine is also found, in one form or another, even if only sporadically in some cases, in the sapiential esoterisms of all the great religions, and this must necessarily be so in that every normal—and thus intrinsically orthodox—religion is itself an indirect and symbolic expression of the eternal *sophia*." ("The Perennial Philosophy", 244)

[3] Letter dated January, 1996, quoted in James Cutsinger, "Introduction", in *Prayer Fashions Man*, xviii.

[4] From Shankara's hymn *Cudgel for Illusion*, quoted in *Stations of Wisdom*, "Modes of Prayer", 125n. Schuon also cites the following from Shankara's *Stanza on the Yellow Robe* (of *sannyāsins*), "Singing *Brahma*, the word of Deliverance, meditating uniquely on 'I am *Brahma*', living on alms and wandering freely, blessed, certainly, is the wearer of the ochre robe."

[5] "No Activity without Truth", 13.

[6] "Invocation of the Divine Name"; also cited as letter dated April 24, 1961, quoted in *Prayer Fashions Man*, "Appendix", 187-188. See also, Whitall Perry (ed.), *A Treasury of Traditional Wisdom*, "Colophon: Invocation", 1001-1042.

[7] See the Introduction, xxvi, 166, for more details on this point.

[8] Schuon comments in parentheses on the following Koranic verse: "'Verily, prayer (the exoteric practice) preventeth man from committing what is shameful (degrading) and blameworthy; and certainly remembrance (invocation) of God (the esoteric practice) is greater' (*Sūrah* "The Spider" [29]:45)" (*Sufism: Veil and Quintessence*, "The Quintessential Esoterism of Islam", 118)

[9] The Arabic name Nūr ad-Dīn means "light of the religion".

[10] Letter to Johann Jakob Jenny, February 20, 1932, quoted in *Frithjof Schuon: Life and Teachings*, 15.

[11] Hans Küry (1906-1987) was one of the many admirers who came to Schuon for counsel during these years. He later recalled the first time he saw Schuon in Basle during the summer of 1932: "Whoever had eyes and came into contact with Frithjof Schuon, even in our youth, could not doubt, even long before he was a spiritual master, indeed before he was a Muslim, that God had intended a mission for him in this regard. . . . Schuon, twenty-four years old, with a bold profile and handsome black beard, strode forward like a whirlwind, with the light of rapture on his forehead. . . . [A]s he flew on like an eagle, it was clear like lightning to me: 'Comfort ends here!'" ("Les jeunes gens dans la Caverne: première rencontre", 382).

[12] Seyyed Hassan Imāmī later became Mufti—*Imām jum'ah*—in Tehran and still remembered Schuon some forty years later.

[13] Letter to Albert Oesch, May 15, 1932, quoted in *Frithjof Schuon: Life and Teachings*, 16.

[14] Schuon made subsequent modifications to the book in 1933 and it was eventually published in 1935. The book is written in Schuon's mother tongue of German and was originally entitled *Leitgedanken zur Urbesinnung.* A second German edition, entitled *Urbesinnung: Das Denken des Eigentlichen*, was published with a new preface by the author in 1989 and was brought out in English translation in 2008 as *Primordial Meditation: Contemplating the Real.*

[15] Letter dated January 24, 1932.

[16] In the preface to the second edition of Schuon's first German work he describes it "more as the diary of an unfolding than as a doctrinal book of the same as my later writings. As in all early works, here, too, much is expressed too angularly or too sharply: certainly, principial Truth is incorruptible and hence changeless, but with time one becomes better acquainted with the multi-layered complexity of the Real, if one has the necessary keys at one's disposition. . .". (*Primordial Meditation*, 22)

[17] This *Tarīqah* is named after the thirteenth century Sufi master Abu'l Hasan ash-Shādhilī (1196-1258) and Mūlay al-'Arabī ad-Darqāwī (1760-1823). The story of Ahmad al-'Alawī's life is told in Martin Lings', *A Sufi Saint of the Twentieth Century.*

[18] Letter written in Mostaghanem, dated December 1932. Based on an interview with Lucy von Dechend, Jean-Baptiste Aymard further describes their meeting: "A man of Indian appearance came in. At the request of Schuon, who still dreamed of going to India, he sat down at their table. At that moment a child came up to Schuon and insisted that he write something. To satisfy the child, Schuon wrote the *Shahādah* in Arabic on the piece of paper that he then held out to him—something that did not fail to surprise their new friend, who having thus gained confidence in them, explained that he was an Indian Muslim, and that he had just returned from Mostaghanem where his master, the venerable

Shaykh al-'Alawī, lived." (*Frithjof Schuon: Life and Teachings*, 17)

[19] The *'Alawiyyah zāwiyah* consisted of a large prayer hall with various outbuildings.

[20] Letter to Lucy von Dechend, early December, 1932.

[21] Frithjof Schuon, "*Rahimahu 'Llāh*", 135-137. See also *A Sufi Saint of the Twentieth Century*, 116-117 and *Frithjof Schuon: Life and Teachings*, 17-18.

[22] Shortly after his arrival in Mostaghanem, Schuon received a letter from René Guénon that was forwarded by Lucy von Dechend. "I would advise you to go to Mostaghanem", Guénon wrote, "and see Shaykh Ahmad ibn 'Alīwa. . .". As one of Schuon's biographers further relates: "At the beginning of January 1933, Schuon, who had in the meantime replied to Guénon, received another letter (whose envelope he kept) addressed directly to Mostaghanem: 'You were perhaps surprised to see that I advised you to go to precisely the place where you are now, and yet this "coincidence" has nothing strange about it.' Then, after giving some details about the Darqāwī and the Shādhilī Orders and expressing his concern for the state of the Shaykh's health, Guénon adds: '. . . in any case, the first essential is affiliation with the Order: the rest can come afterwards, often in an unexpected way. . .'." (*Frithjof Schuon: Life and Teachings*, 18)

[23] "Initiation is a pact with God / With a view to the highest Reality: a promise / That the initiate be faithful unto death, / And betray not his word to the Most High — / His word to himself. God never says 'no' to a soul, / Except when this soul itself chooses to break its word." (*World Wheel*, First Collection, CLVI, 52)

[24] "The term *tarīqah* has two meanings: first of all it designates a spiritual method based on a metaphysical doctrine; then it designates . . . an initiatory order." (personal paper, 1992)

[25] Letter to Lucy von Dechend, late January, 1933. Additional information about Schuon's initiation may be found in *Frithjof Schuon: Life and Teachings*, 18-19.

[26] "L'aspect ternaire de la Tradition monothéiste" ("The Ternary Aspect of the Monotheistic Tradition"). The article begins, "The transcendent unity of the traditional forms is illustrated in a particularly instructive manner by the reciprocal relationships existing between the three great so-called 'monotheistic' Traditions; and this is precisely because these three Traditions alone present themselves in the form of irreconcilable exotericisms." Schuon also continued to work on the manuscript for *Leitgedanken zur Urbesinnung* during his sojourn in Algeria.

[27] Letter to Lucy von Dechend, early December, 1932.

[28] Schuon's poem "Al-Mu'ammar" speaks of him further: "Sidi Tāhir al-Mu'ammar — 'the Fulfilled' — / A holy man whose being I revered. / He came and he was silent, and there was much blessing — / Fulfilled he was, because emptied of delusion. / He was one of those who are deeply absorbed, / And in whose silence one forgets time; / One of those who do not give long speeches, /

Because their being's radiance is everything." (*Autumn Leaves & The Ring*, 113)

Schuon also wrote about his encounters with a mysterious stranger in a poem entitled, "Sidi Ahmad": "It was in Mostaghanem. Somber mood / Oppressed me as I stood in the open / By the mosque. An Arab came, / In black burnous, and took me by the hand / And said to me: 'Thee have I known for long; / Say thrice: "lead us on the straight path." / I thank thee; good-bye, *salām*.' — / And left. I was filled with a blessèd strength. / I met him later in Oran. He said: / 'If thou becomest *Allāh*'s friend, thou wilt never be / Alone; thou wilt have all that thou needest. / They call me Ahmad. Listen to me, and see!'" (*Autumn Leaves & The Ring*, 111) These encounters are described in *Frithjof Schuon: Life and Teachings*, 44-45 and in the section entitled "An Esoteric Lineage", 67-70.

29 *World Wheel*, Fourth Collection, XXVI, 9.

30 *Songs without Names*, First Collection, XLI, 18. Schuon wrote thus of his participation in the dance of the dervishes, a practice of invocatory prayer that takes on various forms in different Sufi orders: "When I attended the dance of the dervishes for the first time, the circle remained open on the side opposite the prayer-niche; that is where the Shaykh sat, his gaze directed unwaveringly towards the niche, towards Mecca, his head moving slowly up and down; the expression on his prophet-like face was profoundly mysterious and majestic, while at the same time there was a certain severity in his features. After the dance he began to speak with soft, disconnected words, let fall like drops of water." (letter to Lucy von Dechend, early January, 1933)

31 *Autumn Leaves & The Ring*, "*'Ayn al-Qalb*", 113.

32 *Adastra & Stella Maris*, "Shaykh Ahmad", 57. In another poem Schuon recalls: "It was at my high school in Basle: I said to my / Classmates: 'On Christmas Day 1932 / Let us all meet at the Cathedral Pfalz; / In the meantime, let us work hard.' / In the aforesaid year, I was with the Shaykh — / And was received into his Order. / On Christmas Day, I walked along the shore, / And, not without longing, I looked toward the north. / It was not lack of gratitude for Heaven's gift —/ But a man likes to have a homeland." (*Songs without Names*, Eleventh Collection, CV, 226) See also *Autumn Leaves & The Ring*, "Al-'Alawī", 191, *Songs without Names*, Sixth Collection, LXXXIV, 280, *Songs without Names*, Tenth Collection, XCVIII, 182, *Songs without Names*, Eleventh Collection, CIII, 225, *World Wheel*, First Collection, CXXX, 44, and *World Wheel*, Seventh Collection, LXXIV, 152.

33 Letter to Lucy von Dechend, late January, 1933.

34 Letter to Lucy von Dechend, October 13, 1933, quoted in *Frithjof Schuon: Life and Teachings*, 67.

Chapter 7: Descent of Responsibility

1 During this time he met with a number of intellectuals, including the renowned scholars of Islam, Louis Massignon (1883-1962) and Émile Dermenghem (1892-1971).

[2] One reason Schuon chose to write in French rather than his native German is that French, being based upon Latin, has an extensive vocabulary of nuanced philosophical terms that allows greater precision in formulating and explaining metaphysical concepts. "For speaking, the best European language is Italian; for writing, Latin. With a language like German, in which there are hardly any words with a definite meaning, there is nothing to be done without complications and lyricism." (letter to Johann Jakob Jenny, November 15, 1931, quoted in *Frithjof Schuon: Life and Teachings*, 15) See also *Language of the Self*, "The Meaning of Race", 161 and *World Wheel*, Sixth Collection, L, 103.

[3] Schuon did not publish his first book until 1935. His first three published articles were: "L'aspect ternaire de la Tradition monothéiste" (*Voile d'Isis*, June, 1933), "Shahadah et Fatihah" (*Voile d'Isis*, July, 1933), and "L'Oeil du cœur" (*Voile d'Isis*, November, 1933). As previously noted, Schuon wrote the first of these articles while staying in Mostaghanem; it was later included in his first major French book, *De l'Unité transcendante des religions* (1948) (*The Transcendent Unity of Religions*, 1953). The second article was incorporated many years later into his classic *Comprendre l'Islam* (1961) (*Understanding Islam*, 1963), while the third article was included in his book of the same name, *L'Oeil du cœur* (1950). More than sixty years after this article was written, it was published for the first time in English in *The Eye of the Heart* (1995).

[4] At this time Schuon was living in the Hôtel de Lodi, 69 Rue Dauphine, Paris.

[5] Letter to Leo Schaya, January 23, 1983. See also *Frithjof Schuon: Life and Teachings*, 20.

[6] Letter to Hans Küry, July 1934. See also *Frithjof Schuon: Life and Teachings*, 20.

[7] *Songs without Names*, First Collection, XL, 17.

[8] *Songs without Names*, Sixth Collection, CLX, 306.

[9] Letter to Titus Burckhardt, April 2, 1944.

[10] Jean-Baptiste Aymard, *Frithjof Schuon: Life and Teachings*, 158.

[11] Letter to Hans Küry, February, 20, 1935. "During those days in that dark cell behind the prayer-niche", Schuon relates further, "I had in a dream seen all the Prophets and their voices were sometimes like rushing water; the Buddha Amitābha also arose, golden, before my inward eye." (letter to Titus Burckhardt, April 2, 1944) For a discussion of this dream and its significance, see Renaud Fabbri, "The Milk of the Virgin: The Prophet, the Saint, and the Sage", 249.

[12] For further details on this authorization see *Frithjof Schuon: Life and Teachings*, 21-22.

[13] Titus Burckhardt (1908-1984) was a German Swiss, born in Florence, Italy and raised in Basle. He was the son of the sculptor Carl Burckhardt and the great-nephew of the famous art historian, Jakob Burckhardt. Titus Burckhardt was an expert on the sacred and traditional art of both Christianity and Islam. He lived for many years in Fez, Morocco and was later an integral part of the

Moroccan government's successful preservation of the ancient medina of Fez as a UNESCO World Heritage City in 1981. The Moroccan government sponsored an international symposium in honor of Burckhardt's work in Marrakech on May 5-9, 1999 entitled, "Sagesse et Splendeur des Arts islamiques—Hommage à Titus Burckhardt". The proceedings were published with the financial assistance of UNESCO in 2000. As an author, he devoted himself to the study and exposition of the different aspects of traditional arts and wisdom. His works include: *Sacred Art in East and West, Siena: City of the Virgin, An Introduction to Sufi Doctrine, Alchemy: Science of the Cosmos, Science of the Soul, Fez: City of Islam, Chartres and the Birth of the Cathedral, Moorish Culture in Spain*, and *Art of Islam: Language and Meaning. The Encyclopedia of Religion* (ed. Mircea Eliade) refers to Burckhardt as one of the "great European Sufi masters" (vol. 7, 424). For more on the relationship between Burckhardt and Schuon, see chap. 21, "Reflections", 125-126.

[14] Schuon would later insist that his bibliography not mention articles that also appeared in his books; however, at this time none of his French articles had yet appeared in any book. All but one of Schuon's articles published before 1935 appeared in the French journal *Le Voile d'Isis* ("Veil of Isis"). Late in 1935 the publisher changed the journal's name to *Études traditionnelles* ("Traditional Studies"). For the next half century, *Études traditionnelles* became the pre-eminent French language journal for authors whose interests converged on "the true traditional spirit". Schuon contributed eleven additional articles to this journal during the second half of the 1930s and remained a prominent contributor for more than fifty years.

[15] The function of Shaykh and the initiatic name of Nūr ad-Dīn given to Schuon by the Shaykh al-'Alawī evoke the premonition Schuon received at the International Exhibition at Vincennes in 1931, when he found himself involuntarily repeating the Islamic name "Shaykh Nūr ad-Dīn" without knowing why.

[16] Letter to Martin Lings, March 7, 1956.

[17] Thus, while Schuon's written message is meant to communicate the Truth to the world, his function as a spiritual master was limited to those whom destiny guided to him. Nor was it in his nature to wish for disciples. Schuon was approached, for example, in the 1980s by Vincent Rossi, director of an organization of Christian spiritual seekers known as the Holy Order of MANS, and asked if he would accept as disciples the more than one thousand group members. Before responding, Frithjof Schuon asked his neighbor, Whitall Perry, to learn more about their spiritual practices. When Perry concluded that the Holy Order of MANS was not following an orthodox form of Christianity, Schuon declined to accept them as disciples and advised them to find an orthodox religion. Based in part on this counsel, Vincent Rossi and many members of the group subsequently converted to the Eastern Orthodox Church. Schuon never considered these seekers as his disciples, but he remains an important influence in Vincent Rossi's life. (See, for example, Rossi, "Presence, Participation, Performance: The Remembrance of God in the Early Hesychast Fathers", 66-70.)

[18] "There is no misfortune worse than having disciples", Guénon wrote to Martin Lings. "I would never have wanted to have any, not for anything in the world!" (letter to Martin Lings, July 26, 1950)

Guénon was initiated into another branch of the *Shādhiliyyah* Sufi order, which traces its lineage through the Egyptian Shaykh 'Abd ar-Rahmān Ilaysh al-Kabīr (1869-1917). For Guénon, access to a valid initiation was a key factor in his choice of a religious form. "I cannot let it be said", Guénon tells a correspondent, "that I 'converted to Islam' for this way of presenting things is completely false; whoever is aware of the essential unity of traditions is therefore 'unconvertible' . . . but one may 'settle', if one may say so, in such or such a tradition depending upon circumstances, and above all for reasons of an initiatory order." (quoted in Alain Daniélou, "René Guénon et la tradition hindoue", 138) See also *René Guénon: Some Observations*, "René Guénon: A Note", 6-7.

[19] Letter dated January, 1996, quoted in James Cutsinger, "Introduction", in *Prayer Fashions Man*, xviii.

[20] See *The Transcendent Unity of Religions*, "The Ternary Aspect of Monotheism", 96 and Titus Burckhardt, *Introduction to Sufi Doctrine*, 19.

[21] *Roots of the Human Condition*, "Outline of the Islamic Message", 81, 81n. On the meaning of this Vedantic phrase and on metaphysical discernment in general, see the Introduction, xxii-xxiv.

[22] *Sufism: Veil and Quintessence*, "The Quintessential Esoterism of Islam", 103. "The fundamental Testimony, or the First *Shahādah*, ['There is no divinity except the (sole) Divinity'] contains a negative part, which rejects false divinities, and a positive part, which affirms the true God. . . . [T]his is the distinction between *Māyā* and *Ātmā*. The Second *Shahādah*, that of the Prophet ['Muhammad is the Messenger of God'], adds that *Māyā* is not other than *Ātmā*, in its 'not unreal' substance." (*Form and Substance in the Religions*, "The Human Margin", 211n) For more on the meaning of the *Shahādah*, see *Understanding Islam*, "Islam", 5-7, "The Koran", 61-65, and "The Path", 150-153, *Sufism: Veil and Quintessence*, "The Quintessential Esoterism of Islam", 104-108, *Form and Substance in the Religions*, "The Five Divine Presences", 56-57, *Survey of Metaphysics and Esoterism*, "Two Esoterisms", 116, and *In the Face of the Absolute*, "Transcendence and Immanence in the Spiritual Economy of Islam", 192-193.

[23] Text, "Islam and *Fitrah*". In the same document he notes, "Islam possesses an essentiality, a simplicity, and universality that renders it particularly apt to convey a direct manifestation of the *Religio Perennis*."

[24] One also notes that Islam is, in principle, more inclusive of other religions than Christianity.

[25] Letter to Leo Schaya, December 19, 1980.

[26] *Understanding Islam*, "Islam", 1.

Chapter 8: War Years

[1] Quoted in part in *Frithjof Schuon: Life and Teachings*, 24.

[2] Quoted in Patrick Laude, "René Guénon: Traditional Sources and Contemporary Contexts", 146.

[3] *Frithjof Schuon: Life and Teachings*, 24. See also *René Guénon: Some Observations*, "Definitions", 1-5 and "Conclusion", 48-49.

[4] The "blessing of the *Tarīqah Qādiriyyah*" refers to Schuon's initiation into a second Sufi lineage, a common practice within Sufism.

[5] See Paul Chacornac, *The Simple Life of René Guénon*, 84.

[6] Quoted in *Frithjof Schuon: Life and Teachings*, 25.

[7] Catherine Schuon, "Frithjof Schuon: Memories and Anecdotes, 52.

[8] Catherine Schuon, "Frithjof Schuon: Memories and Anecdotes, 52.

[9] *Autumn Leaves & The Ring*, "India", 117.

[10] "Communion and Invocation" first appeared in *Études traditionnelles* in May 1940, and was recently published in English translation in *Pray Without Ceasing: The Way of the Invocation in World Religions*, edited by Patrick Laude.

[11] His mother's ancestral home was in the Alsace region, which was repeatedly disputed by Germany and France between the time of the French-Prussian War of the 1870s and the end of Second World War. Germany reclaimed the Alsace region when it invaded France early in World War II, but today the Alsace region is part of France.

[12] Film interview with a journalist, 1991.

Chapter 9: A Heavenly Gift

[1] *Songs without Names*, Third Collection, CVII, 145.

[2] "[A]ll at once, almost overnight, gently and unexpectedly came the great Peace. . .".

[3] Not long after Schuon's own marriage in 1949, Madeleine "made friends most warmly with my young wife". The two women have remained friends and occasionally meet when Mrs. Schuon visits Lausanne.

[4] *Songs without Names*, Sixth Collection, LV, 271.

[5] See *Stations of Wisdom*, "Stations of Wisdom", *Eye of the Heart*, "On Meditation", *In the Face of the Absolute*, "The Mystery of the Prophetic Substance", and *The Transfiguration of Man*, "Dimensions of Prayer". See also *Frithjof Schuon: Life and Teachings*, 27, 94-96 and William Stoddart, *Remembering in a World of Forgetting*, 60.

[6] *Frithjof Schuon: Life and Teachings*, 27. See also: "The Spirit gave six guiding thoughts: / Renunciation, Act, Contentment, Trust, / Discernment and Selfhood; thou needest nothing more." (*Autumn Leaves & The Ring*, "Six Thoughts", 207); and: "Six — in this, two and three combine; / Passivity and activity; on each side / Are three spiritual powers: Fear, Love, then Knowledge, / Which, with His

grace, may lead thee to the Most High. / Two pillars with three levels: Six ways to invoke the One Lord." (*World Wheel*, Sixth Collection, XXXIII, 99)

[7] "Invocation of the Divine Name"; also cited as letter dated April 24, 1961, quoted in *Prayer Fashions Man*, "Appendix", 187-188. In reference to the more metaphysically oriented fifth and sixth Themes, Schuon observes elsewhere that "[M]an must not make use of intentions that surpass his nature; if he is not a metaphysician, he must not believe himself obliged to be one. . . . This means that in prayer there are dimensions that are imperative for every man, and others that he may as it were greet from afar; for what matters in this confrontation is not that man be great or small, but that he stand sincerely before God." (*Transfiguration of Man*, "Dimensions of Prayer", 99)

[8] *Autumn Leaves & The Ring*, "Keys", 105. And: "If God is purity, I am sobriety; / If God is power, I will cultivate the best of acts; / If God is the treasure, I am contentment; / If God is salvation, I will trust in Him. / If God alone is real, the world cannot be; / If God is Identity, then He is mine." (*Songs without Names*, Seventh Collection, XCIV, 35) See also *Autumn Leaves & The Ring*, "Guiding Themes", 125, *World Wheel*, Second Collection, LXI, 79, and *World Wheel*, Fourth Collection, CIX, 36.

[9] *Eye of the Heart*, "Microcosm and Symbol", 152.

[10] "Communion and Invocation", 74n. See also *Logic and Transcendence*, "Nature and Function of the Spiritual Master".

[11] *Autumn Leaves & The Ring*, "Condition", 35.

[12] *In the Face of the Absolute*, "The Ambiguity of Exoterism", 36. In this same article Schuon continues, "One may be surprised at this coincidence between what is most elementarily human and what pertains quintessentially to the highest wisdom, but what is most simple retraces precisely what is highest; *extremitates aequalitates*, 'extremes meet.'"

[13] Schuon has written that "our position is well known: it is fundamentally that of metaphysics, and the latter is by definition universalist, 'dogmatist' in the philosophical sense of the term, and traditionalist; universalist because free of all denominational formalism; 'dogmatist' because far from all subjectivist relativism—we believe that knowledge exists and that it is a real and efficacious adequation—and traditionalist because the traditions are there to express, in diverse ways, but unanimously, this quintessential position—at once intellectual and spiritual—which in the final analysis is the reason for the existence of the human spirit." (*From the Divine to the Human*, "Preface", 1)

[14] "There are diverse viewpoints in the Spirit's realm — / The paths that God blesses are of equal value." (*World Wheel*, First Collection, XX, 8)

[15] Martin Lings, "Frithjof Schuon and René Guénon", 22, from a talk given at the Temenos Academy. Martin Lings (1909-2005) was Schuon's disciple and friend for more than 60 years. He was born in Burnage, Lancashire and received both a BA and an MA in English Literature from the University of Oxford. For four years, starting in 1935, he lectured on Anglo-Saxon and Middle English at the

University of Kaunus, followed by a twelve year lectureship in English Literature, primarily Shakespeare, at Cairo University. He returned to England in 1952 and continued his education, earning a PhD from the School of Oriental and African Studies (University of London). In 1955 he joined the British Library as Keeper of the Arabic Library, eventually becoming the Keeper of Oriental Manuscripts at the British Museum and the British Library before retiring in 1973.

Lings is the author of more than fifteen books. As Jean-Claude Petitpierre, who knew Lings for almost fifty years, has noted, "Martin Lings approached tradition with an emphasis on Islam." (film interview, 2005) Among his works on Islamic mysticism are, *The Book of Certainty: The Sufi Doctrine of Faith, Vision, and Gnosis* (as Abū Bakr Sirāj ad-Dīn), *A Sufi Saint of the Twentieth Century: Shaikh Ahmad al-'Alawī*, and *What is Sufism?*, the last two of which have been published in many languages. He is also the author of *The Secret of Shakespeare: To Take Upon Us the Mystery of Things, Ancient Beliefs and Modern Superstitions*, two volumes of poetry, and the beautifully illustrated *Splendours of Quran Calligraphy and Illumination.* His biography, *Muhammad: His Life Based on the Earliest Sources* has been internationally acclaimed as a masterpiece. Lings' last book, *A Return to the Spirit: Questions and Answers*, contains several chapters that describe Schuon's influence in his life. After Schuon's death, Lings was recognized as a spiritual guide (*shaykh*) in his own right, with disciples and admirers on five continents. According to Petitpierre, "He was like a magnet to the people who knew him."

Martin Lings died in May of 2005. H.R.H the Prince of Wales wrote in memory of him: "One of Martin Lings' greatest legacies—apart from his insights into the true significance of Shakespeare's plays and his remarkable biography of the Prophet Muhammad—must surely be his timely reminder to us that Sufism, of which he was such a distinguished proponent, has always been at the spiritual heart of Islam. . .".

16 "I am neither a Jew, nor Muslim, nor Christian / Rūmī said; and my Islam is not / Dogmatic belief; it is that which is." (*Adastra & Stelle Maris*, "*Gnosis*", 69) Kabīr insisted that while one person might recite a Hindu Name of God and another a Muslim Name of God, there is in reality only one God.

17 It is well documented, for example, that many shaykhs in the *Naqshabandiyya Tarīqah* and numerous Sufi masters in the Jammu and Kashmir regions of India have Hindu disciples.

18 Letter to Rama Coomaraswamy, December 5, 1970. And also: "A question arises that has often been debated: can the function of a spiritual master extend beyond the boundaries of a given religion? This cannot be ruled out categorically, but it is nevertheless a very precarious possibility because of the high degree of spirituality it demands on the part of the master as well as because of the difficulty with which he may be faced in assessing facts situated in a traditional world other than his own; moreover, in such a case he would act as the vehicle of a foreign *barakah*, and this presupposes a spirituality concretely transcending the world of forms; it is necessary to add the word "concretely", because universalist

verbiage is one thing and realization of the Essence is another." (*Logic and Transcendence*, "Nature and Function of the Spiritual Master", 194-195)

[19] *Spiritual Perspectives and Human Facts*, "*Vedānta*", 122. James Cutsinger discusses how a Christian can accept the idea of a "transcendent unity of religions" and how, in addition, a Christian can seek spiritual counsel from a non-Christian: "I am myself a Christian, a member of the Eastern Orthodox Church, and as a professor of theology at a large university in the American South, I teach mostly Christian students. Because of my publications, including a recent book on Schuon, it is only natural that other Christians should from time to time . . . wonder what I could possibly be thinking. How could I compromise my allegiance to Christ and my fidelity to His Church by supposing that other religions are equally true and by looking to a non-Christian for spiritual counsel? . . . In my first meeting with the Shaykh, almost his very first words to me were an admonition that 'Christ is your master'.

"But what about the larger matter of other spiritual forms? How in good conscience can a traditional Christian accept the idea that there is a 'transcendent unity of religions'? The first thing to stress about Schuon's answer to these questions is that it requires no diminution in our conviction as to the stature of Christ. . .". ("The Mystery of the Two Natures", 112-113)

In order to better appreciate Schuon's remark that "Christ is your master", we must recall that he did not provide an initiation to his non-Muslim disciples. In the case of Christianity, initiation is conferred by baptism, confirmation, communion, and the personal vow of the spiritual seeker. In consequence, as Patrick Laude has observed, "the relationship between Schuon and his Muslim *fuqarā'* was of a different nature, in terms of modality", than was his relationship to his non-Muslim followers, who were not directly affiliated with his Islamic *Tarīqah* (Patrick Laude, "Quintessential Esoterism and the Wisdom of Forms", 160n).

[20] Letter to a Christian disciple, January 28, 1983, quoted in *Christianity/Islam*, "Appendix", 204. Schuon was opposed to diluting and blending the forms of the various religions, as is the case, for example, in sanctuaries intended for inter-faith worship. "I am against the construction of an abode for the faithful of all the religions, because this amounts to improvisation and dilettantism. . .". (letter dated April 30, 1976) Schuon extended these principles to his followers, who, if they were practitioners of separate religions, did not say their canonical prayers together. On an exceptional basis, an individual who was traveling might be allowed to attend the group prayer gathering of followers of another religion, always sitting in a separate area and praying silently in his own manner.

Chapter 10: Essentiality and Universality

[1] *Esoterism as Principle and as Way*, "The Religion of the Heart", 232-233. "[T]he perspective of the Religion of the Heart or of Love", Schuon affirms, "is above all intellective and thereby universal".

[2] *Transcendent Unity of Religions*, "Preface", xxxi.

[3] See 2 Corinthians 3:6. In the context of Islam, Schuon notes that the *sharī'ah* "is characterized by its flexibility: it takes into account a legal minimum—what is indispensable, *fardh*." (letter to Hans Küry, October 15, 1953) While an al-Ghazzālī (1058-1111), for example, recommended the observation of the *sunnah* in its minutest ramifications, Schuon writes that the "opposite opinion also exists, namely that the legal minimum suffices for going to Paradise provided there is either great purity of soul, or great virtue, or profound inner knowledge. In this context let us recall that Muslims divide actions into five categories: 1. what is indispensable (*fardh* or *wājib*); 2. what is recommended (*sunnah, mustahabb*); 3. what is indifferent (*mubāh*); 4. what is inadvisable (*makrūh*); 5. what is forbidden (*harām*)." (*Understanding Islam*, "The Quran", 70n) See also *Esoterism as Principle and Way*, "Religion of the Heart", *Sufism: Veil and Quintessence*, "Human Premises of a Religious Dilemma" and "The Quintessential Esoterism of Islam", and *Survey of Metaphysics and Esoterism*, "Enigma and Message of Islamic Esoterism".

[4] Quoted in *Understanding Islam*, "Remarks on the *Sunnah*", 100. There is also the saying of the Shaykh al-'Alawī, "Remembrance (*dhikr*) is the most important rule of the religion. The law was not imposed upon us nor the rites of worship ordained except for the sake of establishing the remembrance of God (*dhikru 'Llāh*)." (quoted in *Sufism: Veil and Quintessence*, "The Quintessential Esoterism of Islam", 117n)

[5] Martin Lings, "Frithjof Schuon and René Guénon", 15. In a letter dated September 13, 1987 Schuon states that "Our *Tarīqah* was founded in the West by a Westerner for Westerners; we did not start with the assumption that Easterners would need us. The great majority of the aspirants were *a priori* seekers coming from Christianity, who based themselves on the *Vedānta*, and who wished to enter the *Tarīqah* because of the initiation and the invocation; they were not Muslims who wished to deepen their religion esoterically. At all events, it is not possible that the passage into Islam be for God the only solution offered Western seekers, because that would be an incomprehensible negation of Christianity—which, however, is willed by God—and just as incomprehensible a victory of Islam. . .".

It should, however, be obvious given the essentiality and universality of Schuon's perspective that his *Tarīqah* could not exist for Christian-born Westerners alone; many Muslim-born Easterners, in particular those who have undergone Western influence, have benefited from attachment to Schuon's spiritual community, which in their case serves to re-awaken or increase awareness of the values in their own tradition. See also chap. 9, "A Heavenly Gift" and chap. 22, "The Close of Two Cycles".

[6] Patrick Laude has written that "Schuon places all the methodical emphasis, as a spiritual teacher, on the Form *par excellence* . . . that is the invocation of the Name of God, which means that under some circumstances, like sickness or the pressure of the most extreme tensions of modern life, the practices of the religion may be reduced to a strict minimum." ("Quintessential Esoterism

and the Wisdom of Forms", 186-187) See also *Sufism: Veil and Quintessence*, "Appendix", 135-136.

[7] Letter to Mcleod Matheson, January 28, 1956, quoted in part in *Sufism: Veil and Quintessence*, "Appendix", 134. Later in this same letter, Schuon notes that "The circumstantial simplifications that I am led to envisage, for some disciples, on the plane of the *sharī'ah*, may be founded on this verse: '. . . and indeed the invocation of *Allāh* is greater', and also on the following: 'God wants for you what is easy, not what is difficult'; one can also base oneself on the *hadīth* that says that at the end of times, 'he who accomplishes one tenth of the Law will be saved', or yet this *hadīth*: 'The end of the world will not come as long as somebody on earth says: *Allāh, Allāh*.'" However, "I do not", Schuon underlines, "forbid the difficulties that the *sharī'ah* or the *sunnah* may entail, that is obvious." (letter to Hans Küry, December 21, 1949)

In a 1968 interview, French author Jean Biès (b. 1933), asked Schuon, "What do you understand as being the 'tenth part of the Law' which is mentioned in a *hadīth* and which is demanded of men at the end of the cycle?" Schuon responded, "At the beginning of the cycle, one had to accomplish nine-tenths of the Law as indicated in the *Shāstra*. At the end of the cycle the tenth part obviously refers to the minimum: in Islam, it is the five daily prayers and almsgiving; for Christians, it is to go to confession once a year and to participate in the Eucharist at Easter. . .". ("A Face of Eternal Wisdom: An Interview with Frithjof Schuon", 15-16). Schuon's indication here of the depths of divine Mercy obtaining at the end of times should not be confused with his own practice, nor that of his disciples, which in fact went well beyond this minimum, especially in its emphasis upon quintessential prayer or prayer of the heart.

[8] See also *Sufism: Veil and Quintessence*, "The Quintessential Esoterism of Islam", 117-119.

[9] A number of Schuon's articles and poems demonstrate his special interest in the teachings of Hōnen Shōnin (1133-1212), the founder and guiding light of Japanese Amidism. In his article "David, Shankara, Hōnen", Schuon writes: "David, Shankarāchārya, and Hōnen are spiritual personalities who are in many respects quite different, but who have in common the fact that they each represent an altogether fundamental mode of spirituality, and that they do so in a perfect, unsurpassable, and incisive manner. . . . If David incarnates the meeting with God and Prayer, and Shankara metaphysical Truth, Intellection, and Meditation, Hōnen for his part will be like the incarnation of Faith and Invocation. . .". (*To Have a Center*, 131, 137) See also *Treasures of Buddhism*, "Dharmakāra's Vow" and "Synthesis of the *Pāramitās*", 141-142, 145-146, *Songs without Names*, Sixth Collection, XLVI, 269, and *Songs without Names*, Sixth Collection, XLIV, 268.

[10] *Understanding Islam*, "Remarks on the *Sunnah*", 101-102. In contrast, "a born Muslim living in *Dār al-Islām* will hardly be satisfied with the legal minimum, for he has little reason for this: he has been raised in Islam and masters its forms with ease, and in fact has learned hardly anything other than those forms; in addition, he is backed by the rhythms of the entire social life." (letter to Hans

Küry, October 15, 1953)

[11] Titus Burckhardt, *Mirror of the Intellect*, 252. In a related context, Patrick Laude has stated that "In a world that is threatened by the bitter corrosiveness of religious fanaticism parading as orthodoxy and tradition, and—in a more tepid and smiling but in fact no less destructive way—by wide segments of New Age spirituality ignorantly and lightly claiming to free the 'essentials' of spirituality from 'obsolete' or 'oppressive' forms, Schuon's remarkably profound and nuanced views provide us with an integral understanding of spirituality that situates each reality, whether essential or formal, in its proper context and at its adequate degree." ("Quintessential Esoterism and the Wisdom of Forms", 192)

[12] "An example of excessive formalism—and of a conventionalism which is definitely superstitious—is provided by certain garments of Muslim women: in Islamic India there are certain ways of veiling women that have something truly sinister about them—they are like walking prisons or phantoms—which, to say the least, is contrary to nature, and which demonstrates to what extent the exoteric spirit can be pedantic, blind, and desiccated; by contrast, the veil of Moroccan women is morally and aesthetically acceptable, being so to speak 'one point of view among others'. In the Maghrib, Berber women go unveiled—this should be recalled here—and the same is true for many Muslims of the black and yellow races, not to mention other examples difficult to categorize; which shows that this convention of dress is in no way essential from the point of view of the Law." (*In the Face of the Absolute*, "The Ambiguity of Exoterism", 33)

[13] *Understanding Islam*, "Remarks on the *Sunnah*", 98. A vexing question for many of today's spiritual and religious leaders is, "What are the most appropriate ways to practice certain religious observances in the midst of the hostile conditions of the modern world?" Spiritual guides from diverse religions come to very different conclusions about the extent to which their Western followers should observe various religious prescriptions, and it is important to recognize that their decisions are often applied on an individual basis and based on a myriad of considerations, both individual and principial.

Chapter 11: At Variance with Guénon

[1] *Songs without Names*, Fourth Collection, XXII, 163.

[2] Film interview, 1993.

[3] Marco Pallis (1895-1989) was born in England to Greek parents. His devotion to mountain climbing led him to the Himalayas, where he became fascinated by Buddhism in its Tibetan form. His first book, *Peaks and Lamas*, describes both the course of his Himalayan mountaineering expeditions as well as the path that he took to commit himself to the Tibetan Buddhist tradition. His two later works, *The Way and the Mountain* and *A Buddhist Spectrum* are each collections of essays on diverse topics of a traditional nature, often with a focus on the Buddhist tradition. In addition to his own writings, Pallis translated into English several works by René Guénon and Frithjof Schuon. See chap. 15, "Noteworthy

Encounters", 79, for more details on Pallis.

[4] For a discussion of the important role they played in altering Guénon's views, see Marco Pallis, "A Fateful Meeting of Minds: A.K. Coomaraswamy and R. Guénon", 12-13. Guénon cited Coomaraswamy's writings on Buddhism as containing the decisive information upon which he changed his opinion. Ananda Kentish Coomaraswamy (1887-1947), described by Heinrich Zimmer (1890-1943) as "That noble scholar upon whose shoulders we are still standing" and by Mircea Eliade (1907-1986) as "one of the most learned and creative scholars of the century", was one of the world's greatest art historians and scholars of traditional iconography. While serving as a curator to the Boston Museum of Fine Arts in the latter part of his life, he devoted his work to the explication of traditional metaphysics and symbolism. Coomaraswamy was responsible for creating the collections of oriental art for the Freer Museum, Washington D.C., as well as for the Boston Museum of Fine Arts. The Princeton University Bollingen Series LXXXIX presented three volumes by Roger Lipsey: *Traditional Art and Symbolism*, *Metaphysics*, and *His Life and Work*. Coomaraswamy was the author of several hundred articles and numerous books.

[5] Letter to a Christian woman, November 21, 1975, quoted in *Gnosis: Divine Wisdom*, "Appendix", 139-140. Guénon was of the opinion that after Christianity had lost its esoteric nature in the third or fourth century, its central teachings and mysteries were kept alive—to this day—by certain secret initiatic organizations such as the Templars, Free-Masons, and various Guilds; he also believed that these organizations still possessed the ability to provide a valid initiation—a secret initiation of which the Church was unaware. Schuon disagreed with each point of Guénon's thesis. (See *René Guénon: Some Observations*, "René Guénon: Some Observations", 37-47.) Schuon's point of view on Catholic initiation is summarized in a letter: "In Christianity, it is baptism, confirmation, and communion that constitute what can be termed initiation; the total character of these sacraments excludes the existence, alongside them, of more or less secret initiatic rites that could be superimposed on them—initiatic rites such as are found in Orphism. . .". (letter to a Christian woman, May 31, 1955)

[6] "The inspiration I had when I wrote 'Mystères Christiques' ['Christic Mysteries'] was twofold: Firstly, that Catholics should pray the rosary fervently, with reference to the old teachings; and secondly, that the sacraments as such are initiations." (letter to Titus Burckhardt, November 29, 1949)

[7] For Schuon's critiques of Guénon see *René Guénon: Some Observations*. See also *World Wheel*, Fourth Collection, XCIII, 30.

[8] In his 1988 Preface to the second edition of *Spiritual Perspectives and Human Facts*, Schuon affirms that his works, taken as a whole, "contain a complete doctrine—the *sophia perennis* or, if one prefers, integral traditionalism" (xi). The term "Perennialism", when used to refer to the "school of thought" associated with Guénon and Schuon, has the advantage of expressing a direct relationship with this school's presiding idea, that of the *philosophia perennis* and the related ideas of the *sophia perennis* and *religio perennis*. (See Introduction, 29 for the

relationship between these terms.) Because this eternal and sacred wisdom, once revealed, is outwardly transmitted through time by the vehicle of tradition (from *tradere*, "to hand down"), the use of the classificatory term "Traditionalism" is also justified. In this context it is important to recall that "there is certainly nothing pejorative about the word ['Traditionalism'] itself. . . ; as a matter of fact, however, it has come to be associated—arbitrarily and reprehensibly so—with an image that inevitably devalues its meaning, namely, 'nostalgia for the past'. . . . If to recognize what is true and just is 'nostalgia for the past', it is clearly a crime or disgrace not to feel this nostalgia. The same applies to other accusations prompted by the idea of tradition, such as 'Romanticism', 'aestheticism', 'folklore'; far from disclaiming any affinity for these things, we adopt them precisely insofar as they have a relationship with either tradition or virgin nature, thus restoring their legitimate and—at the very least—innocent meanings." (*Logic and Transcendence*, "Introduction", 5) However, one must keep in mind the following reservation: "This is not to say that the sacred coincides in an absolute manner with the traditional in the strict sense of the word: that is 'traditional' which is transmitted from a divine source; now we do not say that the latter can manifest outside of the traditional framework, but it can do so independently of inherited formulations, otherwise there would be neither inspiration nor diversity of schools. That is, in the sacred there is a 'vertical' and discontinuous manifestation as well as a 'horizontal' and continuous manifestation." (*From the Divine to the Human*, "The Sense of the Sacred", 109) One must also recognize the fact that the terms "Traditionalism" and "Perennialism" have been applied as labels to widely divergent schools of thought, whose core beliefs often conflict with one another.

[9] Letter to Jean-Pierre Laurant, April 1976, quoted in *Frithjof Schuon: Life and Teachings*, 31.

[10] Schuon's decision, for example, to accept women as disciples went against the recommendations of Guénon, who had proposed that Schuon neither accept female disciples nor allow women to attend prayer gatherings with men. Catherine Schuon recalls that her husband "was completely against that; he said 'there are intelligent women in the world; why shouldn't they be able to come?' And he wrote all of this to Guénon; but there were discrepancies between what Guénon thought the spiritual path should be and what my husband thought the spiritual path should be." (film interview, 2005)

[11] Letter to Michel Vâlsan, October 9, 1960.

[12] Letter to Jean-Pierre Laurant dated 1976, quoted in *Frithjof Schuon: Life and Teachings*, 34.

[13] An extreme example of such a personal attack on Schuon came in 1991, when a man tried to coerce him to give a supposed "esoteric benediction" to an adulterous relationship. Schuon refused, and the man sought revenge by making false accusations against him to an assistant prosecutor. On the basis of these allegations, criminal charges were filed against the eighty-four year old philosopher. However, when the chief prosecutor looked at the evidence, he became aware

of the accuser's criminal record, his court-ordered psychological counseling, and the fact that Schuon's accuser had received large amounts of money from the married woman. The chief prosecutor thus immediately dismissed the charges and forced the resignation of the assistant responsible for the case. The police investigator was reassigned to another town. The local newspaper quoted the prosecutor as saying that other than the testimony of one individual "there is not one shred of evidence . . . against Schuon. Insofar as Schuon has been labeled (by the allegations), a miscarriage has occurred." (Bloomington *Herald Times*, November 21, 1991) The prosecutor added that Schuon's accuser "has come under a very large cloud of credibility." (Bloomington *Herald Times*, November 21, 1991) Later the prosecutor acknowledged that "Schuon is owed an apology. . . . A mistake was made by my office . . . and the system broke down." (interview on WTHR Channel 13, November 21, 1991) A few days later the local newspaper's lead editorial, "Schuon Case a Travesty", was strongly critical of the prosecutor's inattention to the case while he was campaigning for a state-wide political office (Bloomington *Herald Times*, November 26, 1991).

It is regrettable that Schuon's humiliated accuser subsequently disseminated a document containing the same perverted allegations that had been discredited by the legal authorities. However, a positive result of this ordeal occurred when, within a week of the charges being dismissed, Schuon agreed to two filmed interviews with a local newspaper reporter. These interviews later provided the basis for the documentary film on his life. His extemporaneous responses to the interview questions help place both his message and his private life—including his spiritual vocation—in a more accessible context. This broader accessibility to the man and his message are a direct result of the incident.

[14] See *World Wheel*, Fifth Collection, C, 76.

[15] *Roots of the Human Condition*, "Cosmic Shadows and Serenity", 110.

Chapter 12: Marriage and a New Home

[1] Catherine Feer (b. 1924) became a disciple of Schuon in 1946. Gifted in languages, she became fluent in English and conversant in Italian, in addition to the three languages of her youth: German, French, and Spanish. She accompanied her husband on all of his travels and assisted him with receiving visitors and answering correspondence from spiritual seekers who asked for his counsel. She is also a gifted painter. Since her husband's death in 1998 she has spent several months each year traveling throughout the world to visit many of her late husband's admirers, while maintaining as her permanent residence the home she shared for 18 years with Schuon in the forests of Southern Indiana.

[2] In a letter dated May 10, 1949 Guénon expresses his sadness on learning of the death of Schuon's mother and his pleasure at Schuon's marriage, adding, "We very much hope that we will soon see her here with you!"

[3] Catherine Schuon, "Frithjof Schuon: Memories and Anecdotes", 41.

[4] Catherine Schuon, "Frithjof Schuon: Memories and Anecdotes", 41.

[5] Whitall Perry (1920-2005) and his wife, Barbara Perry (b. 1923), are among the few people who had close personal relationships with A.K. Coomaraswamy, René Guénon, Titus Burckhardt, and Frithjof Schuon—the four most important writers of the Perennialist school. Whitall Perry placed himself at Schuon's call in varying capacities, ranging from practical assistance to answering certain correspondence on Schuon's behalf. Whitall Perry's books include the monumental *A Treasury of Traditional Wisdom*, a compendium of spiritual doctrine spanning all history and every spiritual tradition. Barbara Perry translated a number of Schuon's personal papers and poems from German into English and is the author of a biographical article first written in 1981, "Frithjof Schuon: Metaphysician and Artist", that she later reworked for publication in a number of different contexts. For more on their life and their close relationship with the Schuons, see Whitall Perry, "Perspectives", 32-46.

[6] Catherine Schuon, "Frithjof Schuon: Memories and Anecdotes", 41. Schuon once remarked: "I have always given a higher significance to living spaces, and forms in the broadest sense, than is usually done. The body is the first form; dress the second; living space the third; the house the fourth; landscape the fifth. Each thing has its respective meaning." (letter to Hans Küry, January 12, 1942) See also *The Transcendent Unity of Religions*, "Concerning Forms in Art".

[7] *Autumn Leaves & The Ring*, "Lac Léman", 151. See also *Autumn Leaves & The Ring*, "Encounters", 121.

Chapter 13: A View of Daily Life

[1] Catherine Schuon, "Frithjof Schuon: Memories and Anecdotes", 53-54. As a further example of the simplicity with which they lived, Catherine Schuon mentions that they did not have a telephone in their house in Switzerland. "The idea of having such a device in his house occurred to my husband as little as having a typewriter." (56)

[2] Mark Perry (b. 1951) moved next door to Schuon in 1952, and has spent the rest of his life in Schuon's proximity, both in Switzerland and America. Perry is an author and is also working with other editors and translators in preparing new translations for Schuon's metaphysical writings, in addition to translating Schuon's letters from both French and German into English.

[3] "[F]or many years", Schuon writes in a letter, "I have had a particular and completely involuntary relationship with the Name *Hari Om*; I pronounce these words fairly often, but only notice it afterwards. . . . It goes without saying that I would not allow anyone to imitate me on this point, all the more as the initiative does not come from me." (letter dated November 27, 1976)

[4] Mark Perry, "La compassion intellective", 219n, 215, 222-223.

[5] Quoted in part in *A Return to the Spirit*, 11-12, together with a commentary by Martin Lings.

[6] Matthew 5:48.

[7] *From the Divine to the Human*, "To Refuse or to Accept Revelation", 146.

Schuon also wrote of the related idea of dignity: "There is endless talk about 'human dignity', but it is rather too often forgotten that '*noblesse oblige*'; dignity is invoked in a world that is doing everything to empty it of its content, and thus to abolish it. In the name of an indeterminate and unconditional 'human dignity', unlimited rights are conceded to the basest of men, including the right to destroy all that goes to make our real dignity, that is to say, everything on every plane that attaches us in one way or another to the Absolute. Without doubt truth obliges one to stigmatize the excesses of the aristocracy, but one can see no reason at all why it should not also confer a right to judge contrary excesses." (*Light on the Ancient Worlds*, "Light on the Ancient Worlds", 10)

[8] *Autumn Leaves & The Ring*, "On Nobility", 205.

[9] Letter to Titus Burckhardt, June 11, 1983.

[10] Whitall Perry, "Perspectives", 45.

[11] Whitall Perry, "Perspectives", 45. "I am reminded here", Perry continues, "of a story in the *Collations* of Cassianus Eremita about St. John the Evangelist, who was chided by a hunter who came upon him gently stroking a partridge, imagining that with a man of such holiness and fame a loftier manner of passing the time would be more in character. St. John then asked the hunter why he did not keep his bow taut. To the answer that it would in the long run weaken the capacity of the wood to project the arrows with the force necessary, the Evangelist replied that he too needed repose in order that his intellectual faculties be at the proper intensity when needed."

[12] "One cannot know all animals equally well; / Those I like best, I will mention here: / The lion, the tiger, and the puma; / Also the little cat that often delights us; / And then the deer, the noble horse, the lama; / In the realm of birds, the eagle and the swan; / And the little birds that sing in the trees — / With this enumeration, let it suffice." (*World Wheel*, Third Collection, LXXI, 123)

[13] Film interview with Barbara Perry, 2008.

[14] "One is almost ashamed to take pleasure in little things — / They gladden the soul, even though we know / That they are but trifles, and that we must nonetheless / Taste each day the earnestness of life. / Ye who are ashamed, do not forget / That even in little things, sparks of God's Presence appear." (*World Wheel*, Second Collection, XXXVIII, 72)

[15] *Songs without Names*, Second Collection, XXI, 64. Schuon wrote of another form of childlike pleasure: "I know not who discovered the soap bubble — / Neither Copernicus nor Paracelsus, / Nor a philosopher brimful of ideas — / It must come from the fairy-tale land of children / And yet it is full of wisdom. For it shows / How a host of souls ascends to heaven, / Or how graces descend upon us, / Vivifying the earthly world with heavenly light; / And also how the soul, resplendent in its colors — / Each one unto itself — goes its own way." (*World Wheel*, Third Collection, LXX, 123)

[16] Text, "The Elements of the *Religio Perennis*", quoted in *Light on the Ancient Worlds*, "Appendix", 130.

[17] Letter dated March, 1985.

[18] See, for example, *Eye of the Heart*, "Transgression and Purification", 103-106, and *Form and Substance in the Religions*, "The Five Divine Presences", 65-66, and "The Two Paradises", 243-245.

[19] Text, "Empirical Ego and Intellectual Ego", quoted in *Prayer Fashions Man*, "Appendix", 195.

[20] *World Wheel*, Fourth Collection, XXIX, 11. See also *Autumn Leaves & The Ring*, "Art of the Dwelling-Place", 21. "We would like to say a few words", Schuon explains in a general way, "concerning the integration of a foreign element into a particular traditional formalism; this problem places us between syncretism, which is intrinsically heterodox, and esoterism, which in certain cases can admit such coincidences. This is because, in principle, esoterism is 'open to all forms', as Ibn 'Arabī expressed himself in speaking of his heart; but in fact, such exceptions depend upon certain subjective as well as objective conditions; therefore we must ask, not only what has been done, but also by whom and for what reason." (*In the Face of the Absolute*, "The Ambiguity of Exoterism", 29)

[21] "Do not do several things at once; / Do one thing after the other, as the dignity / Of things, and of thyself, demands — / Therefore be orderly, and make thy choice. / Even God allotted to each day its burden, / When He created things without number. / Thou canst not sow different things at the same time; / For every seed wills to be wholly itself." (*Songs without Names*, Third Collection, XIX, 117) And: "Music from time to time; for music cannot be / The 'always' of the soul — let the soul be silent in God. / For if thou desirest God's presence, / Thou too must show Him thy heart and thy soul." (*Songs without Names*, Eighth Collection, LXXXVIII, 84)

[22] See *Autumn Leaves & The Ring*, "Sound and Stillness", 161.

[23] One of Schuon's poems offers this insight concerning Cossack and Red Indian music: "Why, in the songs of Red Indians and Cossacks, / Is there a primordial power / That combines melancholy and joy of living? / What is it that creates this savage beauty? / The heroic soul combines opposites: / A storm that sweeps over prairies and waves; / Then contemplativity, a noble longing — / An inward vision, profound and motionless." (*Songs without Names*, Eleventh Collection, XXIV, 201) See also *Songs without Names*, First Collection, XCIII, 36 and *World Wheel*, Seventh Collection, LIX, 148.

[24] *Songs without Names*, First Collection, XLVIII, 20.

[25] *Songs without Names*, Second Collection, CIII, 93. See also *Adastra & Stella Maris*, "Gypsy Melody", 171, *Autumn Leaves & The Ring*, "The Language of Sounds", 21, *Songs without Names*, First Collection, XCIV, 37, *Songs without Names*, Fifth Collection, XXXVII, 218, *World Wheel*, First Collection, LXII, 22, *World Wheel*, Second Collection, XVII, 65, and *World Wheel*, Seventh Collection, LVIII, 147.

[26] Catherine Schuon, "Frithjof Schuon: Memories and Anecdotes", 55-56.

[27] After their move to America, the Schuons annually attended a Thanksgiving feast in recognition of the first meeting of Europeans with Indians on American soil.

[28] One of Schuon's poems recalls an early childhood memory of a Christmas tree: "As a child, I once imagined I was in / A dark, cold forest, and before me in the distance, / I saw a Christmas tree, / And above it a sweet choir of angels; / I drew near this golden warmth / Of pine boughs, richly hung with ornaments / And red candles — and I thought to myself: / It is thus that, one day, I would like to enter Paradise." (*Songs without Names*, Second Collection, XXVI, 66) And in another poem he says: "The Christmas tree — a miracle from the forest, / On which candles shine and small globes hang; / It is no effort for a child's heart / To make of this an image of Paradise. / For us too, the little tree has meaning — / It evokes gratitude and innocence." (*World Wheel*, Fifth Collection, XXV, 54) See also *Songs without Names*, Second Collection, CXI, 96, and *World Wheel*, First Collection, CLVII, 53.

[29] *World Wheel*, Fifth Collection, CXVIII, 81.

Chapter 14: Travels

[1] "[W]e arrived", recalls Catherine Schuon, "at the moment of the opening of the season so that during one week we were the only guests at the hotel and we had the whole big park entirely to ourselves. Every day we went for lengthy walks, enjoying the flower-covered meadows and resting by rushing streams, observing the deer running and frolicking on the mountain pastures and the marmots playing like children in front of their burrows. For the Shaykh, who had always lived in cities, it was a wonderful experience. I felt that he was drinking in with all of his being what was offered to his senses. We almost always walked in silence." ("Frithjof Schuon: Memories and Anecdotes", 47)

[2] Travel journal, 1959.

[3] This excerpt is from a paper entitled, "A Metaphysic of Virgin Nature", which Schuon wrote shortly after his first trip to the American West in 1959. Copies were often given to American Indians over the next thirty years. It was later published as a chapter in *The Feathered Sun*.

Catherine Schuon writes that the respect which her husband had for all of creation manifested itself in small things. "For example, when crossing a meadow he would avoid stepping on daisies, or if sparrows were picking up crumbs on a sidewalk, he would wait till they flew away or make a detour not to disturb them. He would never kill an insect: if a spider or a centipede showed up in his room, he would get a drinking glass, put it upside down over the beast, glide a postcard under it and throw the thus imprisoned insect out of the window. . . . After we had moved into our new house in Pully, the Shaykh was helping me plant flowers in the garden, when all of a sudden he stopped, turned pale, and said: 'I cannot go on with this task—with the spade I have cut a worm in two. . .'" ("Frithjof Schuon: Memories and Anecdotes", 42)

[4] Barbara Perry, "Frithjof Schuon: Metaphysician and Artist".

[5] *The Feathered Sun*, "The Shamanism of the Red Indians", 41. Frithjof Schuon loved all manifestations of virgin nature, including changes in the weather. His wife wrote that her husband "loved thunderstorms and he would watch them from his balcony. The more lightning flashes and thunderclaps, the happier he was." (Catherine Schuon, "Frithjof Schuon: Memories and Anecdotes", 58) One of Schuon's poems speaks of the symbolism inherent in weather: "A thunderstorm bears witness to God's wrath; / Hail is like His punishment. Mild rain / Shows His mercy; and pure snow / Is heavenly light — and may its blessing, / Like a white veil, cover our homeland; / The stillness of pure Being, as far as I can see." (*Songs without Names*, Tenth Collection, CIX, 185)

[6] Harry Oldmeadow, *Frithjof Schuon and the Perennial Philosophy*, 7.

[7] *Spiritual Perspectives and Human Facts*, "The Spiritual Virtues", 228.

[8] In my own experiences traveling with Schuon, I was struck by his constant ability to combine discernment between beauty and ugliness, or between nobility and ignobility, with a simultaneous and unwavering concentration on whatever was most beautiful and noble.

[9] Whitall Perry, "Perspectives", 43. Although in a different context, Perry offers an example of a diagram that Schuon used in a conversation with Titus Burckhardt: ". . . Schuon asked for a pencil and paper. He drew a line across the middle, and then turning to Burckhardt said 'It's as simple as that. Everything below this line represents the world of becoming and of change, of flux and agitation and suffering. It is in its nature to be that way, and nothing can make it otherwise. Above the line is the supraformal realm of eternal beatitude and peace, which is always the same without change. Our sole task is to transfer the center of our being from the space below to the one above!'"

[10] On board the San Giorgio, Schuon noted: "I feel a special affinity with the mosques of the Maghrib because here, an austere and crystalline richness is combined with a marvelous simplicity always near to Nature." (travel journal, May 8, 1968)

[11] Whitall Perry relates the following anecdote from one of their trips to England: "One afternoon we were driving out of London on our way back to Dover to cross the English Channel for home: Kingsway, Aldwych, Waterloo, Elephant and Castle, Southwark, Bermondsey, Eltham, Sidup, Bexley—the pressing metropolis and interminable drone of tight-wedged traffic would never end. And then suddenly we hit the greenbelt and freedom; it was as though the city had never been. 'That is how the modern civilization will end', said Schuon, 'something seemingly lasting forever, and all at once it is no more!'" ("Perspectives", 43)

[12] In addition, Schuon made two visits to Bloomington, Indiana, prior to settling there in September 1980.

Chapter 15: Noteworthy Encounters

[1] Hans Küry, "Les jeunes gens dans la Caverne: première rencontre", 383.

[2] Letter to Marco Pallis, June 9, 1982.

[3] A more comprehensive list of trips and meetings can be found in *Frithjof Schuon: Life and Teachings*, 36-37. Three foreign-language anthologies contain tributes to Schuon from admirers in many religions and from throughout the world: *Frithjof Schuon: Connaissance et Voie d'Intériorité, Biographie études et témoignages* (1999), *Les Dossiers H: Frithjof Schuon* (2002), and *Frithjof Schuon (1907-1998): Notas biográficas, estudios, homenajes* (2004).

[4] Letter to Hans Küry, August 7, 1982, quoted in *Frithjof Schuon: Life and Teachings*, 10.

[5] Fr. Anthony Bloom (1914-2003), Metropolitan of Sourozh, was the author of such works as *Beginning to Pray*, *Courage to Pray*, and *God and Man*.

[6] Archimandrite Sophrony's (1896-1993) works include *Wisdom from Mount Athos: The Writings of Staretz Siloan* and *Saint Silouan, the Athonite*.

[7] In a letter to Marco Pallis, one of Schuon's Buddhist followers, Merton (1915-1968) wrote: "I think Schuon has exactly the right view. . . . I have the impression that I am perhaps going along parallel to him, and once in a while I will get a glimpse of what he means in terms of my own tradition and experience. I liked very much his essay on prayer, for instance." (*Hidden Ground of Love*, 468-469) After receiving a subsequent message from Schuon, Merton wrote in his personal journal, "That I can be accepted in a personal and confidential relationship [with Schuon], not exactly as a disciple but at any rate as one of those who are entitled to consult him directly and personally. This is a matter of great importance to me. . . . It can have tremendous effects. I see that already." (journal entry, June 16, 1966, quoted in *Merton and Sufism*, 220-221)

[8] Rama P. Coomaraswamy (1929-2006) was the son of A.K. Coomaraswamy. Although raised within the Hindu tradition, Rama converted to Catholicism after the death of his father in 1947. Dr. Coomaraswamy was a practicing physician as well as an ardent student of Church history and theology; in later life he was Professor of Ecclesiastical History at the St. Thomas Aquinas (Lefebrist) Seminary. His book *Destruction of the Christian Tradition* provides an in-depth critique of the subversive innovations of the Second Vatican Council, which disavowed almost two thousand years of inspired Church doctrine.

[9] James S. Cutsinger (b. 1953) is Professor of Theology and Religious Thought at the University of South Carolina. Cutsinger's projects include an anthology of Schuon's writings entitled *The Fullness of God: Frithjof Schuon on Christianity*. He has also edited an anthology of Schuon's writings entitled, *Prayer Fashions Man: Frithjof Schuon on the Spiritual Life*.

[10] Schuon also had prominent Christian admirers in Europe, including Bernard Kelly (1907-1958), Phillip Sherrard (1922-1995), Jean Borella (b. 1930), and Jean Hani (b. 1917), all of whom contributed articles to the *festschrift* in celebration of

his eightieth birthday, entitled *Religion of the Heart*. Sherrard and Gerald Palmer (1904-1984), one of Schuon's Christian followers, are well known for their work in translating the *Philokalia* and other writings of the Eastern Church.

[11] Shojun Bando (1932-2004), a Shin Buddhist priest, was co-translator, with Harold Stewart, of selected passages from the *Tannishō*, a commentary on the *nembutsu* by Shinran (1173-1263), the founder of Shin Buddhism (*Jōdo Shinshū*). A number of Shojun Bando's writings in English can be found in *Studies in Comparative Religion*, including "Shinran's Indebtedness to T'an-luan" and "Significance of the *Nembutsu*".

[12] The works in English of Sohaku Ogata (1901-1973), the Zen Buddhist priest, include *Zen for the West*.

[13] The works in English of Shinichi Hisamatsu (1889-1980), a Zen Buddhist scholar and master of the Japanese tea ceremony, include *Zen and the Fine Arts* and *Critical Sermons of the Zen Tradition*.

[14] Lobsang Lhalungpa (1924-2008), a prominent Tibetan Buddhist scholar, is well known for his translation of *The Life of Milarepa*.

[15] Shanti Sadan, the *āshram* founded by Hari Prasad Shastri (1882-1956), remains active to this day. (See www.shantisadan.org.) Schuon later wrote to a friend that Shastri had remarked to him that his "explanation of *Māyā* was the only correct one he had ever found in a European book." An extensive list of Shastri's works have been published by Shanti Sadan of London. Shortly before Pandit Shastri's death, Schuon wrote to the venerable Hindu, "I feel that when I am invoking the Name of God, wherever I may be, I am with you; for in this state there are no more spatial distances, and in the holy Names of the Infinite we are all one." (letter to Hari Prasad Shastri, September, 1955) Shortly after Shastri's death, Schuon wrote to his wife: "We know that death is not a real separation, that it is but an illusory and fleeting veil, and that in God souls meet, even here-below. We cannot be closer to those whom we love than by clinging to God, and in losing ourselves in Him. It is in losing ourselves in Him that we find ourselves in Him again, along with those whom we love." (letter dated February 28, 1956)

[16] For further details on the life and work of Swami Ramdas (1884-1963), see www.anandashram.org.

[17] Swami Ramdas, *World is God*, 103-107.

[18] This first meeting with Swami Ramdas took place in the home of two of Schuon's Buddhist disciples, Marco Pallis and Richard Nicholson (1905-1995).

[19] *Autumn Leaves & The Ring*, "Ramdas", 117. And: "In his youth, Swami Ramdas was / A fine and earnest-looking ascetic; / When I met him, he was almost an old man — / And yet he was like a child out of a book. / How can one explain such a change? / Ram does not teach everyone in the same way — / Blessèd the man who goes to Heaven as a child." (*World Wheel*, Second Collection, XXIV, 68)

[20] Film interview, 2006. Ramachandran (d. 2006) lived in southern India and first

visited Schuon in Lausanne in 1964. This film interview was taken during his annual visit to Bloomington.

[21] In the same 2006 film interview, Ramachandran also spoke of the Jagadguru reading *Language of the Self*: "The Jagadguru read the book from cover to cover and was absorbed in the book for a long time." Schuon also dedicated an article called "His Holiness and the Medicine Man" to the Jagadguru.

[22] Petitpierre knew Schuon for more than forty years. A retired Swiss diplomat, he was formerly a Director of the United Nations.

[23] Private correspondence, 2007.

[24] *Autumn Leaves & The Ring*, "The Jagadguru", 117.

[25] *Understanding Islam* was published in French in 1961. The first English translation was published by Penguin Books in 1963. This work is one of the few books Schuon wrote on a single religion, as most of his books consist of articles written on diverse themes and subjects. Praise for *Understanding Islam* includes: "Schuon's book shows the essence of Islam. . . . [O]ne often finds passages which touch the heart." (Annemarie Schimmel, Harvard University); "The best work in English on the meaning of Islam and why Muslims believe in it." (Seyyed Hossein Nasr, the George Washington University); and, "A masterpiece of comparative religion. . . . Such objectivity as Frithjof Schuon's . . . is exceedingly rare." (*Islamic Quarterly*)

[26] *Publishers Weekly* has described Nasr (b. 1933) as "a living legend in Islamic Studies. . .". Dr. Nasr is the only intellectual figure to deliver the Gifford Lectures in Edinburgh (established in 1888) and be included in the Library of Living Philosophers series (*The Philosophy of Seyyed Hossein Nasr*), which commenced in 1939.

[27] Yusuf Ibish (1926-2003) was an internationally known expert in Middle Eastern politics and Islamic studies, the author of two dozen books, and a professor at universities that included the American University in Beirut, the American University in Washington D.C., and Cambridge University in the United Kingdom.

[28] Jean-Louis Michon (b. 1924) is a French scholar who specializes in Islam in North Africa, Islamic art, and Sufism. He has received numerous awards within the Islamic world for his prolonged efforts to preserve their cultural heritage, in particular their architecture and traditional crafts. His work has been performed under the auspices of UNESCO and directly for various governments. He is the author, among other works, of *Introduction to Traditional Islam: Illustrated*. In a paper entitled, "The 'True Man': Myth or Reality?", Michon reflects on his relationship to Schuon, recalling their first meeting in 1946.

[29] Victor Danner (1926-1990) was a professor of Islamic Studies at Indiana University and translated a number of Sufi texts from Arabic into English. His books include *The Islamic Tradition: An Introduction*.

[30] Letter to Martin Lings, January 22, 1951.

[31] Personal paper, 1954. Perry's account includes these additional comments made by Shaykh Mahdi to Schuon's followers: "He, Shaykh 'Īsā, is like a sun, and you are the mirrors. But it is for you to turn your mirrors toward the sun to capture its light. Only he who turns his mirror fully to the sun can benefit from all the sun has to give."

[32] See *Frithjof Schuon: Life and Teachings*, 37 for further details.

[33] Letter to Titus Burckhardt, May 21, 1965.

Chapter 16: The American Indian Spirit

[1] *World Wheel*, Sixth Collection, LXXXVII, 116. Also: "What art thou? German — also somewhat French, / Then also Arab — and finally Indian, / By adoption into the circle of the tribe. / Thus did the goddess of destiny cast her lots — / Thou knowest not how, for the Lord alone knows. / Also Mother India didst thou early encounter — / She blessed thee with the light of Wisdom." (*World Wheel*, Seventh Collection, XXXIII, 141) See also *Songs without Names*, Fifth Collection, CVIII, 239.

[2] Schuon had a special interest in the Plains Indians, in part due to their metaphysical doctrine, their artistic expressivity, and their practice of perpetual prayer. See especially *The Feathered Sun*, "A Metaphysic of Virgin Nature".

[3] Letter to Chief Medicine Robe, 1947. In the closing paragraph of his letter, Schuon states, "I have been very happy to hear that Chief Medicine Robe has given Mr. Brown several strands of braided sweet grass for me; I pray every day for him and his wife and their work, and I have told my community to do the same."

[4] Film interview with Johann Jakob Jenny, 1992.

[5] Schuon added these precisions after viewing the film interview with his childhood friend.

[6] Film interview with a journalist, 1991.

[7] Yellowtail (1903-1993) received the function of Sun Dance Chief of the Crow tribe in 1963, a role he fulfilled for the last thirty years of his life. The story of his life and his efforts to preserve the Crow-Shoshone Sun Dance is published in *Yellowtail: Crow Medicine Man and Sun Dance Chief*. Prior to its publication, Schuon wrote of the manuscript to his brother: "Yellow Tail (= Hawk with the Yellow Tail Feathers) dictated a book that in a certain way completes the two books of Black Elk [*Black Elk Speaks* and *The Sacred Pipe*]." (letter to Father Gall, July 21, 1984)

[8] Susie Yellowtail (1903-1981) was the first American Indian registered nurse and a tireless advocate for her tribe. In 1983 she was enshrined in the Montana Hall of Fame in the State Capitol Building at Helena.

[9] Thomas and Susie Yellowtail were the Schuon's first guests in their new home in Lausanne. In 1971 Susie Yellowtail told me of Schuon's astonishing ability, after only a few brief encounters, to describe the character of each of

the members of her traveling dance troupe—insights she concluded could only be gleaned as a result of reading their minds. When I later told Schuon of Susie Yellowtail's recollection and opinion, he indicated that he could not read minds; but he acknowledged that he possessed an ability to judge a person's character based upon a short encounter, while recognizing that each person has a spectrum of human possibilities and the ability either to rise above or fall below their inherent potential.

[10] Thomas Yellowtail, "Introduction", in *The Feathered Sun*, xiii-xiv.

[11] Film interview, 1991. One month after this 1953 encounter, Schuon wrote to Titus Burckhardt, who had accompanied the Schuons on this trip: "Assuredly, the meeting with the Indians was a decisive experience."

[12] Catherine Schuon, private correspondence, 2007. The night of the full moon is the preferred time for the monthly Sun Dance prayer meetings held by many Plains tribes. "Towards midnight", Burckhardt wrote of this event, "[Yellowtail] sent a messenger who directed us to his room where he had lit a ritual fire on a copper tray that he had found in the hotel. . . . He burnt some sweet grass and said: 'With this eagle's feather, which I pass over the sacred fire, I shall purify each one of you; then I shall raise my voice to the Great Spirit, that he may give you an understanding of our religion. You will receive this understanding in the form of a dream.'. . . Each of us later had a dream which symbolically revealed one or other aspect of the tradition of the Plains Indians." (*Mirror of the Intellect*, 164-165). Burckhardt's article, "The Sun Dance", provides a description of this encounter and his subsequent experiences with Yellowtail at the Crow-Shoshone Sun Dance.

[13] At the request of Marco Pallis, the Schuons were accompanied in 1959 by Paul Goble (b. 1933), who was then a young artist with a great love of the American Indians. Goble has since written and illustrated many books on the American Indians. The Schuons were accompanied in 1963 by Whitall and Barbara Perry.

Schuon's travel journal for his first trip to the American West ends with this postscript: "Two months after our return home from America, Reginald Laubin wrote me the following lines: 'In September a few of our Arapaho and Sioux friends came over to put on a *Yuwipi* ceremony for us. In the sweat tipi they said prayers for their friends and they included "Mr. Schuon, for help and guidance in his wonderful work in bringing about an understanding and realization that so many religions are alike." We never dreamed that they knew of you, so you can imagine our surprise and delight when they mentioned your name and even had a copy of your splendid article on Indian religion. They were very much impressed by your good words.' And all help is from God alone!" (quoted in part in Whitall Perry, "Corrigendum", 141)

[14] *The Feathered Sun*, "Journeys to America", 129-130, 142-145, 120, 119.

[15] *Autumn Leaves & The Ring*, "Red Cloud", 115.

[16] Shortly after the ceremony Ben Chief presented Schuon with a feathered war bonnet. His wife also received a name from Chief Red Cloud and another

at Sheridan, but she gives preference to her first Indian name, "Eagle People Woman", given to her by old Black Elk through the intermediary of Joseph Brown. See Barbara Perry, "Foreword: Frithjof Schuon: Metaphysician and Artist", in *The Feathered Sun*, xvii.

[17] Travel journal, August 11, 1959. The story of the Schuons' adoption and their receipt of Indian names was published in the local newspaper, along with a photograph of the Schuons and Joe Medicine Crow taken during the adoption ceremony. ("Foreign Visitors Recognized", *The Sheridan Press*, Monday, August 10, 1959). Joseph Medicine Crow (b. 1913) is the Crow tribal historian, the last traditional Plains Indian war chief, and a recipient of the Presidential Medal of Freedom, the highest civilian honor bestowed by the United States. I often meet Medicine Crow at the annual Crow Sun Dance. Until the time of Schuon's death, he invariably inquired about his good friend and asked me to convey his prayers and best wishes to him; these, in turn, were always reciprocated from Schuon to Medicine Crow.

[18] Letter dated November 23, 1983. In 1987 Thomas Yellowtail adopted Frithjof Schuon into his family and the Crow tribe. See chap. 20, "The Move to America", 118, 215.

[19] In his travel journal Schuon also recalls that "Last Bull urged us to pray for him; this we promised to do, and also confided to him that for the last few years, at each full moon, we had been praying for the Indians in the manner which Yellowtail had taught us."

[20] *The Feathered Sun*, "His Holiness and the Medicine Man", 114. Schuon's article is also posted on the Internet site of the Jagadguru's *āshram*, www.kamakoti.org/souv/5-24.html.

[21] Joseph Epes Brown (1920-2000) played an important role in helping to preserve the ancestral traditions of the Lakota and became one of the most influential scholars of American Indian spirituality in the twentieth century. Among other endeavors, he helped establish the "Indigenous Religions Traditions Group" of the American Academy of Religions and served as the group's first chairman.

[22] Film interview, 1991.

[23] Letter to William Stoddart, August 8, 1984.

[24] See Joseph E. Brown, *The Spiritual Legacy of the American Indian: With Letters While Living with Black Elk*, 117.

[25] Schuon's letters to Black Elk covered many subjects, including a description of his own spiritual quest: "I wished not only to love God, I wished also to know Him, and the Christianity of our time teaches only the love of God, never the knowledge. . . . And so, with regard to the knowledge of God which I was seeking—because it is a need of my nature, and God wishes to be worshipped by every man according to the nature He gave him—I found this sacred knowledge through a holy man of the Arab people, whose name was Ahmad al-'Alawī. He was a spiritual Master and had many disciples. There I found what I was searching for: the knowledge of God, and the means to realize God." (letter to

Black Elk [in care of Benjamin Black Elk], October 7, 1947, quoted in *Frithjof Schuon: Life and Teachings*, 62)

[26] Joseph Epes Brown, letter to Frithjof Schuon, October 28, 1947.

[27] Joseph Epes Brown, letter to Frithjof Schuon, November 19, 1947. The publication of *The Sacred Pipe* achieved one part of Schuon's intention when he recommended to Brown that he find Black Elk: the preservation and dissemination of sacred wisdom. Schuon also hoped to stimulate a resurgence in traditional spiritual practices at a time when they were in danger of being lost. Joseph Brown's letters to Lausanne sent while living with Black Elk detail the Lakota holy man's renewed efforts to continue the old-time beliefs and ways of his people, efforts which were facilitated by Brown's assistance. Schuon collected and preserved Brown's letters, and excerpts were recently published in the Appendix to the 2007 commemorative edition of Brown's *The Spiritual Legacy of the American Indian.*

[28] Martin Lings notes: "[T]he Sioux Indians who adopted Schuon into their tribe would refer to his followers as 'the eagle people'." ("Frithjof Schuon and René Guénon", 17) Catherine Schuon later explained: "Black Elk gave me the name Wámbli Oyáte Win after Joseph Brown explained to him about the *Tarīqah* and the method of invoking the Divine Name, which was used by all of my husband's disciples; so Black Elk called these the 'Eagle People'." (personal correspondence, 2007)

[29] "My late brother was a monk, / From his childhood a friend of the Red Indians. / Once a troupe of Red men came from across the sea; / He made firm friends of some of them. / He learned Lakota and, all his life, / He wrote letters in this language; / To his monastery Indians came several times — / He learned many wondrous Indian songs." (*World Wheel*, Second Collection, LXXXV, 87)

[30] It was Father Gall's wish that, after his death, the gifts he received from Black Elk be returned to the Black Elk family. In 1991 my wife and I accompanied Catherine Schuon to the Black Elk family in Manderson, South Dakota, to return these sacred objects. During our visit, members of the Black Elk family recalled that he often spoke of Father Gall, always calling him by the Lakota name given to him by Black Elk: Lakota Ishnala ("Solitary Lakota").

[31] Joseph Epes Brown, letter of November 17, 1947. Brown's letters also correct certain errors in the ongoing debate about the Lakota holy man's relationship to both traditional Lakota spirituality and Christianity; for example, some scholars have alleged that Black Elk completely abandoned his ancestral Lakota spiritual traditions after he entered Catholicism in 1904. Brown's letters, however, make it clear that Black Elk continued to participate in the sweat lodge ceremony and the prayer with the sacred pipe throughout his life. (See *The Spiritual Legacy of the American Indian*, 99-125.) Additional information about Black Elk's and other American Indians' relationship with Christianity is presented in an article entitled, "Frithjof Schuon and the American Indian Spirit: Interview with Michael Fitzgerald".

[32] Joseph Epes Brown, letter to Frithjof Schuon, October 8, 1954. Lucy Looks Twice, Black Elk's daughter, recalled her father's account of these events: "As he [Black Elk] waited for death, he told me, 'Do not worry, there is a man who comes to see me everyday at three o'clock. He is from overseas, and he comes in to pray with me—so I pray with him. He is a sacred man.'" (Michael F. Steltenkamp, *Black Elk: Holy Man of the Oglala*, 129)

[33] *The Feathered Sun*, "Journeys to America", 125.

[34] "The Perennial Philosophy", 247.

[35] *The Feathered Sun*, "Journeys to America", 147.

[36] *The Feathered Sun*, "Publisher's Preface", xii.

Chapter 17: A Spiritual Patroness

[1] Port Vendres (*Portus Veneris*, the port of Venus) lies on the Mediterranean coast between Perpignan, France, and the border with Spain.

[2] *World Wheel*, Sixth Collection, LX, 107.

[3] *Adastra & Stella Maris*, "*Stella Maris*", 135. He also wrote: "Port Vendres — here I had a dream-vision, / On the ship that was carrying me south; / It was in full daylight — my senses were not asleep — / The heavenly message approached clearly and sweetly / In a feminine form; as if she would say: / 'I will take care of thee and thy preoccupations.' / What could my soul expect after such a greeting? / It knew that it was in a heavenly garden. / True graces never vanish — / They help thee find thy true self." (*World Wheel*, Second Collection, XXII, 67) See also *Songs without Names*, Seventh Collection, XL, 17. And see generally, *Autumn Leaves & The Ring*, "El Pilar", 213, *World Wheel*, Fifth Collection, CXXIX, 85, and *World Wheel*, Sixth Collection, LXIII, 108.

[4] Also, "And (remember) she who guarded her chastity, We breathed into her of Our spirit, and We made her and her son a sign for all peoples." (21:91) The many other Koranic verses about the Virgin Mary include: 2:253; 3:35-59; 4:156-159 and 171; 5:17 and 46-116; 19:16-35; 61:6; 66:12. Likewise, many sayings of the Prophet (*hadīth*) testify to Mary's exalted status, among them: "Except Mary and her son (Jesus), no human being is born without the devil touching him, so that he raises his voice crying out because of the devil's touch."

[5] Schuon also writes: "The Blessed Virgin is inseparable from the incarnate Word, as the Lotus is inseparable from the Buddha, and as the Heart is the predestined seat of immanent wisdom. In Buddhism there is an entire mysticism of the Lotus which communicates a celestial image of an unsurpassable beauty and eloquence, a beauty analogous to the monstrance containing the real presence, and analogous above all to that incarnation of Divine Femininity that is the Virgin Mary. The Virgin, *Rosa Mystica*, is like the personification of the celestial Lotus; in a certain respect, she personifies the sense of the sacred, which is the indispensable introduction to the reception of the Sacrament." (*In the Face of the Absolute*, "*Sedes Sapientiae*", 137)

[6] *Christianity/Islam*, "Alternations in Semitic Monotheism", 88.

[7] Frithjof Schuon, quoted in part in James Cutsinger, "The Virgin", 156.

[8] Catherine Schuon, "Frithjof Schuon: Memories and Anecdotes", 36. Whitall Perry's account of his first meeting with Schuon in the Spring of 1948, includes the following description: "He had just one room, opening onto a balcony full of geraniums, and a kitchen where he had his worktable. Fine Afghan rugs of sober beauty lined the floor, while on the walls were Sumatran hangings and various Oriental inscriptions. The décor included Arabic and Tibetan artifacts and standing on a medieval chest, a Romanesque statuette of the Virgin and Child." ("Perspectives", 38)

[9] Catherine Schuon recalled an event that took place not long after his mother moved to Lausanne in the mid-1940s: "She had, after a stroke, lost the ability to speak. The Shaykh brought her his statuette of the Virgin and said to his mother: 'Look at this statue and try to say "*Ave Maria*"; if you persevere, you will be able to speak again.' And this is what happened: after three days, she could speak normally and was telling everybody that her son had cured her—whereas the Shaykh knew very well that it was the Virgin who did so." ("Frithjof Schuon: Memories and Anecdotes", 42-43)

[10] Frithjof Schuon, quoted in James Cutsinger, "The Virgin", 158. Cutsinger's article contains insights from his conversations with Schuon and additional excerpts from Schuon's published writings and private papers. Cutsinger explains, for example, that "Schuon was to benefit from Mary's presence and graces throughout the rest of his life, though he would remain circumspect in speaking about them. . .". He adds, "We do know, however, that he was granted additional visual experiences, that the Virgin would speak to him in his native German, and that he sometimes received presentiments of a tactile order when Mary clasped his hand." ("The Virgin", 158)

[11] Schuon has written in numerous places about the meaning of celestial apparitions, notably in *Esoterism as Principle and as Way*, "Celestial Apparitions" and *Transfiguration of Man*, "Characteristics of Voluntaristic Mysticism".

[12] *Logic and Transcendence*, "Nature and Function of the Spiritual Master", 191-192.

[13] Letter dated July 6, 1977.

[14] Letter dated September 28, 1985, partially quoted in James Cutsinger, "The Virgin", 159. Jean-Louis Michon reports Schuon's warning that "'When a man experiences a spiritual state or favor, or when he has a vision or audition, he must never desire this to happen again; and above all he must not base his spiritual life on such a phenomenon, nor imagine that the happening has conferred on him any kind of eminence. The only important thing is to practice what takes us nearer to God. . . . Life is a dream, and to think of God is to wake up.'" (film interview, 2005)

Schuon also noted that if one wants to impart a mystical certitude to another, the import or message should be capable of being coherently expressed: "You may often keep silent about a certitude, / But if you wish to impart it, you must support it / With clear logic; for those who hear you / Want to see a meaning in what you are saying. / You must not say: I am certain of this — / And then withdraw in proud obscurity. / Finally: what is of no use to anyone, / You are not obliged to preach in the streets." (*World Wheel*, Fifth Collection, CXXX, 85)

[15] It is important to recall that Schuon did not want the occurrence of his mystical experiences to divert attention away from his primary message. "I do not wish my person to be made the object of symbolist and mystical speculations which—apart from their possibly problematical character—create supplementary preoccupations and divert the mind from that which alone matters. . .". (personal paper dated 1981) Schuon's descriptions of his spiritual graces often stand in marked contrast to speculations based on third- and fourth-hand sources.

[16] Schuon wrote to one of his Christian followers: "It is true that I received from the part of the Blessed Virgin some extraordinary graces, the nature of which I have described to no one. The authenticity of such graces is proven by the fact that they leave durable traces in the soul, to the point that we are no longer the same man as before; they remove one from the world and draw us toward Heaven. And there is a kind of vision or inward presence that remains." (letter to Rama Coomaraswamy, December 5, 1970)

[17] Travel journal, May 12, 1968.

[18] Schuon's own spiritual master named his *Ṭarīqah* the *'Alawiyyah*, and adopted the surname al-'Alawī following a visionary experience of 'Alī, the cousin and son-in-law of the Prophet Muhammad and the fourth Caliph of Islam. 'Alawī is the Arabic adjective formed from 'Alī. See Martin Lings, *A Sufi Saint of the Twentieth Century*, 65.

[19] Martin Lings, *A Return to the Spirit*, 6. "It is not I who have chosen the Virgin", Schuon wrote, "it is she who has chosen me. A few years ago, I was in my prayer room invoking the two names of Mercy [*ar-Rahmān, ar-Rahīm*]; and meanwhile I felt something totally unexpected invade my whole being, and it was the blessed Presence of Sayyidatnā Maryam. . . . From this blessed moment on, I advised the recitation of both Names; but I did not attach further importance to this event. Later, while going to Morocco, she saved me from deepest distress. . . . Yet, I had never thought of the Holy Virgin when she interceded out at sea; *Stella Maris*!" (letter to Martin Lings, March 23, 1967, quoted in *Frithjof Schuon: Life and Teachings*, 75)

[20] Martin Lings, *A Return to the Spirit*, 6. As Schuon has written elsewhere: "[T]he Virgin, in that she personifies both the universal *Shakti* and the *Sophia Perennis*, belongs exclusively neither to Christianity nor to Islam, but to both religions at the same time. . . . [S]he constitutes the link between the two." (*Form and Substance in the Religions*, "The Virginal Doctrine", 115)

[21] Text, "Meeting the Logos: Virtue", quoted in James Cutsinger, "The Virgin", 141. According to Martin Lings, "it is generally accepted, in Sufism, that every

great Master, in addition to being a mysterious prolongation of the Prophet [Muhammad], prolongs also in a certain way, one of those spiritual lights who preceded Islam." (*A Return to the Spirit*, 7) In his book *A Sufi Saint of the Twentieth Century* (199-203), Lings explains how one can consider the Shaykh Ahmad al-'Alawī as a prolongation of Jesus. In this light, when Schuon was asked if "one could consider him to be, like his own Master, a prolongation of Jesus", Schuon's reply was, "'No, I am *Maryamī*', that is, a prolongation of Mary." (Martin Lings, *A Return to the Spirit*, 7) See also *Christianity/Islam*, "Appendix", 205.

22 Schuon's disciples in religions other than Islam periodically use the word *Maryamī* ("of Mary") to refer to themselves, and the word *Tarīqah* ("spiritual path") to refer to their spiritual way, even though they are not, strictly speaking, attached to his Islamic *Tarīqah.*

Chapter 18: An Artistic Dimension

1 Barbara Perry, "Foreword: Frithjof Schuon: Metaphysician and Artist", in *The Feathered Sun*, xix.

2 Michael Pollack, "Editor's Introduction", in *Images of Primordial and Mystic Beauty*, 1-2.

3 Frithjof Schuon, quoted in Michael Pollack, "Editor's Introduction", in *Images of Primordial and Mystic Beauty*, 3-4. For a more complete description of Schuon's views on the Eternal Feminine see *Roots of the Human Condition*, "*Mahāshakti*" and *Esoterism as Principle and as Way*, "The Problem of Sexuality".

4 *The Feathered Sun*, "The Sun Dance", 100.

5 Letter to Leo Schaya, October 10, 1981.

6 Letter to Leo Schaya, December 27, 1982, quoted in *Frithjof Schuon: Life and Teachings*, 42. "The painted images", Schuon explains, "should not be the object of worship; their function consists uniquely in suggesting existentially our connection with the Sovereign Good." (personal paper, 1993) Renaud Fabbri observes: "These paintings do not directly concern his *tarīqah* and Schuon explicitly forbade that they become a support of concentration or devotion." ("The Milk of the Virgin", 259)

7 Barbara Perry, "Foreword: Frithjof Schuon: Metaphysician and Artist", in *The Feathered Sun*, xix. "The divine imprint in supra-formal or luminous manifestation also comprises, by cosmic repercussion, a psychic imprint . . . and it is this psychic imprint that is 'Mary' in her human form. This is why the universal Prototypes, when they manifest themselves in that portion of humanity for which Mary lived on earth, do so by way of the psychic, hence individual and human, form of the Virgin." Schuon draws analogies to similar manifestations in other spiritual traditions: "In other sectors of humanity, the same Prototype—at once divine and angelic—takes the form appropriate to the respective ambiences; it appears most often in the form of a beautiful woman, as is the case in the apparitions of the *Shekhīnah* in Judaism, of Durgā, 'the Mother', in Hinduism, or of Kwan Yin or Tārā in the Far East; similarly, in the Sioux Indian tradition, the

Calumet—the pre-eminent sacred instrument—was brought from Heaven by Pté San Win, a marvelously beautiful celestial maiden. . . ." (*Treasures of Buddhism*, "*Nirvāna*", 92, 92n)

8 Michael Pollack, "Editor's Introduction", in *Images of Primordial and Mystic Beauty*, 2. In a letter, Schuon writes of the connection between his paintings and Mahayanic art: "The meaning of these images is the actualization of the Presence of the Sacred, then it is holy immobility, silence and inwardness; thus the remembrance of God. Hence in my pictures of Mary there is something of the golden, earth-remote *barakah* of the Buddhist spiritual message; it is as though something of that world of the Spirit had also to be present in our spiritual way. This kinship I observe *a posteriori*, for my paintings flow forth from the depths of my heart, and imitation of any kind is foreign to me; nonetheless, I must mention that the image of the Buddha was for me a kind of revelation even in my childhood and that something of it lies in my very nature. Moreover, there is in my pictures something too of the Tārā of Brahmanism and the *Mahāyāna* and—beyond that—something of the 'Eternal Feminine', of the Primordial Feminine: of the Divine Femininity. Or again: something of the merciful, liberating *Māyā*." (letter to Leo Schaya, August 28, 1985)

9 *World Wheel*, Fifth Collection, CXXVII, 84.

10 The exhibit ran from January 24, 1981 through March 8, 1981. Barbara Perry's article, "Frithjof Schuon: Metaphysician and Artist", was first written to appear in the catalog for this exhibition. It was later revised to appear as the Foreword to *The Feathered Sun* and then subsequently revised as the Introduction to *Art from the Sacred to the Profane: East and West*.

11 Barbara Perry, "Frithjof Schuon: Metaphysician and Artist".

12 None of the nineteen American Indian paintings reproduced in *The Feathered Sun* are included amongst the more than one hundred and twenty paintings reproduced in *Images of Primordial and Mystic Beauty*. During his lifetime, Schuon created over 200 oil paintings; however, many were sold or given as gifts without ever being photographed, making it impossible to quantify or compile a complete catalogue of his works.

13 Michael Pollack, "Editor's Introduction", in *Images of Primordial and Mystic Beauty*, 3.

14 Michael Pollack, "Editor's Introduction", in *Images of Primordial and Mystic Beauty*, 2. The following statement from the beginning of this same book clarifies Pollack's comment about Schuon's partial acceptance of the work of various modern artists: "In the case of 'post-Impressionist' painters such as Gauguin, Van Gogh, and Hodler, one may sense the lack of an interesting choice of subjects, but one cannot deny the fascinating message of their styles. Conversely, one may reject the naturalistic style of the 'academic' artists from Michelangelo to Ingres, but one must nevertheless accept those works whose content shows nobility and grandeur. . . . In these cases the aesthetic, psychological, and moral qualities of the subject excuse or even neutralize the errors of a totally naturalistic style". (Sharlyn

Romaine, "Intention and Style", in *Images of Primordial and Mystic Beauty*, 6) Romaine is the first among several later painters whom Schuon instructed and who thereafter adopted his style of painting. Thus there are paintings that appear at first glance to be by Schuon, but which are by one or another of his students. In the parlance of art historians, one would speak of works that are of "the school of Schuon".

[15] Barbara Perry, "Introduction", in *Art from the Sacred to the Profane*, xiii.

[16] Notes from a private interview with Titus Burckhardt, 1979.

[17] See the painting *The White Buffalo Woman*, 1965, in *The Feathered Sun*, 137, and the painting of the Pté San Win in *Images of Primordial and Mystic Beauty*, 125, which was created in 1978.

[18] See James R. Walker, *Lakota Belief and Ritual*, edited by Raymond DeMallie and Elaine A. Jahner, 109-112, 148-49.

[19] Personal interview, 1990.

[20] Since the DeMallie-Jahner edition of Walker's work there have been other accounts published that corroborate the nakedness of the Buffalo Calf Woman. Several scholars have joined Schuon in opining that when the first Christian missionaries heard this account they were horrified because they considered nudity sinful, with the result that Lakota elders subsequently described the Pté San Win as clothed in white buckskin robes, which is the most often preserved account. (See Marla Powers, *Oglala Women: Myth, Ritual and Reality*, 43, for further details.) Some of the same Lakota elders who recorded the history of the naked Pté San Win bringing the Sacred Pipe to the chief also mentioned that she was clothed in white robes during the time she subsequently spent in the camp instructing the tribe about the performance of sacred rites. Schuon wrote to his close friend, Leo Schaya, of a dream in which a celestial woman appeared to him clothed in a white robe: "The inward experience which you relate in your letter reminds me of a sacred dream I had . . . about two years ago. I saw", he recounts, "a beautiful young American Indian woman standing in a white robe; she came towards me, and when she stood very close in front of me, she ascended gently, and I ascended with her." (letter dated November 14, 1984)

[21] Barbara Perry, "Frithjof Schuon: Metaphysician and Artist". See also "The Basis of Religion and Metaphysics: An Interview with Frithjof Schuon", Appendix II, 146-151.

[22] Frithjof Schuon, quoted in Michael Pollack, "Editor's Introduction", in *Images of Primordial and Mystic Beauty*, 4.

Chapter 19: Expanding Readership

[1] The steering committee for the colloquium included Msgr. George Khodr (b. 1923), Metropolitan of Mount Lebanon, Seyyed Hossein Nasr, Director of the Imperial Iranian Academy of Philosophy, and A.K. Saran (1922-2003), Professor of sociology and philosophy at the University of Jodhpur. The colloquists presented papers on diverse faith traditions including Judaism, Christianity

(Eastern and Western churches), Islam, American Indian spirituality, African Yoruba spirituality, Hinduism, and Buddhism (Tibetan, *Jōdo Shinshū*, and Zen branches).

[2] Ileana Marculescu, "Afterword", 259. Dr. Ileana Marculescu was a specialist in the theological principles in biology. She taught in both the biology and theology departments at the University of Bucharest, in addition to the University of California, the Union Theological Seminary, and Sweet Briar College.

[3] Jacob Needleman (b. 1934) is also a professor emeritus at San Francisco State College.

[4] *Studies in Comparative Religion* was founded in Britain in 1963 by F. Clive-Ross (1921-1981) and is the earliest and most influential English-language journal of traditional studies. The journal was published under the name *Tomorrow* until 1967, when it was changed to its present name. Its publication was interrupted in 1987 and has recently resumed as both an on-line and paper journal. www.studiesincomparativereligion.com intends to upload an on-line archive of all the issues of *Studies* dating to 1963.

[5] Jacob Needleman, "Foreword", in *Sword of Gnosis*, 9. *Sword of Gnosis* was reprinted by Penguin numerous times throughout the 1970s, '80s and early '90s.

[6] Jacob Needleman, "Foreword", in *Sword of Gnosis*, 14-15

[7] "If we sometimes refer to these perennialists as a 'school' or 'movement'", one of Schuon's commentators remarks, "this is merely an expedient: their unanimous testimony about the *sophia perennis* could not be encompassed by a mere 'school' or 'movement'." (Harry Oldmeadow, *Frithjof Schuon and the Perennial Philosophy*, xiii)

[8] Founded in 1909, the American Academy of Religion (AAR) is the world's largest association of academics who research or teach topics related to religion.

[9] From 1986 to 1989 there was a designated group called Esotericism and Perennialism that met for multiple sessions during the annual meetings of the AAR. The ongoing discussion now takes place under the auspices of different groups. Important elements of the debate were summarized in Huston Smith's defense of the perennial philosophy in his article, "Is There a Perennial Philosophy?"

[10] Our scope only allows us to mention the existing English language journals with a Perennialist orientation. As previously discussed, *Studies in Comparative Religion* dates its origin to 1963 and is now both an on-line and paper journal. The *Temenos Academy Review* is the journal of the Temenos Academy and is the successor to the journal *Temenos*, first published in 1981and founded by Keith Critchlow (b. 1933), Brian Keeble (b. 1941), Kathleen Raine (1908-2003), and Philip Sherrard. HRH the Prince of Wales (b. 1948), who is now the Patron of the Temenos Academy, has written that the Academy and its review are "committed both to the perennial philosophy and to the notion that Man is, at root, a spiritual creature with spiritual and intellectual needs which have to be

nourished if we are to fulfill our potential." ("Introduction to the Sacred Web Conference", 17-18) The journal *Sophia* was founded in 1995 by the Foundation for Traditional Studies, whose initial board members included Seyyed Hossein Nasr, Huston Smith, James Cutsinger, Rama Coomaraswamy, and Joseph E. Brown. *Sacred Web: A Journal of Tradition and Modernity* was founded by M. Ali Lakhani in 1998, while *The Eye of the Heart* published its first issue in 2008 under the auspices of Latrobe University in Bendigo, Australia with Timothy Scott as its executive editor.

[11] James W. Morris, "Ibn 'Arabī in the 'Far West': His Contribution to the Emerging Science of Spirituality", lecture presented at Kyoto University, January 20, 2001. Schuon was asked in a 1991 interview why his books are often neglected in academic circles. "The reason", Schuon responded, "is that I am not a relativist. . . . I am an absolutist. I believe in Truth, and the official scholars do not believe in Truth."

[12] "[I]n our century only individuals can be saved from modernism, not collectivities; in a way, modern man is the creature which stubbornly doesn't want to be saved. All this means that we have information to give, but nothing to preach." (letter to Jacob Needleman, March 1, 1990)

[13] It was once suggested to Schuon that he enter into academia. "[I]t strikes me as impossible", he responded, "that I would sacrifice myself for several years to studies that would occupy me fully—and all that for the sake of a profession that would devour me for the rest of my life more totally than all other possible professions." (letter to Hans Küry, November 27, 1934)

[14] Letter dated July 12, 1950. "Tradition speaks to each man the language he can understand, provided he be willing to listen; this reservation is essential, for tradition, we repeat, cannot become bankrupt; it is rather of man's bankruptcy that one should speak, for it is he who has lost the intuition of the supernatural and the sense of the sacred." (*Play of Masks*, "No Initiative without Truth", 77)

[15] Back cover quote on *Survey of Metaphysics and Esoterism.*

Chapter 20: The Move to America

[1] *Songs without Names*, Second Collection, XXVII, 66.

[2] The Schuons' long-time friends and neighbors, the Perrys, and Mr. and Mrs. John Murray, also moved from Switzerland to become their neighbors in America. John Murray (1910-1999), one of Schuon's most trusted friends, first visited him in Lausanne in 1947, and remained his neighbor for the rest of his life, both in Switzerland and America. The close friendship that Schuon and his wife shared with these two American couples was such that they were, in effect, part of their extended family.

[3] Catherine Schuon, "Frithjof Schuon: Memories and Anecdotes", 59.

[4] Letter to Martin Lings, June 12, 1980. One of the outward reasons for the move was the city of Lausanne's steady expansion around the Schuons' originally remote chalet-style home. Their former dwelling was demolished in 1994 to

make way for condominiums.

[5] Letter to Hans Küry, October, 1980. Some months following, Schuon wrote, "I must often reflect that our *Ṭarīqah* is not a *Ṭarīqah* like the others; or rather, that it cannot be like them at all. . . . One should be clearly aware of the grounds for this: there is, first of all, our purely esoteric perspective; then the fact of the contents of our consciousness, given us by our Western origin; and then the *Vedānta* as a metaphysical foundation. . . . Our point of departure is the quest after esoterism and not after a particular religion; after the pure and total Truth. . . ." (letter to Hans Küry, May, 1981)

[6] Thomas Yellowtail came to Bloomington, Indiana, for periods of two or three weeks every October from 1975 until his death in 1993, each time staying in our home. Yellowtail also came to Bloomington in March 1993 for a visit that included a celebration of his ninetieth birthday. Martin Lings recounts that "Schuon once remarked to me that some people might find these regular visits surprising but that the explanation was very simple. In his own words: 'Yellowtail is profoundly conscious of being a priest by his very nature and he senses the same consciousness in me, despite the many outward differences between us.'" ("Frithjof Schuon and René Guénon", 17)

[7] Letter to Leo Shaya, October 20, 1980. Patrick Laude has correctly observed that "The Crow Medicine Man and Sun Dance Leader Thomas Yellowtail performed healing ceremonies pertaining to 'white magic' during his regular visits to the Schuons in Indiana. These sessions were in no way part of the spiritual method of Schuon's *ṭarīqah.*" ("Quintessential Esoterism and the Wisdom of Forms", 190n) See also *World Wheel*, Second Collection, XX, 66.

[8] The headdress Schuon wore on this occasion was the one given to him when he was adopted into the Sioux tribe. Schuon wrote about his reluctance to wear a headdress: "During my adoption [into the Sioux tribe], the Indians gave me the gift of a feathered headdress, which I did not put on for eight to ten years; then, I put it on two or three times, but never in front of several people. . . . When I arrived in America, at the time of our emigration, one of the friends of Bloomington, the adopted son of Yellowtail since many years, gave me the gift of another headdress, of Sioux origin, ornamented with a feathered train; I wore it just once, outdoors near my tipi. This gift was like the welcome from the red race in this continent which fundamentally belongs to it. . .". (letter to William Stoddart, October 10, 1983)

[9] Letter to Titus Burckhardt, December 7, 1983.

[10] Schuon specified that "[o]ur Indian dancing is not a rite", and further affirmed that "the fact that we practice from time to time Indian dances", is "independent and outside" of the spiritual method that he had founded (personal papers dated 1991 and March, 1997). Among his diverse followers there were naturally, therefore, some who shared his personal interests to a greater degree than others, this being solely a matter of individual affinity. At the same time, Schuon notes, "Given that our perspective is essentialist, and thus universalist and primordialist,

it is entirely plausible that we have fraternal relations with the world of the American Indians, which integrates Virgin Nature into religion; furthermore, it can give to us—we who live in an unwholesome universe made of artificiality, ugliness, and pettiness—a refreshing breath of primordiality and grandeur." (personal paper, "Concerning our Perspective", quoted in part in *Frithjof Schuon: Life and Teachings*, 47)

Schuon also spoke of the need, in a "world of agitation and ugliness, a technocratic and exhausting world", for "something that does not take an effort of concentration but on the contrary provides a refreshing expansion, a return to Nature that allows one to breathe and, in a sense, to forget." Indian dancing, he observed, "provide[s] a noble and aesthetic form of recreation, which is spiritually healthy given that, like all traditional dances, they have in principle an interiorizing and unitive quality on account of their reference to the archetypes." (personal paper, January 1992) As one of his poems explains: "In a world where everything is ugly / For the first time in history, / One cannot ask a wise man / To renounce the solace of recreation. / All the sages of the past / Lived in beauty; for there was nothing else / In lands where Revelation dominated — / And with this, the sense of God and bliss." (*Songs without Names*, Seventh Collection, LXXVI, 29)

[11] Over a period of years more dances and songs were added to these events. Some were based on suggestions from Yellowtail, but the vast majority followed what Schuon had witnessed decades earlier when many of the old-timers were still living. While the dances at the Indian Days were inspired by traditional Plains Indian costumes and dances, these gatherings were different in several ways from contemporary American Indian powwows. Yellowtail commented on a number of occasions that the Indian Days were more similar to the powwows from the days of his youth.

[12] Schuon later wrote of this event: "Now, what does it signify for our spiritual order that the Shaykh was solemnly adopted into a tribe of Red Indians and that, at an Indian Day, the priest of the Sun Dance adopted all those present into his clan? What do our Indian Days signify, where everyone dances and in which, once a year, Indian friends participate? First of all: like every religious tradition that has no historical founder and that has not undergone a serious deviation, the tradition of the Red Indians is a branch of the Primordial Tradition, of which, in its essential elements, it conveys the spiritual perfume or the *barakah*; now, in pure esoterism, non-confessional and untainted by theology, the contacts with such a climate or such a *barakah* can have a meaning, without for that being indispensable to the Method. Usefulness is not necessity, any more than an optional character is uselessness; and in virtue of its transcendence, authentic esoterism allows of much more liberty than does exoterism." (personal paper, c. 1990)

[13] Notes from a personal conversation, 1987. In a 1992 film interview, Yellowtail said of Schuon: "I think that he is a great man. . . . I know that people come over here to see him from other countries—from all over the world. I regard him as

a holy man. . . . Considering this and because he is a good friend, I did something well worth doing by adopting a great man into the family."

[14] *World Wheel*, Second Collection, XXVIII, 69.

[15] These occasions provided an opportunity to pose questions to the sage, and there were often one or more queries on a wide range of topics, either intermittently during the meal or just after it. While the resulting conversation was always essentialized and brief, this did not prevent him from presenting penetrating insights on a staggering range of subjects—personal, spiritual, metaphysical, and political.

While Schuon did not read world news on a regular basis, he asked to be informed of important world events. Whitall Perry and I, amongst others over the years, provided him each month with a number of news articles and from time to time he would ask for more information on certain current events and subjects of interest. His occasional private comments of a political nature demonstrated an in-depth understanding of historical causality, theory, and practical reality; he rarely chose to publish observations on current events, however, lest any attention be diverted from his timeless message. For similar reasons, he also avoided any association with a person or group promoting a political agenda. For example, in the late 1970s a publisher requested permission to translate and publish one of his books. After making inquiries about the publisher, Schuon responded: "Sir, I have just received the list of your publications and I note that for the most part they are racist, fascist, and nazi in spirit and thus in no sense traditionalist in the proper and authentic sense of this word. I do not wish to appear in such a context, and I cannot give my consent to the publication of one of my books under your imprint. The public would place me in a modern political category, whereas I am engaged in nothing of the kind, being a true traditionalist, and thus identified with a scale of values that escapes modernists, even those of the right." (letter to a publisher, late 1970s)

[16] "They built for me a veranda, / A walkway with wall and roof by my house — / So that each day I can walk peacefully / Protected from rain and rushing wind. / It is a symbol of solitary wayfaring. / Be alone with God — and thou wilt be one with the Self / And with everything good. He whose soul / Rests in the True is embraced by the Sovereign Good." (*Songs without Names*, Twelfth Collection, CXVI, 277) See also *World Wheel*, Second Collection, III, 59.

[17] In 1935, when Leo Schaya (1916-1985) was nineteen years old, he attended a lecture given by Schuon at the Basle Museum on the subject of "Religion, Philosophy, and Metaphysics". Such was the impact of Schuon's lecture—the first and only time he spoke in public—that Schaya immediately became one of Schuon's disciples. One of Schaya's friends recorded that, "As [Schaya] told me later, the content of what was said passed him by without his being quite aware of it, so much did Schuon's appearance and the sound of his voice demand Schaya's visual and aural attention." (Hans Küry, "Les jeunes gens dans la Caverne") Founder of the French journal *Connaissance des religions*, Schaya contributed several articles on Judaism to *Studies in Comparative Religion*, while

his book, *The Universal Meaning of the Kabbalah*, provides important insights into Jewish mysticism from the Perennialist point of view.

[18] Letters dated October 10, 1981 and November 29, 1981.

[19] Letters dated October 10, 1981 and November 29, 1981.

[20] *Autumn Leaves & The Ring*, "Home", 123. And also: "I was born on the Rhine, where it / Bends upwards, and flows towards the North Sea; / Now, in my old age, I live / In a forest, which shields me from the world. / The green Rhine is a symbol — it is the soul/ Moving toward the Limitless; / And the forest: it is my final home — / The shelter on which God's Peace descends." (*World Wheel*, Second Collection, XV, 64)

Chapter 21: Reflections

[1] Letter to Marco Pallis, June 26, 1987.

[2] Letter to Max Schray, November 3, 1989. Schray first met Schuon in primary school, became one of his earliest disciples, and remained a lifelong follower. In a 1926 letter to Lucy von Dechend, the eighteen year old Schuon recalled the first time he met Max Schray: "I am glad you met Frau Schray and her son; the first time I saw him was when my father played that wonderful, heart-wrenching Hungarian dance of Brahms to [Aunt] Gisela's accompaniment; we boys were in the next room, Erich [Schuon's brother] stood on the table and gave an inimitable impression of an affected opera singer, Max laughed; I sat in my corner and wept, so overcome was I by that dance, which my father played with veritably fanatical hot-bloodedness, like a gypsy." (letter dated February, 1926)

[3] *Songs without Names*, Fifth Collection, CVIII, 239.

[4] *Songs without Names*, Sixth Collection, LXXXIV, 280. See also: "I knew, very early, the *Bhagavad Gītā*; / And before that, the Psalms and the Sermon on the Mount; / And then the core saying of Islam, the *Shahādah*; / Each came at its proper time and place. / God has sown many seeds for salvation in this world — / Blessèd are those into whose hearts the seed falls." (*World Wheel*, First Collection, LII, 18)

[5] *Adastra & Stella Maris*, "Life's Work", 235. Schuon has elsewhere explained: "Thus the symbolist mentality can be a unilateral tendency of the intelligence and the sensibility, but it can also be a spiritual realism on the plane of phenomena, in which case it gives rise to a sanctity based, not on negation, rejection, and sacrifice, but on the concrete analogy between earthly phenomena and heavenly archetypes. This is the *distinguo* between a Shankara and an Abhinavagupta or a Krishna, or between a Desert Father and David or Solomon; what is involved is not the cosmic scope of the holy personages, but only their manner of combining their already heavenly station with the phenomena of earthly life. The ascetics turn away from creatures because creatures are not God; others on the contrary have the capacity to accept creatures because they manifest Him, and to the extent that they do so, this being the perspective of tantrism." (*Roots of the Human Condition*, "The Twofold Discernment", 101)

[6] Martin Lings was one of the few lifelong friends of Schuon to live longer than him.

[7] Letter to Richard Nicholson, 1989, in reference to the passing of Marco Pallis. The Buddhist *mantra* quoted by Schuon is from the *Heart Sutra*.

[8] Letter to Hans Küry, January 21, 1984. Schuon's 1935 book, *De quelques aspects de l'Islam* ("Some Aspects of Islam"), contained this dedication: "To my brother Ibrāhīm 'Izz ad-Dīn ad-Darqāwī", which is the traditional name of Titus Burckhardt.

[9] *Songs without Names*, Ninth Collection, LXXII, 128. See also *Autumn Leaves & The Ring*, "Yellowtail", 113, and *World Wheel*, Fourth Collection, LX, 20.

[10] *World Wheel*, Fifth Collection, LXIV, 65.

Chapter 22: The Close of Two Cycles

[1] See *In the Face of the Absolute*, "The Human Margin". The Countess Valentine de Saint Point (1870-1953) provides a colorful example of the diversity of human types among Schuon's followers. Jean-Baptiste Aymard has described the first phase of her life: "The great-great-niece of Lamartine, she had lived in Cairo since the 1920s and had known Guénon since his arrival [in 1930]. A prolix and capricious poetess in her youth (she read one of her *Poèmes d'orgueil* in a cage of lions), blessed with an impeccable figure (she posed for Rodin and was the inspiration of several poets), eccentric and feminist (she published some rather questionable manifestos in 1912), the first woman to cross the Atlantic by air, the organizer of dance performances for the Metropolitan Opera in New York, and the friend of Gabriele d'Annunzio, she had been converted to Islam in the 1920s under the name Ruhīya, and had become a militant Arab nationalist." (*Frithjof Schuon: Life and Teachings*, 145)

The second phase of her life began when she came under the interiorizing influence of Guénon in the 1930s and then renounced her political activities. Through Guénon she met Schuon, with the result that, "in her old age, she became an unconditional disciple of Schuon, whom she visited every year." (*Frithjof Schuon: Life and Teachings*, 145) Catherine Schuon recalls: "The Countess de Saint-Point came from Cairo to Lausanne every June to spend the entire month in the proximity of my husband. She asked my husband if she could come and just sit quietly in his presence, so the Shaykh allowed her to visit quite often from 11 o'clock until noon. The Countess explained that, 'I am only truly alive when I am able to feel his *barakah*'; so many times when I knocked on the door at noon to end the *darshan*, she remarked with a smile, 'Here comes the angel of death'." (personal interview, 2007)

[2] Although many decided to remain within Christianity, by far the majority of Schuon's followers chose Sufism as their spiritual path. As mentioned before, Schuon also had a number of followers in other religions, including Hinduism, Buddhism, and Judaism. For various reasons, however, it is impossible to know the precise number of Schuon's followers, all the more so in that he did not

approve of such attempts at quantification. A spectrum of possibilities also exists in each person's relationship with him: some seekers have considered him as their spiritual master; others have considered themselves Schuonian, meaning that his writings have become one of the most important influences in their lives; while yet others have simply been influenced by his philosophy in a significant manner. Those familiar with his teachings are not overly preoccupied with specifying where others might place themselves on that spectrum.

[3] "Frithjof Schuon: A Small Word of Homage and Celebration", 55. Schuon wrote of the value of spiritual company: "'Tell me whom thou frequentest, and I will tell thee who thou art.' / Frequent people who honor the sacred; / *Sat-Sangha* — the "company of the pure" — / Will increase the purity of thy soul. . .". (*World Wheel*, First Collection, XLV, 16)

[4] Personal paper, "Declaration".

[5] Schuon's designation of representatives included a small number in Christianity in addition to those within Sufism.

[6] Martin Lings has written about Schuon's retirement and Lings' own branch of spiritual followers in his article, "How Did I Come to Put First Things First?" (*A Return to the Spirit: Questions and Answers*, 78-79)

[7] René Guénon, *The Great Triad*, 122n.

[8] Schuon subsequently reviewed a number of his articles that had been previously published in his French books but which had not yet appeared in his English-language books. The result was the English-language publication of *Eye of the Heart* in 1997, a book that first appeared in French in 1950. While Schuon edited a number of the articles for this English edition, the great majority of the work on these articles was completed prior to the publication of *Transfiguration of Man*.

[9] The present book contains a list of Schuon's current and planned English-language works. In accordance with his preference we have not listed either *Dimensions of Islam* or *Islam and the Perennial Philosophy* among his English-language compilations. "My doctrinal message is in my French books and their translations. It is only indirectly and imperfectly in the English compilations *Dimensions of Islam* and *Islam and the Perennial Philosophy*, which were produced for contingent reasons and do not correspond to my intentions." (personal paper, "Remarks on the Appendix", quoted in *Frithjof Schuon: Life and Teachings*, 178) The contents of these two compilations can be found within one or another of Schuon's "French books and their translations".

We recall here Schuon's emphasis on the importance of his published corpus. "I want to place the accent on my books and not on the *Tarīqah*. . .". In the same letter he explains, "My message is in my books; it is not in the *Tarīqah*, at least not *a priori* so; what I mean by this is that my books constitute a 'predication', they are directed to the public, whereas the *Tarīqah* is not the object of any propaganda. I could say that the *Tarīqah* is only a message in terms of my books and inasmuch as it extends my written message." (letter dated January 6, 1988)

[10] Harry Oldmeadow, *Frithjof Schuon and the Perennial Philosophy*, 13-14.

[11] Martin Lings has explained that these texts form "a series of messages or instructions concerning the spiritual path . . . set down on behalf of his disciples." ("Preface", in *The Underlying Religion*, ix-x) Schuon referred to them collectively as *The Book of Keys*. As Jean-Baptiste Aymard has remarked: "His *Book of Keys*, made up of over one thousand texts of one to three pages, is in itself, by its density and depth, a genuine monument of spiritual, esoteric, and methodic teaching." (*Frithjof Schuon: Life and Teachings*, 157) "I think Schuon's great gift was the wisdom of spiritual direction", notes Rama Coomaraswamy, one of his Catholic followers. "[H]is spiritual texts . . . are a tremendous source of spiritual insight that can be used by people of any viable tradition. They touch on a variety of facets of the Truth and the spiritual life. I turn to them as a source of spiritual wisdom even more often than his books." (film interview, 2005) One of Schuon's books, *Echoes of Perennial Wisdom*, is a compilation of his writings that contains many excerpts from his texts.

[12] *Transfiguration of Man*, "Excerpts from Correspondence", 125.

[13] Letter dated November 8, 1929.

Chapter 23: A Profusion of Songs

[1] *World Wheel*, First Collection, CXIV, 39.

[2] *Songs without Names*, Eleventh Collection, XLV, 207.

[3] *Sulamith* and *Tage-und Nächtebuch*. Schuon's *Images of Primordial and Mystic Beauty* includes an English translation of the final poem of each volume ("Confession" and "Layla"). *The Essential Frithjof Schuon* also includes translations of these and two additional poems from *Tage-und Nächtebuch* ("Shaykh Ahmad" and "Mostaghanem").

[4] Schuon continues, "With the poet, his work must be the expression of an inner nobility; the work must express the man himself, and not just an isolated and over-accentuated corner of the man." In a letter to Martin Lings, Schuon speaks further of the nature of poetry and of the duties of the poet: "Poetry is the 'language of the gods'; and 'noblesse oblige'; what I mean by this is that the poet has certain responsibilities. In poetry, the musicality of things, or their cosmic essentiality, erupts onto the plane of language; and this process requires grandeur, hence also authenticity, both of the image and of the sentiment. The poet spontaneously has the intuition of the underlying musicality of phenomena; under the pressure of an image or an emotion—the emotion, moreover, being naturally combined with concordant images—the poet expresses an archetypal beauty; without this pressure, there is no poetry, which implies that true poetry always has an aspect of inward necessity, whence its irreplaceable perfume." (letter dated January 1971, quoted in *Spiritual Perspectives and Human Facts*, "Appendix", 233)

[5] While Schuon was not immune to the normal physical ailments for a person of his age, he nevertheless manifested a remarkable vitality during this period: "I

know a man who is ninety years old. / His body is as if he had drunk nectar — / It is almost young; with new black hairs in his beard, / With a sharp glance and a strong voice, / He comes forth, immersed in the Eternal Now." (*Songs without Names*, Fifth Collection, CXII, 241)

[6] *Autumn Leaves & The Ring*, "Midwest", 151.

[7] William Stoddart, "Introduction", in *Adastra & Stella Maris*, ix.

[8] Annemarie Schimmel (1922-2003) is among the twentieth century's foremost Rūmī scholars and interpreters. Schimmel also wrote a Foreword for Schuon's *Understanding Islam.*

[9] Annemarie Schimmel, "Foreword", in *Adastra & Stella Maris*, vii-viii.

[10] *Songs for a Spiritual Traveler*, "Editors' Foreword", x. And also: "A ray comes over thee and makes thee write poetry / At early dawn, and deep into the night; / Thou weary one, who wouldst repose — thou must accomplish / The work, which the Spirit ever kindles anew. / Let me then harken to the Spirit's voice —/ And my despondency may God forgive. / I do not wish to interfere with a God-given gift — / What He expects of me, that I will be." (*Adastra & Stella Maris*, "The Poet", 229)

[11] *Songs for a Spiritual Traveler*, "Editors' Foreword", xii-xiii. Schuon himself has said: "Why all these didactic poems / After all that I have said in my books? / Because poetry speaks a language / That is for everyone — educated and uneducated alike — / Because it goes directly to the heart. / However, what I have to say here / Has different levels, according to Heaven's gift." (*Songs without Names*, Twelfth Collection, CXXV, 280) Schuon, for example, wrote a number of articles exploring the subtle questions of the posthumous states of being, while a didactic poem pierces through to an essential teaching in just a few words: "Earth, Heaven, and hell; purgatory, / And transmigration. Do not rack / Your brain over these. / The good go to Heaven and the wicked go to hell. / You would like to know what no eye can see; / God knows best what will happen with you — / What lies in the destiny of creatures, / In Eternity. And that He knows, suffices." (*World Wheel*, First Collection, LXXX, 28) His articles on this subject include: *Survey of Metaphysics and Esoterism*, "Universal Eschatology", *Eye of the Heart*, "Concerning the Posthumous States", *Form and Substance in the Religions*, "Comments on an Eschatological Problem", and *Treasures of Buddhism*, "Cosmological and Eschatological Viewpoints".

[12] *World Wheel*, Seventh Collection, CXXX, 167.

Chapter 24: Departure

[1] *Road to the Heart*, "Treasures", 86. The remainder of the poem was not read on this occasion.

[2] John Pretty On Top, a Crow Sun Dance chief, came from Montana to the funeral to render his homage. He first visited Schuon in the company of Thomas Yellowtail in 1985.

Afterword

[1] Mark Perry, "Frithjof Schuon Seen Through His Handwriting", 132.

[2] Catherine Schuon writes that people generally reacted towards her husband with respect or with a respectful inquisitiveness. "His dignity and his recollected expression could not but attract the attention of certain persons. . . . People would ask him who he was, or tell him that he had a strong radiance or that they felt a state of well-being in his presence. . . . During a stay in Morocco, we were invited to lunch by a merchant who was living in the middle of the medina of Fes. We went there dressed in traditional garments and the Moroccans started following us through the narrow lanes of the old city, forming an even longer line behind us. The Shaykh accelerated his pace in order to escape them, but to no avail; they pursued us to the very door of our host and settled themselves, imperturbable, in front of it in the hopes of seeing us when we left. . . . We had to wait until the time of the afternoon prayer, when everyone would go to the mosque, in order to be able to return to our hotel without hindrance." ("Frithjof Schuon: Memories and Anecdotes", 44)

It could also happen that, "When in the street, his proud bearing and piercing gaze could intimidate passersby; some even took offense at it. This is as much as to say that the riveting nobility of his presence implied a kind of existential judgment of which not all men were accepting. . . . One notes, however, that the outward appearance manifesting the indwelling spiritual presence underwent a change over the years, such that the ferocious expression of Schuon's youth became in later years an aura of imperturbable serenity. Nonetheless, his gravity of mien, when he retreats into the silence of his inwardness, never changes." (Mark Perry, "La compassion intellective", 212-213)

[3] Swami Ramdas, *World is God*, "Visit to a Sufi Saint", 104.

[4] Schuon describes the possible modalities of charismatic power belonging to extraordinary individuals: "The saint, the sage, the hero and / The martyr; each has his particular radiance, / And is a consolation for this poor world. / The saint: he is the image of virtue; / From the sage radiates the Truth, that delivers; / The hero is our sword and our shield; / The martyr bears the suffering of all men. / Thus each, with his particular gift, shines / Into this vale of tears; may God grant / That every man may have in him something of each one." (*Songs without Names*, Second Collection, LXXI, 82) Of the sage he also writes: "The true sage is a sacrament, / Placed in this lowly world by God; / Fully aware of the essential Truth. / Woe unto him who does not appreciate his spiritual power; / This world has always hated the Light — / But blessèd the man who has grasped Its radiance!" (*Songs without Names*, Fifth Collection, XCVI, 235)

[5] Huston Smith "Providence Perceived: In Memory of Frithjof Schuon", 31. Huston Smith (b. 1919), Professor Emeritus at Syracuse University, is the author of one of the most widely used textbooks on world religions: *The Religions of Man*, now retitled *The World's Religions.* Smith has also written: "Ever since I came upon his writings 20 years ago, Mr. Frithjof Schuon has been the most important intellectual and spiritual influence in my life. . . . I regularly begin

each day by reading, first a passage from sacred scripture, and follow this with something written by Mr. Schuon, for he 'feeds my soul', as the saying goes, as does no other living religious thinker." (Bloomington *Herald Times*, November 1, 1991)

[6] Film interview, 1993. Lings' observation concerning the person of Schuon is echoed by Tage Lindbom's observation concerning the writings of Schuon: "Looking back in time, we like to pause before historical figures who have produced a legacy of spiritual work that is characterized by timelessness, the Eternal. We pause before three names: Plato, Shankara, Frithjof Schuon." ("Frithjof Schuon and Our Times", 89) Tage Lindbom (1909-2001) was one of the intellectual architects of the Swedish Welfare State. In middle age, he underwent a profound intellectual and spiritual change, in large part due to the writings of Frithjof Schuon. After meeting Schuon, Lindbom resigned from all political activity and dedicated himself to a life of prayer and to writing on themes relating to tradition and the perennial philosophy.

[7] Schuon also discourages his readers from seeking to define his function: "Several lives, but within one life — / This was my path; and within it, several deaths; / And may God grant — since I have seen so much — / That others may inherit my message. / And ask not who I am. For every striving / On High is given by the Holy Spirit." (*Songs without Names*, Second Collection, CXXXVI, 105) See also *Road to the Heart*, "Confession", 27.

[8] Renaud Fabbri includes a discussion of the concept of the "seal" of wisdom in his article entitled, "The Milk of the Virgin: The Prophet, the Saint, and the Sage", 252-254.

[9] Whitall Perry, "Perspectives", 33. John Murray provides an insight into the providential timing of Schuon's birth: "[Schuon's] writings are a vast synthesis of those fundamental perspectives, crystallizations of universal and essential truths, which preceded it in history, including Primordial religion and the idea of *Sophia Perennis*, total synthesis in other words. This synthesis was only possible, moreover, at this particular moment in the last four hundred years. Had Schuon been born a century earlier, it would have been too early, and a century later, too late. It would have been too early because the key notion in this perspective, namely the idea of *Sophia Perennis,* was unknown in the West at that time. . . . It was Guénon who brought the idea of *Sophia Perennis* to the attention of his contemporaries. It would have been too late a century later because first of all Schuon would have missed contacts with Guénon. . . . Secondly he would have missed his contacts with the Plains Indians of North America—with the 'Old Timers', such as James Red Cloud, Black Elk, Black Elk's son, and Thomas Yellowtail.... Without these contacts there would have been no synthesis properly speaking. In short this synthesis was a matter not only of destiny, but also of Providence." ("Le maitre de la primordialité", 386-387)

[10] *In the Face of the Absolute*, "Preface", 5.

[11] *World Wheel*, Seventh Collection, CXXIX, 167. "What is the proof, I might

be asked, / That thou art right when thou speakest of the One / Who is All — of the Great Unseen? / Might we not think that this is mere dream? / In answer, I could remain silent — or I could say: / These truths I have not received from outside; / I believe in them because I am, in the spirit, what I believe — / God help me to bear it with humility." (*Songs without Names*, Ninth Collection, LXXIII, 128) See also *World Wheel*, Fifth Collection, CXIII, 80.

[12] Thomas Merton, *Disputed Questions*, 194.

[13] Walter James, the 4th Lord Northbourne (1896-1982) was educated at Oxford and was for many years a Provost of Wye College, which became the Agricultural College of London University. His interest in the environment and "organic farming" (he coined the term) led him into contact with Schuon's writings. Lord Northbourne was the author of three books, and translated Perennialist works by the likes of Schuon, Guénon, and Burckhardt from French into English.

[14] Lord Northbourne, *Looking Back on Progress*, 11, 11n.

[15] Letter to Hans Küry, December 20, 1951.

[16] *Light on the Ancient Worlds*, "The Universality and Timeliness of Monasticism", 102.

[17] *Play of Masks*, "Foreword", vii.

[18] Letter to Father Gall, January 1991.

Appendix I: *Sophia Perennis*

[1] *The Essential Frithjof Schuon*, 534-539.

Appendix II: The Basis of Religion and Metaphysics: An Interview with Frithjof Schuon

[1] This interview with Deborah Casey was first published in *Quest Magazine* in 1996. Casey was for many years the managing editor of World Wisdom; in that capacity she had the opportunity to meet frequently with Schuon regarding the publication of many of his books in English translation.

Appendix III: Selected Texts on the Spiritual Life

[1] *Transfiguration of Man*, 119-120.

[2] *The Essential Frithjof Schuon*, 529-530.

[3] *Transfiguration of Man*, 114.

[4] *Echoes of Perennial Wisdom*, 78-79.

[5] *Transfiguration of Man*, 112.

[6] *Echoes of Perennial Wisdom*, 56-57.

[7] *Echoes of Perennial Wisdom*, 73.

[8] *The Essential Frithjof Schuon*, 530-531.

[9] *Transfiguration of Man*, 107.

GLOSSARY OF FOREIGN TERMS AND PHRASES

adastra (Latin): "to the stars"; symbolically, spiritual striving.

advaita (Sanskrit): "non-duality". See also *Advaita Vedānta* and *Vedānta*

Advaita Vedānta (Sanskrit): the "non-dualist" interpretation of *Vedānta*; the Hindu doctrine according to which the seeming multiplicity of things is the product of ignorance, the only true reality being *Brahma*, the One, the Absolute, the Infinite, which is the unchanging ground of appearance. See also *Vedānta*

agapē (Greek): selfless "love", as of God for man and man for God; human compassion for one's neighbor; equivalent of Latin *caritas*. See also *eros*

Agathón (Greek): the Sovereign Good.

'ain al-qalb (Arabic): "eye of the heart", or intellect; the supra-rational faculty of knowledge that sees the truth directly through intellectual intuition.

'Alawiyyah Tarīqah (Arabic): a branch of the *Shādhiliyyah-Darqāwiyyah* Sufi order (*tarīqah*) founded by Ahmad al-'Alawī (1869-1934). See also *Darqāwiyyah Tarīqah* and *Shādhiliyyah Tarīqah*

Allāh (Arabic): "God"; a term used by both Muslims and Arab-speaking Christians to refer to the One God.

Allāh karīm (Arabic): "God is gracious".

Amida (Japanese). *See* Amitābha

Amitābha (Sanskrit): the Buddha of "Infinite Light" (Japanese: Amida), who as a *bodhisattva* named Dharmakāra vowed not to enter *Nirvāna* until he had brought all who invoked his Name into the paradise of his Pure Land, also known as *Sukhāvatī* ("place of bliss") or the Western Paradise.

Ānanda (Sanskrit): "Bliss", "Beatitude", "Joy"; one of the three essential aspects of *Brahma*, together with *Sat*, "Being", and *Chit*, "Consciousness".

a posteriori (Latin): "from after"; proceeding from effect to cause or from experience to principle.

a priori (Latin): "from before"; proceeding from cause to effect or from principle to experience.

āshram or *āshrama* (Sanskrit): in Hinduism, a center for meditation and religious study, often located near the hermitage of a saint or sage, whether living or dead.

Ātmā or *Ātman* (Sanskrit): the supreme "Self"; in the perspective of *Advaita Vedānta*, identical with *Brahma*, the Supreme Reality or Absolute.

Avatāra (Sanskrit): the earthly "descent", incarnation, or manifestation of God, especially of Vishnu in the Hindu tradition.

Ave Maria (Latin): "Hail, Mary"; traditional prayer to the Blessed Virgin, also known as the Angelic Salutation, based on the words of the Archangel Gabriel and Saint Elizabeth in Luke 1:28, 42.

barakah (Arabic): spiritual "blessing" or grace; in Islam, a spiritual influence or energy emanating originally from God, but often attached to sacred objects and spiritual persons.

Bhagavad Gītā (Sanskrit): "the Song of the Lord"; a Hindu sacred text consisting of a dialogue between prince Arjuna and his charioteer, the *Avatāra* Krishna, concerning the different paths to God.

bodhisattva (Sanskrit, Pali): "enlightenment-being"; in *Mahāyāna* Buddhism, one who postpones his own final enlightenment and entry into *Nirvāna* in order to aid all other sentient beings in their quest for Buddhahood.

Brahma or *Brahman* (Sanskrit): the Supreme Reality, the Absolute. *See also* Brahmanism

Brahmā (Sanskrit): God in the aspect of Creator, the first divine "person" of the *trimūrti*; to be distinguished from *Brahma* or *Brahman*, the Supreme Reality.

brahman or *brāhmana* (Sanskrit): in Hinduism, a priest or teacher; a member of the highest of the four castes. *See also* Brahmanism

*Brahma Sūtra*s (Sanskrit): a collection of 555 aphorisms and verses, traditionally ascribed to Bādarāyana, in which the philosophy of *Vedānta* is tersely articulated; also referred to as the *Vedānta Sūtra*s.

Dār al-Islām (Arabic): "abode of Islam"; geographically, those areas where Islam is the predominant religion.

Darqāwiyyah Tarīqah (Arabic): a branch of the *Shādhiliyyah* Sufi order (*tarīqah*) founded by Mūlay al-'Arabī ad-Darqāwī (1760-1823). See also *Shādhiliyyah Tarīqah*

darshan (Sanskrit): "view", "sight"; the visual assimilation of celestial qualities; the contemplation of saintly persons; the contemplation of the Divine in nature or in art.

dharma (Sanskrit): law, norm, vocation, religion; in Hinduism, the underlying law or "order" of the cosmos as expressed in sacred rites and in actions appropriate to various social relationships and human vocations; in Buddhism, the practice and realization of Truth. See also *Sanātana Dharma*

dhawq (Arabic): "taste"; in Sufism, direct, mystical knowledge of transcendent realities.

dhikr (Arabic): "recollection" or "remembrance"; in Sufism, the rite of methodical invocation.

dhikr Allāh (Arabic): "recollection" or "remembrance of God"; in Sufism, methodical invocation of the Name of God.

distinguo (Latin): "I distinguish"; as in a medieval or scholastic philosophical "disputation".

Durgā (Sanskrit): a form of the Divine Mother; consort of the Hindu God Shiva.

eros (Greek): romantic love; desire. See also *agapē*

ex nihilo (Latin): "(creation) out of nothing"; the doctrine that God Himself is the sufficient cause of the universe, needing nothing else; often set in contrast to emanationist cosmogonies.

ex Oriente Lux (Latin): "from the East, the light"; symbolically, the wisdom emanating from the Orient.

ex-voto (Latin): an offering to a saint or divinity, given in fulfillment of a vow; derived from the Latin, *ex voto suscepto*, "from the vow made"; typically placed in churches or chapels where the worshipper seeks grace or wishes to render thanks.

Fātihah (Arabic): the "opening" *sūrah*, or chapter, of the Koran, recited in the daily prayers of all Muslims.

fiat lux (Latin): "Let there be light" (cf. Gen. 1:3).

fitrah (Arabic): "primordial nature" or primordial norm; in Islam the natural predisposition of man, as created by God, to act in accordance with the will of Heaven; the original uprightness of humanity (cf. *Sūrah* "The Romans" [30]:30).

fuqarā' (Arabic, singular *faqīr*): the "poor ones"; in Sufism, followers of the spiritual path, whose "indigence" or "poverty" (*faqr*) testifies to complete dependence on God and a desire to be filled by Him alone.

ghaflah (Arabic): "forgetfulness" or "negligence" with regard to God and the spiritual life.

Golgotha (Aramaic: *Gûlgaltâ*): "place of the skull"; the site where Christ was crucified in Jerusalem; symbolically, a place of suffering or sacrifice.

gopuram (Sanskrit): massive ornamental entrance structure, measuring ten or more stories high and in the form of an enormous pyramid, each storey decorated with a wealth of sculptures; characteristic of South Indian Hindu temples in the Dravidian style.

gompa (Tibetan [*dgon-pa*]): "place of quiet study"; a Buddhist complex typically containing a fortification, monastery (or nunnery), and university; located in areas of Tibet, Ladakh (India), Nepal, and Bhutan.

gnosis (Greek): "knowledge"; spiritual insight, principial comprehension, divine wisdom.

guru (Sanskrit): in Hinduism, a spiritual master; one who gives initiation and instruction in the spiritual path and in whom is embodied the supreme goal of realization or perfection.

hadīth (Arabic): "saying", "narrative"; an account of the words or deeds of the Prophet Muhammad, transmitted through a traditional chain of known intermediaries.

hanīf (Arabic): "pure", "upright"; those who, by the purity and uprightness of their nature, practiced the pristine monotheism of Abraham before the coming of Islam, not succumbing to the prevailing polytheism in the Arabian Peninsula.

Haqq (Arabic): Truth, Reality; in Islam, a Name of God.

Hari (Sanskrit): "dispeller of sins"; a name of Vishnu or Krishna.

Hari Om (Sanskrit): a sacred formula or *mantra.* See also *Om*

ijāzah (Arabic): a formal certificate issued upon successful completion of a course of study; in Sufism, a certificate authorizing a disciple to represent and initiate disciples into a Sufi order.

'Īsā (Arabic): Jesus.

jagadguru (Sanskrit): "universal master"; in *Advaita Vedānta*, the unbroken line of "Shankarāchāryas" or "great teachers" of the Shankara tradition, who perpetuate the intellectual and spiritual legacy of the Hindu sage Shankara (788-820); their role as spiritual authorities is located at the *pītha*s ("religious seats") that Shankara established in India during his lifetime.

jai Ram (Sanskrit): "hail" or "glory to Rāma", the seventh incarnation (*Avatāra*) of the Hindu God Vishnu.

japa-yoga (Sanskrit): the method of "union" (*yoga*) based upon the repetition (*japa*) of a *mantra* or sacred formula, often containing one of the Names of God.

janna (Arabic): "garden"; in Islam, the celestial paradise.

jnānī or *jnānin* (Sanskrit): a follower of the path of knowledge (*jnāna*); a person whose relationship with God is based primarily on sapiential knowledge or *gnosis*; often contrasted with followers of the path of love or devotion (*bhakti-yoga*) and the path of action or works (*karma-yoga*).

Jōdo (Japanese): "pure land"; the untainted, transcendent realm created by the Buddha Amida (Sanskrit: Amitābha), into which his devotees aspire to be born in their next life.

Jōdo Shinshū (Japanese): "true pure land school"; a sect of Japanese Shin, or Pure Land, Buddhism founded by Shinran (1173-1263), based on faith in the power of the Buddha Amida and characterized by use of the *nembutsu.*

Kali-yuga (Sanskrit): the "dark age"; in Hindu cosmology the disgraced "iron" age wherein the tenets of religion are transgressed and violated. See also *yuga*

kalpa (Sanskrit): world cycle, the duration of a world; in Hindu cosmology, a "day of Brahmā", totaling 1,000 *mahā-yugas*. See also *mahā-yuga*, *para*, and *yuga*

karma-yoga (Sanskrit): the path of action; the method of "union" (*yoga*) based upon right "action, work" (*karma*).

khalīfah (Arabic): a "vicegerent" or "representative" of God; man as the mediator between Heaven and earth; in Sufism, the designated representative of a Shaykh.

kōan (Japanese): "precedent for public use", case study; in Zen Buddhism, a question or anecdote often based on the experience or sayings of a notable master and involving a paradox or puzzle that cannot be solved in conventional terms or with ordinary thinking.

Krishna (Sanskrit): the eighth *Avatāra* (incarnation) of the Hindu God Vishnu; hero of the epic *Mahābhārata* and instructor of prince Arjuna in the *Bhagavad Gītā*; also known for his dalliance (*krishna-līlā*) with the *gopīs* (cowgirls).

Krita-yuga (Sanskrit): "perfect age"; in Hindu cosmology, the pure "golden" age wherein the tenets of religion are followed naturally. See also *yuga*

Kwannon or Kannon (Japanese): the *bodhisattva* of mercy and compassion (Sanskrit: Avalokiteshvara; Chinese: Kwan Yin); one of the two main attendants of Amida Buddha.

Kwan Yin (Chinese). *See* Kwannon

lactatio (Latin): "nursing", "suckling"; according to Christian tradition, while St. Bernard of Clairvaux was praying before a statue of the Blessed Virgin nursing the Child Jesus, the statue miraculously came alive, and the Virgin pressed her breast, causing a stream of milk to come forth and wet the lips of Bernard, which were dry from singing her praises.

Lakshmī (Sanskrit): the Hindu Goddess of prosperity, beauty, generosity; the consort of Vishnu.

Logos (Greek): "word", "reason"; in its uncreated aspect, the transcendent Principle of creation and revelation (cf. John 1:1); in its created aspect, the various prophets insofar as they transmit the Word of God to humanity.

Mahāshakti (Sanskrit). See *Shakti*

Mahāyāna (Sanskrit): "great vehicle"; the branch of Buddhism, including such traditions as Tibetan Buddhism, Zen, and *Jōdo Shinshū* (Shin Buddhism), distinguished by the idea that *Nirvāna* is not other than *samsāra*, and by the ideal of the compassionate *bodhisattva*; contrasted with *Theravāda* Buddhism, the "teaching of the elders", which emphasizes the ideal of the *pratyeka* Buddha ("solitary awakened one") and the *arhat* (solitary saint).

mahā-yuga (Sanskrit): a great age or eon; in Hindu cosmology, the four ages of the *Krita-* or *Satya-yuga*, *Tretā-yuga*, *Dvāpara-yuga*, and *Kali-yuga*; analogous to the Greco-Roman Golden, Silver, Bronze, and Iron Ages. See also *yuga*

Mani mantra (Sanskrit). See *Om mani padme hum*

mantra (Sanskrit): "instrument of thought"; a word or phrase of divine origin, often including a Name of God, repeated by those initiated into its proper use as a means of salvation or liberation. See *japa-yoga*

Maryamiyyah Tarīqah (Arabic): a branch of the *Shādhiliyyah-Darqāwiyyah-'Alawiyyah* Sufi order (*tarīqah*) founded by 'Īsā Nūr ad-Dīn Ahmad (1907-1998). See also *'Alawiyyah Tarīqah, Darqāwiyyah Tarīqah*, and *Shādhiliyyah Tarīqah*

Māyā (Sanskrit): universal illusion, relativity, appearance; in *Advaita Vedānta*, the veiling or concealment of *Brahma* in the form or under the appearance of a lower, relative reality; when viewed positively as "productive power", the unveiling or manifestation of *Ātmā* as "divine art" or theophany.

muqaddam (Arabic): the representative of a Sufi *shaykh*; authorized to give instruction and initiate disciples into the spiritual order.

murshid (Arabic): "guide", "instructor"; in Sufism, a spiritual master capable of guiding disciples on the path.

nāma-japa (Sanskrit): repetition (*japa*) or invocation of a Name (*nāma*) of God.

nembutsu (Japanese): "remembrance" or "mindfulness of the Buddha", based upon the repeated invocation of his Name.

Nirvāna (Sanskrit): "blowing out, extinction"; in Indian traditions, especially Buddhism, the supremely blissful state of liberation resulting from the extinction of the fires of passion, egoism, and attachment.

noblesse oblige (French): "nobility obligates"; the view that nobility constrains to honorable behavior and that privilege entails responsibility.

Nūr ad-Dīn (Arabic): "light of the religion".

O *beata solitudo, o sola beatitudo* (Latin): "O beatific solitude, O sole beatitude".

Om (Sanskrit): in Hinduism, the sacred monosyllable symbolizing *Brahma* or the Absolute; also prevalent in Buddhism as a mantric syllable.

Om mani padme hum (Sanskrit): "Om, jewel in the lotus, hum"; an invocatory formula, or *mantra*, used extensively in Tibetan Buddhism.

para (Sanskrit): the "life of Brahmā", the Hindu creator God; in Hindu cosmology, totaling 100 "years of Brahmā". See also *kalpa*

pāramitās (Sanskrit): virtues, "perfections"; "that which has reached to the other shore" of *Nirvāna*.

petitio principii (Latin): "assuming the initial point", or begging the question. A logical fallacy in which the proposition to be proved is assumed implicitly or explicitly in the premises.

Philosophia Perennis (Latin): "perennial philosophy".

pneumátikos (Greek): a "spiritual man"; one in whom the element spirit (*pneuma*) predominates over the soul and the body (cf. 1 Thess. 5:23; 1 Cor. 2:14-15).

Pté San Win (Lakota): the White Buffalo Cow Woman, celestial revealer of the Sacred Pipe to the Sioux Indians.

Rahmah (Arabic): divine "Mercy"; also, divine Goodness, Beauty, Beatitude.

Rāma (Sanskrit): the seventh *Avatāra* (incarnation) of the Hindu God Vishnu; hero of the epic *Rāmāyana.*

Religio Perennis (Latin): "perennial religion".

risālah (Arabic): the message brought by an envoy or messenger (*rasūl*) of God.

Risālat al-Ahadiyah (Arabic): "message of unity".

Rosa Mystica (Latin): "Mystical Rose"; a title for the Virgin Mary.

sādhu (Sanskrit): a wandering monk, ascetic, or practitioner of *yoga*, solely dedicated to achieving liberation (*moksha*), the fourth and final Hindu goal of life.

salām (Arabic): "peace".

samsāra (Sanskrit): "wandering"; in Hinduism and Buddhism, transmigration or the cycle of birth, death, and rebirth; also the world of apparent flux and change.

Sanātana Dharma (Sanskrit): "eternal law"; in Hinduism, the universal or absolute law or truth underlying specific and relative laws and truths.

sannyāsin (Sanskrit): one who has renounced the world in search of deliverance (*mukti*) from the round of births and rebirths (*samsāra*).

satsangha (Sanskrit): "company of the good"; the company of persons of holy or ascendant nature.

Sayyidnā (Arabic): "our liege lord"; a title of respect, often placed before the name of a prophet or saint.

Sayyidatnā (Arabic): "our liege lady"; a title of respect, often placed before the name of a female prophet or saint.

Sedes Sapientiae (Latin): "Throne of Wisdom"; one of the names given by the litany of Lorette to the Virgin Mary; cf. 1 Kings 10:18-20.

Seishi (Japanese): the *bodhisattva* of wisdom and strength (Sanskrit: Mahāsthāmaprāpta); one of the two main attendants of Amida Buddha.

Shādhiliyyah Tarīqah (Arabic): the Sufi order (*tarīqah*) founded by Abu'l Hasan ash-Shādhilī (1196-1258).

Shahādah (Arabic): the fundamental "profession" or "testimony" of faith in Islam, consisting of the words *lā ilāha illā 'Llāh, Muhammadan rasūlu 'Llāh*: "There is no god but God; Muhammad is the messenger of God."

Shakti (Sanskrit): the efficient energy of the Supreme Principle; creative "power", expressed in Hinduism in the form of divine femininity. *Mahāshakti*, or "great *Shakti*", refers to the feminine aspect of *Brahma* or the Absolute.

Shānti Om (Sanskrit): "Peace, *Om*"; in Hinduism, a sacred formula or *mantra*. See also *Om*

sharī'ah (Arabic): in Islam, the revealed law; the legal prescriptions of the religion; Muslim exoterism.

shaykh (Arabic): "old man" or "elder"; in Sufism, a spiritual master or head of a Sufi order.

Shekhīnah (Hebrew): "dwelling"; in Judaism, the dwelling place, and thus presence, of God in the world.

Shemā (Hebrew): "Hear, O Israel, the Lord our God is one Lord" (Deut. 6:4); also, and by extension, the central prayer of Judaism, recited twice daily, and consisting of passages from Deut. 6:4-9; 11:13-21 and Num. 15:37-41.

Shrī or Śrī (Sanskrit): "venerable one", "eminent one"; an honorific title often placed before the names of Hindu deities and saints.

Shulamite: an epithet applied to the beautiful young bride of the Biblical Song of Solomon, 6:13.

Sidi (Arabic): the Maghrebi form of *Sayyid*, "liege lord". *See also* Sayyidnā

silsilah (Arabic): "chain"; in Sufi orders, an initiatic chain of transmission, beginning with the Prophet Muhammad, and including an unbroken lineage of spiritual masters through the centuries.

Sophia (Greek): "wisdom"; in Jewish and Christian tradition, the Wisdom of God, often conceived as feminine (cf. Prov. 8).

Sophia Perennis (Latin): "perennial wisdom"; the eternal, non-formal Truth at the heart of all orthodox religious traditions.

staretz (Russian): "old man"; in the Christian East, a spiritual father or guide.

Stella Maris (Latin): "Star of the Sea"; a title for the Virgin Mary ("Our Lady, Star of the Sea").

sunnah (Arabic): the sayings and actions of the Prophet Muhammad, serving as a precedent and standard for the behavior of Muslims.

sūrah (Arabic): a chapter of the Koran.

Swami (Sanskrit *Svāmi*): a title of respect placed before the name of a spiritual teacher, revered personage, or monk.

Tao Te Ching (Chinese): the sacred scripture of Taoism, consisting of 81 chapters on the Way (*Tao*) and its power or virtue (*Te*); attributed to the ancient sage Lao Tzu.

Tārā (Sanskrit): "star"; in Hinduism, an epithet for many goddesses, notably Pārvatī, consort of Shiva; in Buddhism, the name given to a diverse group of female Buddhas and *bodhisattvas*.

tarīqah (Arabic): "way" or "path"; the spiritual method leading to union with God; also, a Sufi order or brotherhood.

Tat tvam asi (Sanskrit): "thou art That"; one of the *mahāvākyas*, or "great sentences", from the *Vedas* enunciating the supreme identity, or union with *Brahma*.

Tawhīd (Arabic): "unification", "union"; in Islam, the affirmation of divine unity as expressed in the first phrase of the *Shahādah*, "There is no god but God" (*lā ilāha illā 'Llāh*); in Sufism, the doctrine of mystical union.

trimūrti (Sanskrit): "having three forms"; in Hindu tradition, a triadic expression of the Divine, especially in the form of Brahmā, the creator, Vishnu, the preserver, and Shiva, the transformer.

Upanishad (Sanskrit): "to sit close by"; hence, any esoteric doctrine requiring direct transmission from master to disciple; in Hinduism, the genre of sacred texts that end or complete the *Vedas*.

Uttara Mīmānsā (Sanskrit): the way of knowledge expounded by the philosophy of *Vedānta*, "the end or culmination of the *Vedas*"; contrasted with *Pūrva Mīmānsā*, the way of ritual action.

Veda (Sanskrit): a body of sacred knowledge revealed to ancient Indian seers and transmitted in the *Vedas*, sacred texts composed of hymns, ritual formulas, and metaphysical doctrines regarded in Hinduism as authoritative for both doctrine and practice.

Vedānta (Sanskrit): "end or culmination of the *Vedas*"; one of the major schools of traditional Hindu philosophy, based in part on the *Upanishads*. The three main schools of *Vedānta* are: (1) *Advaita Vedānta* (non-dualism), whose chief representative is Shankara (788-820); (2) *Vishishtādvaita Vedānta* (qualified non-dualism), whose chief representative is Rāmānuja (1017-1137); and (3) *Dvaita Vedānta* (dualism), whose chief representative is Madhva (1199-1278).

vincit omnia Veritas (Latin): Truth conquers all (cf. I Esdras 1:12).

Virgen del Pilar (Spanish): "Virgin of the Pillar"; referring to the miraculous appearance of the Virgin Mary—atop a column or pillar carried by angels—to the Apostle James in Zaragoza, Spain, c. 40 A.D. Today, the Basilica of Our Lady of the Pillar in Zaragoza is said to house the pillar upon which the Virgin stood.

viveka (Sanskrit): discernment, discrimination; a *vivekin* being one who possesses the ability to discern between the Real and the illusory.

al-Wujūd al-Mutlaq (Arabic): "Necessary Being", That which cannot not be, as opposed to contingent or possible being, that which may or may not be.

yoga (Sanskrit): "yoking", "union"; in Indian traditions, any meditative and ascetic technique designed to bring the soul and body into a state of concentration; one of the six orthodox *darshanas*, or perspectives, of classical Hinduism.

yogī (Sanskrit): a practitioner of *yoga*; also, one who has attained the goal or end of *yoga*, that is, union.

yuga (Sanskrit): age or eon; in Hindu cosmology, one of the four ages of the world: (1) the *Krita-* or *Satya-yuga*, (2) the *Tretā-yuga*, (3) the *Dvāpara-yuga*, and (4) the *Kali-yuga*; analogous to the Greco-Roman Golden, Silver, Bronze, and Iron Ages.

Yuwipi (Lakota): a healing ceremony among the Sioux involving the aid of "medicine spirits".

zāwiyah (Arabic): "corner"; a place where Sufi initiates gather together to pray and perform their rites of remembrance.

For a glossary of all key foreign words used in books published by World Wisdom, including metaphysical terms in English, consult: www.DictionaryofSpiritualTerms.org.
This on-line Dictionary of Spiritual Terms provides extensive definitions, examples, and related terms in other languages.

BIBLIOGRAPHY

Aymard, Jean-Baptiste & Patrick Laude. *Frithjof Schuon: Life and Teachings.* Albany, NY: SUNY, 2004.

———. (eds.). *Les Dossiers H: Frithjof Schuon.* Lausanne: L'Âge d'Homme, 2002.

Baker, Rob & Gray Henry (eds.). *Merton and Sufism: The Untold Story.* Louisville, KY: Fons Vitae, 2000.

Bando, Shojun. "Shinran's Indebtedness to T'an-luan". *Studies in Comparative Religion*, Vol. 5, No. 4, Autumn 1971, 221-234.

———. "Significance of the *Nembutsu*". *Studies in Comparative Religion*, Vol. 6, No. 4, Autumn 1972, 211-220.

——— & Harold Stewart (trans.). *Tannisho: Passages Deploring Deviations of Faith and Rennyo Shonin Ofumi: The Letters of Rennyo.* Berkeley, CA: Numata Center for Buddhist Translation and Research, 1996.

Biès, Jean. "A Face of Eternal Wisdom: An Interview with Frithjof Schuon". *Sophia*, Vol. 3, No. 1, Summer 1998, 5-20.

Bloom, Anthony. *Beginning to Pray.* Mahwah, NJ: Paulist Press, 1970.

———. *Courage to Pray.* Mahwah, NJ: Paulist Press, 1973.

———. *God and Man.* Mahwah, NJ: Paulist Press, 1975.

Brown, Joseph Epes. *The Sacred Pipe: Black Elk's Account of the Seven Sacred Rites of the Ogallala Sioux.* Norman: University of Oklahoma Press, 1953.

———. *The Spiritual Legacy of the American Indian: With Letters While Living with Black Elk.* Bloomington, IN: World Wisdom, 2007.

Burckhardt, Titus. *Mirror of the Intellect.* Cambridge, UK: Quinta Essentia, 1987.

———. *Fez: City of Islam.* Cambridge, UK: Quinta Essentia, 1991.

———. *Chartres and the Birth of the Cathedral.* Bloomington, IN: World Wisdom, 1995.

———. *Alchemy: Science of the Cosmos, Science of the Soul.* Louisville, KY: Fons Vitae, 1997.

———. *Moorish Culture in Spain.* Louisville, KY: Fons Vitae, 1999.

———. *Sacred Art in East and West.* Bloomington, IN: World Wisdom/Louisville, KY: Fons Vitae, 2001.

———. *Introduction to Sufi Doctrine.* Bloomington, IN: World Wisdom, 2008.

———. *Siena: City of the Virgin.* Bloomington, IN: World Wisdom, 2008.

———. *Art of Islam: Language and Meaning.* Bloomington, IN: World Wisdom, 2009.

———. "The Sun Dance". In *Mirror of the Intellect*, 164-170.

Casey, Deborah. "The Basis of Religion and Metaphysics: An Interview with Frithjof Schuon". *Quest Magazine*, Summer, 1996, 74-78.

Chacornac, Paul. *The Simple Life of René Guénon.* Hillsdale, NY: Sophia Perennis, 2004.

Charles, HRH The Prince of Wales. "Introduction to the Sacred Web Conference". *Sacred Web*, 17, 2006, 17-22.

Chevilliat, Bernard (ed.). *Frithjof Schuon: Connaissance et Voie d'Intériorité, Biographie études et témoignages.* Paris: Connaissance des Religions, 1999.

Coomaraswamy, Ananda K. *Selected Papers I: Traditional Art and Symbolism*, ed. Roger Lipsey. Princeton: Princeton University Press, 1977.

———. *Selected Papers II: Metaphysics*, ed. Roger Lipsey. Princeton: Princeton University Press, 1977.

Coomaraswamy, Rama P. *The Invocation of the Name of Jesus: As Practiced in the Western Church.* Louisville, KY: Fons Vitae, 1999.

———. *Destruction of the Christian Tradition: Updated and Revised.* Bloomington, IN: World Wisdom, 2006.

——— (ed.). *The Essential Ananda K.Coomaraswamy.* Bloomington, IN: World Wisdom, 2004.

Cutsinger, James S. *Advice to the Serious Seeker: Meditations on the Teaching of Frithjof Schuon.* Albany, NY: SUNY Press, 1997.

——— (ed.). *Paths to the Heart: Sufism and the Christian East.* Bloomington, IN: World Wisdom, 2002.

——— (ed.). *The Fullness of God: Frithjof Schuon on Christianity.* Bloomington, IN: World Wisdom, 2004.

——— (ed.). *Prayer Fashions Man: Frithjof Schuon on the Spiritual Life.* Bloomington, IN: World Wisdom, 2005.

———. "The Mystery of the Two Natures". *Sophia*, Vol. 4, No. 2, Winter 1998, 111-141.

———. "The Virgin". In *Ye Shall Know the Truth: Christianity and the Perennial Philosophy*, ed. Mateus Soares de Azevedo, 107-162.

Danielou, Alain. "René Guénon et la tradition hindoue". In *Les Dossiers H: René Guénon*, ed. Pierre-Marie Sigaud, 136-140.

Danner, Victor. *The Islamic Tradition: An Introduction.* San Rafael, CA: Sophia Perennis, 2005.

de Azevedo, Mateus Soares (ed.). *Ye Shall Know the Truth: Christianity and the Perennial Philosophy.* Bloomington, IN: World Wisdom, 2005.

Eliade, Mircea (ed.). *The Encyclopedia of Religion* (16 vols.). New York: Collier Macmillan, 1987.

Fabbri, Renaud. "The Milk of the Virgin: The Prophet, the Saint, and the Sage". *Sacred Web*, 20, 2007, 225-265.

——— & Timothy Scott (eds.). *Vincit Omnia Veritas: Collected Essays.* Bendigo: La Trobe University, 2008.

Faivre, Antoine. "Foreword". In *The Fullness of God*, ed. James S. Cutsinger, xi-xv.

Fitzgerald, Michael. *Yellowtail: Crow Medicine Man and Sun Dance Chief.* Oklahoma: University of Oklahoma Press, 1991.

———. "Beauty and the Sense of the Sacred: Schuon's Antidote to the Modern World". *Sacred Web*, 20, 2007, 129-154.

———. "Frithjof Schuon and the American Indian Spirit: An Interview with Michael Fitzgerald". In *Vincit Omnia Veritas: Collected Essays*, 13-34.

Guénon, René. *The Great Triad.* Cambridge, UK: Quinta Essentia, 1991.

———. *The Crisis of the Modern World.* Hillsdale, NY: Sophia Perennis, 2001.

———. *East and West.* Hillsdale, NY: Sophia Perennis, 2001.

———. *The Reign of Quantity and the Signs of the Times.* Hillsdale, NY: Sophia Perennis, 2002.

Hani, Jean. "The Rosary as Spiritual Way". In *Ye Shall Know the Truth: Christianity and the Perennial Philosophy*, ed. Mateus Soares de Azevedo, 94-106.

Hisamatsu, Shinichi. *Zen and the Fine Arts.* Tokyo: Kodansha International, 1982.

———. *Critical Sermons of the Zen Tradition*, eds. Christopher Ives & Tokiwa Gishin. Honolulu: University of Hawaii Press, 2002.

Ibish, Yusuf & Ileana Marculescu (eds.). *Contemplation and Action in World Religions: Selected Papers from the Rothko Chapel Colloquium Traditional Modes of Contemplation and Action.* Washington: University of Washington Press, 1979.

Küry, Hans. "Les jeunes gens dans la Caverne: première rencontre" (extrait). In *Les Dossiers H: Frithjof Schuon*, eds. Jean-Baptiste Aymard & Patrick Laude, 382-383.

Laude, Patrick. *Singing the Way: Insights in Poetry and Spiritual Transformation.* Bloomington, IN: World Wisdom, 2005.

——— (ed.). *Pray Without Ceasing: The Way of the Invocation in World Religions.* Bloomington, IN: World Wisdom, 2006.

———. "Quintessential Esoterism and the Wisdom of Forms: Reflections on Frithjof Schuon's Intellectual and Spiritual Legacy", *Sacred Web*, 20, 2007, 159-192.

———. "René Guénon: Traditional Sources and Contemporary Contexts". *Sacred Web*, 21, 2008, 129-149.

Lhalungpa, Lobsang. *The Life of Milarepa.* Boston: Shambhala, 1982.

Lindbom, Tage. "Frithjof Schuon and Our Times". *Sophia*, Vol. 4, No. 2, Winter 1998, 78-90.

Lings, Martin. *Muhammad: His Life Based on the Earliest Sources.* Cambridge, UK: Islamic Texts Society, 1991.

———. *The Book of Certainty: The Sufi Doctrine of Faith, Vision, and Gnosis.* Cambridge, UK: Islamic Texts Society, 1992.

———. *A Sufi Saint of the Twentieth Century.* Cambridge, UK: Islamic Texts Society, 1993.

———. *What is Sufism?* Cambridge, UK: Islamic Texts Society, 1993.

———. *The Secret of Shakespeare: To Take Upon Us the Mystery of Things.* Cambridge, UK: Quinta Essentia, 1996.

———. *Ancient Beliefs and Modern Superstitions.* Cambridge, UK: Archetype, 2001.

———. *The Eleventh Hour: The Spiritual Crisis of the Modern World in the Light of Tradition and Prophecy.* Cambridge, UK: Archetype, 2002.

———. *Splendours of Quran Calligraphy and Illumination.* Vaduz, Liechtenstein: Thesaurus Islamicus Foundation, 2005.

———. *A Return to the Spirit: Questions and Answers.* Louisville, KY: Fons Vitae, 2005.

———. "Frithjof Schuon and René Guénon". *Sophia*, Vol. 5, No. 2, Winter 1999, 9-24.

———. "Preface". In *The Underlying Religion: An Introduction to the Perennial Philosophy*, ix-x.

Lings, Martin & Clinton Minnaar (eds.). *The Underlying Religion: An Introduction to the Perennial Philosophy*. Bloomington, IN: World Wisdom, 2007.

Lipsey, Roger. *Coomaraswamy: His Life and Work*. Princeton: Princeton University Press, 1977.

Merton, Thomas. *Disputed Questions*. New York: Farrar, Straus and Cudahy, 1960.

———. *The Hidden Ground of Love: Letters on Religious Experience and Social Concerns*, ed. William M. Shannon. New York: Farrar, Straus, Giroux, 1985.

Michon, Jean-Louis. *Introduction to Traditional Islam, Illustrated: Foundations, Art, and Spirituality*. Bloomington, IN: World Wisdom, 2008.

———. "The 'True Man': Myth or Reality?". *Sacred Web*, 19, 2007, 57-77.

Morris, James W. "Ibn 'Arabī in the 'Far West': His Contribution to the Emerging Science of Spirituality". Public lecture, Kyoto University, Japan, January 19-23, 2001: "Sufi Thought and Inner Dimensions of the Islamic World: Ibn 'Arabī and His School in Asia and Africa".

Murray, John. "Le maitre de la primordialité". In *Les Dossiers H: Frithjof Schuon*, eds. Jean-Baptiste Aymard & Patrick Laude, 384-387.

Nasr, Seyyed Hossein (ed.). *The Essential Frithjof Schuon*. Bloomington, IN: World Wisdom, 2005.

———. & William Stoddart (eds.). *Religion of the Heart: Essays Presented to Frithjof Schuon on His Eightieth Birthday*. Washington: Foundation for Traditional Studies, 1991.

———. *The Philosophy of Seyyed Hossein Nasr*, eds. Lewis Edwin Hahn, Randall E. Auxier, & Lucien W. Stone, Jr. Chicago, IL: Open Court, 2000.

Needleman, Jacob (ed.). *The Sword of Gnosis: Metaphysics, Cosmology, Tradition, Symbolism*. Baltimore, MD: Penguin, 1974.

Neihardt, John G. *Black Elk Speaks*. New York: William Morrow & Co., 1932.

Northbourne, Lord. *Looking Back on Progress*. Ghent, NY: Sophia Perennis et Universalis, 1995.

———. *Of the Land and the Spirit: The Essential Lord Northbourne on Ecology and Religion*, edited by Christopher James and Joseph A. Fitzgerald. Bloomington, IN: World Wisdom, 2008.

Ogata, Sohaku. *Zen for the West*. New York/London: The Dial Press, 1959.

Oldmeadow, Harry. *Frithjof Schuon and the Perennial Philosophy*. Bloomington, IN: World Wisdom, 2010.

——— (ed.). *The Betrayal of Tradition: Essays on the Spiritual Crisis of Modernity*. Bloomington, IN: World Wisdom, 2005.

Pallis, Marco. *Peaks and Lamas*. Berkeley, CA: Counterpoint, 2004.

———. *A Buddhist Spectrum: Contributions to Buddhist-Christian Dialogue*. Bloomington, IN: World Wisdom, 2003.

———. *The Way and the Mountain: Tibet, Buddhism, and Tradition*, ed. Joseph A. Fitzgerald. Bloomington, IN: World Wisdom, 2008.

———. "A Fateful Meeting of Minds: A. K. Coomaraswamy and R. Guénon". In *The Essential Ananda K. Coomaraswamy*, ed. Rama P. Coomaraswamy, 7-20.

Perry, Barbara. "Frithjof Schuon: Metaphysician and Artist". In *Scenes of Plains Indian Life.* Taylor Museum, Colorado Springs Fine Arts Center, 1981.

———. "Foreword: Frithjof Schuon: Metaphysician and Artist". In *The Feathered Sun*, xvi-xx.

———. "Introduction". In *Art from the Sacred to the Profane: East and West*, ed. Catherine Schuon, xiii-xv.

Perry, Mark. "Frithjof Schuon Seen Through His Handwriting". *Sophia*, Vol. 6, No. 1, Summer 2000, 107-152.

———. "La compassion intellective". In *Les Dossiers H: Frithjof Schuon*, eds. Jean-Baptiste Aymard & Patrick Laude, 210-231.

Perry, Whitall. *A Treasury of Traditional Wisdom.* London: Allen & Unwin, 1971.

———. "Corrigendum". *Studies in Comparative Religion*, Vol. 15, Nos. 3 & 4, Summer-Autumn, 1983, 141.

———. "Perspectives". *Sophia*, Vol. 4, No. 2, Winter 1998, 32-46.

Pollack, Michael. "Editor's Introduction". In *Images of Primordial and Mystic Beauty*, 1-4.

Powers, Marla. *Oglala Women: Myth, Ritual and Reality.* Chicago/London: University of Chicago Press, 1986.

Prats, Josep & Esteve Serra (eds). *Frithjof Schuon (1907-1998): Notas biográficas, estudios, homenajes.* Palma de Mallorca: Sophia Perennis, 2004.

Ramachandran, Mudumbaï. "Frithjof Schuon: A Small Word of Homage and Celebration". *Sophia*, Vol. 4, No. 2, Winter 1998, 47-55.

Ramdas, Swami. *World is God.* Via Kanhangan: Anandashram, 1955.

———. *In Quest of God.* San Diego, CA: Blue Dove Press, 2002.

Romaine, Sharlyn. "Intention and Style". In *Images of Primordial and Mystic Beauty*, ed. Michael Pollack, 5-6.

Rossi, Vincent. "Presence, Participation, Performance: The Remembrance of God in the Early Hesychast Fathers". In *Paths to the Heart: Sufism and the Christian East*, ed. James S. Cutsinger, 64-111.

Schaya, Leo. *The Universal Meaning of the Kabbalah.* Louisville, KY: Fons Vitae, 2004.

Schimmel, Annemarie. "Foreword". In *Adastra & Stella Maris: Poems by Frithjof Schuon*, vii-viii.

Schuon, Catherine (ed.). *Art from the Sacred to the Profane: East and West.* Bloomington, IN: World Wisdom, 2007.

———. "Frithjof Schuon: Memories and Anecdotes". *Sacred Web*, 8, 2001, 35-60.

Schuon, Frithjof. *Adastra & Stella Maris: Poems by Frithjof Schuon.* German-English edition. Bloomington, IN: World Wisdom, 2003.

———. *Autumn Leaves & The Ring: Poems by Frithjof Schuon.* German-English edition. Bloomington, IN: World Wisdom, 2010.

———. *Castes and Races.* London: Perennial Books, 1982.

———. *Christianity/Islam: Perspectives on Esoteric Ecumenism*. Bloomington, IN: World Wisdom, 2008.

———. *Echoes of Perennial Wisdom*. Bloomington, IN: World Wisdom, 1992.

———. *Esoterism as Principle and as Way*. London: Perennial Books, 1981.

———. *The Eye of the Heart*. Bloomington, IN: World Wisdom, 1997.

———. *The Feathered Sun: Plains Indians in Art and Philosophy*. Bloomington, IN: World Wisdom, 1990.

———. *Form and Substance in the Religions*. Bloomington, IN: World Wisdom, 2002.

———. *From the Divine to the Human*. Bloomington, IN: World Wisdom, 1982.

———. *Gnosis: Divine Wisdom*. Bloomington, IN: World Wisdom, 2006.

———. *Images of Primordial and Mystic Beauty: Paintings by Frithjof Schuon*, ed. Michael Pollack. Bloomington, IN: Abodes, 1992.

———. *In the Face of the Absolute*. Bloomington, IN: World Wisdom, 1994.

———. *In the Tracks of Buddhism*. London: Allen & Unwin, 1968.

———. *Language of the Self*. Bloomington, IN: World Wisdom, 1999.

———. *Light on the Ancient Worlds*. Bloomington, IN: World Wisdom, 2006.

———. *Logic and Transcendence*. Bloomington, IN: World Wisdom, 2009.

———. *Memories and Meditations*. Unpublished.

———. *The Play of Masks*. Bloomington, IN: World Wisdom, 1992.

———. *Primordial Meditation: Contemplating the Real*. *Sacred Web*, 20, 2007, 19-120.

———. *Road to the Heart: Poems*. Bloomington, IN: World Wisdom, 1995.

———. *Roots of the Human Condition*. Bloomington, IN: World Wisdom, 2002.

———. *Songs for a Spiritual Traveler: Selected Poems*. German-English edition. Bloomington, IN: World Wisdom, 2002.

———. *Songs without Names: Poems by Frithjof Schuon, Volumes I-VI*. Bloomington, IN: World Wisdom, 2006.

———. *Songs without Names: Poems by Frithjof Schuon, Volumes VII-XII*. Bloomington, IN: World Wisdom, 2006.

———. *Spiritual Perspectives and Human Facts*. Bloomington, IN: World Wisdom, 2007.

———. *Stations of Wisdom*. Bloomington, IN: World Wisdom, 1995.

———. *Sufism: Veil and Quintessence*. Bloomington, IN: World Wisdom, 2007.

———. *Survey of Metaphysics and Esoterism*. Bloomington, IN: World Wisdom, 2000.

———. *To Have a Center*. Bloomington, IN: World Wisdom, 1990.

———. *The Transcendent Unity of Religions*. London: Faber & Faber, 1953; Wheaton, IL: Quest, 1993.

———. *The Transfiguration of Man*. Bloomington, IN: World Wisdom, 1995.

———. *Treasures of Buddhism*. Bloomington, IN: World Wisdom, 1993.

———. *Understanding Islam*. Bloomington, IN: World Wisdom, 1998.

———. *World Wheel: Poems by Frithjof Schuon, Volumes I-III*. Bloomington, IN: World Wisdom, 2006.

———. *World Wheel: Poems by Frithjof Schuon, Volumes IV-VII.* Bloomington, IN: World Wisdom, 2006.

———. "*Rahimahu 'Llāh*". *Cahiers du Sud*, August-September 1935, 135-137.

———. "Mystères christiques". *Études traditionnelles*, juillet-août 1948, n° 269; *Les Dossiers H: Frithjof Schuon*, eds. Jean-Baptiste Aymard & Patrick Laude, 432-439.

———. "Invocation of the Divine Name". *Kalyana-Kalpataru*, Vol. 25, No. 10, October 1961.

———. "No Activity Without Truth". In *The Betrayal of Tradition*, ed. Harry Oldmeadow, 3-14.

———. "Communion and Invocation". In *Pray Without Ceasing*, ed. Patrick Laude, 72-78.

———. "The Perennial Philosophy". In *The Underlying Religion*, ed. Martin Lings, 243-248.

Sigaud, Pierre-Marie (ed.). *Les Dossiers H: René Guénon.* Lausanne-Paris: L'Âge d'Homme, 1984.

Smith, Huston. "Is there a Perennial Philosophy?" *Journal of the American Academy of Religion*, 60:3, 1987, 553-566.

———. "Providence Perceived: In Memory of Frithjof Schuon". *Sophia*, Vol. 4, No. 2, Winter 1998, 29-31.

Sophrony, Athonite. *Wisdom from Mount Athos: The Writings of Staretz Siloan.* Crestwood, NY: St. Vladimir's Seminary Press, 1975.

———. *Saint Silouan, the Athonite.* Crestwood, NY: St. Vladimir's Seminary Press, 1999.

Steltenkamp, Michael F. *Black Elk: Holy Man of the Oglala.* Norman: University of Oklahoma Press, 1992.

Stoddart, William. *Remembering in a World of Forgetting: Thoughts on Tradition and Postmodernism*, eds. Mateus Soares de Azevedo & Alberto Vasconcellos Queiroz. Bloomington, IN: World Wisdom, 2008.

——— (ed.). *René Guénon: Some Observations.* Hillsdale, NY: Sophia Perennis, 2004.

———. "Introduction". In *Adastra & Stella Maris: Poems by Frithjof Schuon*, ix-xi.

Walker, James R. *Lakota Belief and Ritual*, eds. Raymond DeMallie & Elaine A. Jahner. Lincoln: University of Nebraska Press, 1980.

Yellowtail, Thomas. "Introduction". In *The Feathered Sun*, xiii-xv.

INDEX

BIOGRAPHICAL NOTES

MICHAEL OREN FITZGERALD (b. 1949) is an award-winning author, editor, and publisher of books on world religions, sacred art, and traditional culture. He was introduced to Frithjof Schuon in 1971 through Thomas Yellowtail, the Sun Dance Chief of the Crow tribe, who also adopted Fitzgerald into his family and the Crow tribe. Fitzgerald was Schuon's neighbor for the last eighteen years of his life and is the executor of his estate. He has previously written and lectured on aspects of Schuon's life and work. He also recorded Yellowtail's autobiography and description of the Sun Dance Religion, published as *Yellowtail: Crow Medicine Man and Sun Dance Chief*, and has edited more than a dozen other books and produced two documentary films. Several of his books and both of his documentary films are used in university classes. Fitzgerald has taught Religious Traditions of the North American Indians at Indiana University, an institution from which he earned a degree in Religious Studies as well as a doctorate of Jurisprudence. He lives with his wife in Bloomington, Indiana.

WILLIAM STODDART (b. 1925) is an author, editor, and translator of Perennialist writings, who was for many years a close associate of Frithjof Schuon. Stoddart has translated two of Schuon's French language books and co-translated 23 collections of his German poetry into English; he has also edited an anthology of Schuon's writings on René Guénon and co-edited a collection of essays presented to Schuon on his eightieth birthday. Stoddart served for many years as assistant editor of the British journal *Studies in Comparative Religion*, and has written extensively on the world's great spiritual traditions. His essential writings were published in 2008 by World Wisdom as *Remembering in a World of Forgetting: Thoughts on Tradition and Postmodernism.* Born in Carstairs, Scotland, he studied modern languages, and later medicine, at the universities of Glasgow, Edinburgh, and Dublin. Pursuing his interests in comparative religion, he has traveled widely in Europe, North Africa, India, Ceylon, and Japan. He currently lives in Windsor, Ontario.

Titles in the Spiritual Masters: East & West Series by World Wisdom

The Essential Shinran: A Buddhist Path of True Entrusting,
edited by Alfred Bloom, 2007

The Essential Sri Anandamayi Ma: Illustrated,
by Alexander Lipsky and Anandamayi Ma, 2007

The Essential Swami Ramdas: Commemorative Edition,
compiled by Susunaga Weeraperuma, 2005

Frithjof Schuon: Messenger of the Perennial Philosophy,
by Michael Oren Fitzgerald, 2010

The Golden Age of Zen: Zen Masters of the T'ang Dynasty,
by John C.H. Wu, 2003

Honen the Buddhist Saint: Essential Writings and Official Biography,
edited by Joseph A. Fitzgerald, 2006

Introduction to Hindu Dharma: Illustrated
by Jagadguru His Holiness Sri Chandrasekharendra Saraswati Swamigal,
Sankaracharya of Kanchi, edited by Michael Oren Fitzgerald, 2008

The Laughing Buddha of Tofukuji:
The Life of Zen Master Keido Fukushima,
by Ishwar C. Harris, 2004

Messenger of the Heart: The Book of Angelus Silesius,
by Frederick Franck, 2005

Paths to Transcendence: According to
Shankara, Ibn Arabi, and Meister Eckhart,
by Reza Shah-Kazemi, 2006

Samdhong Rinpoche: Uncompromising Truth for a Compromised World:
Tibetan Buddhism and Today's World,
edited by Donovan Roebert, 2006

A Spirit of Tolerance: The Inspiring Life of Tierno Bokar,
by Amadou Hampaté Bâ, edited by Roger Gaetani, 2008

The Sufi Doctrine of Rumi: Illustrated Edition,
by William C. Chittick, 2005

Timeless in Time: Sri Ramana Maharshi,
by A. R. Natarajan, 2006